teenage citizens

**CONSTANCE A. FLANAGAN**

# teenage citizens

## THE POLITICAL THEORIES
## OF THE YOUNG

**HARVARD UNIVERSITY PRESS**   Cambridge, Massachusetts, and London, England
2013

*Library of Congress Cataloging-in-Publication Data*

Flanagan, Constance A.
   Teenage citizens : the political theories of the young / Constance
A. Flanagan.
      p. cm.
   Includes bibliographical references and index.
   ISBN 978-0-674-04862-1
   1. Teenagers—Political activity. 2. Youth—Political activity.
   3. Citizenship. 4. Political sociology. I. Title.
   HQ799.2.P6F65 2013
   303.48'4—dc23                    2012019968

*For*

*Erika and Steve*
*Erin and Jove*
*Maggie, Stevie,*
*and Bampi, of course*

# Contents

Introduction    1

1  Adolescents' Theories of the Social Contract    10

2  Teens from Different Social Orders    35

3  We the People    50

4  Democracy    87

5  Laws and Public Health    112

6  Inequality    134

7  Trust    161

8  Community Service    197

Coda: What Have We Learned?    227

*Appendix: Methods    239*

*Notes    267*

*Acknowledgments    295*

*Index    299*

teenage citizens

# Introduction

THIS BOOK IS about adolescents and politics. Yes, teenagers, most of whom are under the age of eighteen and thus are not yet eligible to vote. Consequently, they are off the radar screen for most political scientists for whom voting is such an important dependent variable. Similarly, politics as an integral aspect of human development has been largely ignored by psychologists. Perhaps these omissions are due to the narrow way in which we typically conceive of politics—as if it were mainly the business of government and the result of electoral contests. This restricted view of politics ignores the roots of the term, which, as the political theorist Michael Walzer notes, refers to the people who are connected to one another via their membership in a civic community:

> A citizen is, most simply, a member of a political community, entitled to whatever prerogatives and encumbered with whatever responsibilities are attached to membership. The word comes to us from the Latin *civis;* the Greek equivalent is *polites,* member of the polis, from which comes our political.[1]

Walzer's definition of a citizen with its emphasis on membership, prerogatives, and responsibilities, offers the science of human development an en-
trée into the political realm. As a developmental psychologist, I have used
his definition to argue that, in the context of adolescent development,
concepts of a political community and the rights and responsibilities associated with belonging to that community are rooted in the relationships
teens form in the settings of everyday life—for example, through the solidarity they feel with fellow students at school, the voice they exercise in a
youth activist project, or the sense of responsibility for public spaces and
natural resources that they develop through environmental programs. I have
called these spaces "mini-polities" to emphasize the fact that it is through their
engagement in these settings that younger generations construct their ideas
and identities about civic membership in the (macro) polity, their nation. This
framework expands the definition of citizenship beyond state-sanctioned adult
rights and obligations (such as voting) and looks instead at the developmental
processes whereby concepts of self, of others, and of the ties that bind them in
a political community evolve.

In exploring young people's views of the political realm, I attempt to
bridge political science and developmental psychology (disciplines that
typically do not interact) by showing that between the early- and late-
adolescent years, young people are forming concepts about topics such as
democracy, authority, self-determination, laws, liberty, loyalty, collective
action, social trust, and the common good that are highly relevant to
politics; that these understandings vary by an adolescent's age and experiences; and that during the adolescent years, young people are developing
identities, dispositions, and values that are logically consistent with their
political theories.

In this book, I argue that politics is about more than party affiliation and
elections. Politics concerns membership in communities and the processes
and practices whereby we work with fellow members of those communities
to determine the kind of communities, society, and world we want to live in.
That process is rooted in development and begins before citizens are old
enough to vote.

For adolescents, politics is embedded in their experiences of membership,
of exercising prerogatives, and of assuming obligations—experiences that are
played out in mediating institutions (schools, community-based organiza-

tions, volunteer work, etc.)—contexts that I call mini-polities because it is in these settings that youth construct their identities as citizens of the larger polity. Constructing a civic identity is an integral part of the process of identity formation, a central task of the adolescent years.

Between early and late adolescence, youth also construct a lay theory about their political-economic order—that is, about the "social contract" that binds members of their society together and about how they fit in that order. These lay theories reflect greater knowledge and broader perspectives that accrue with age and experience. Besides knowledge, adolescence also is a time for developing psychological dispositions of trust, open-mindedness, and tolerance of dissent that enable democracies to work.

Adolescents' political theories are informed by personal experiences that vary according to the opportunities (i.e., discussions of current events, diverse peer networks, community service, etc.) that accrue to individuals and according to the groups (social class, racial or ethnic, immigrant, gender, etc.) to which the adolescent belongs. Political theories are not objective truths but are entangled with a teen's affections for and allegiance to the groups with which she identifies, with the values she lives by, and with her ideas about what constitutes a just society.

In this book, I focus on how adolescents think about political phenomena. In most chapters I use verbatim responses from teenagers to the open-ended questions that I posed to them—for example, about what democracy means to them, about what they learned from doing volunteer work in their community, or about why they think some people in the United States are rich while others are poor.

This book draws from a program of work that I have dubbed "Adolescents' Theories about the Social Contract." In Chapter 1, I will say more about the philosophical foundations for social contract theory. Here I allude briefly to the core idea and to why I have employed the metaphor as an interpretive frame for understanding how young people theorize and try to make sense of their social order. At its core, the social contract refers to the bargain that individuals make to relinquish unchecked freedoms in order to form a society, to gain security, and to live together. Political authority derives from this bargain and people's moral and political obligations depend on the agreement.

The terms of the social contract will vary across societies and even at different periods within a society. However, the underlying principle is the same, that is, every society operates based on some compact, some set of rules and obligations by which the state, the market, the institutions of civil society, and the people live in harmony. The stability of any society will be undermined if actors in any of these spheres violate the terms of the compact. I hasten to add that there is ample criticism of social contract theory based on arguments about power and privilege, that is, that those who make the rules of the social order are more likely to garner the benefits, to the disadvantage of minorities and females.[2]

I happen to agree with these critiques but have decided to use the term because the social contract is a good metaphor for discussing the processes underlying socialization and social change. Concerning the former, I would argue that there is a kind of social compact or bargain conveyed in the messages with which parents and other adults raise and impart values to children. For example, we may tell them that they should work hard in school *if* they want to succeed in life or we may urge our teenage workers to be on time, to be honest, and to be responsible because such qualities in workers are rewarded by employers who stick by them. The underlying message is that if you play by the rules of our social contract, you'll be rewarded by society in the end. However, there are ample signs that the terms of this intergenerational compact have been undergoing change within the United States and in other nations. In fact, observing these changes is what motivated me to begin this program of work.

## BACKGROUND FOR THE PROGRAM OF WORK

My interest in adolescents' theories about the social contract can be traced to the mid-1980s when I was working as a graduate student on a project in communities in southeastern Michigan, communities whose economies and lives were structured around the auto industry. The study, led by Dr. Jacquelynne Eccles at the University of Michigan, concerned the changes in academic motivation and achievement that were associated with early adolescents' transition from elementary to middle school. We wanted to hear from parents about how they were helping children to negotiate this school transition. Consequently, parents completed surveys at four time points over the two years of the study.

At the time there was an unemployment rate of 15 percent in the state and, not surprisingly, many parents of the early adolescents in our study were affected. Over the course of the study, several hundred families reported that one or both parents had either lost their job or had been demoted. Our research team was able to document that these stressors in parents' work lives spilled over into their families: over the two years of the study, patterns of parent-adolescent conflict that were reported by the early adolescents increased in the wake of layoffs or demotions in the work lives reported by their parents. The child's adjustment at school also was affected: according to teachers (who weren't privy to information about parents' employment), kids had more trouble getting along with fellow students and focusing on schoolwork when their parents were dealing with the stress of job loss or demotion.[3]

The ripple effects of parents' job loss on family relationships and children's well-being was hardly an earth-shattering finding. But I began to ponder how the economic changes these families were dealing with reflected deeper changes in assumptions about work and the intergenerational legacy of steady jobs on which families had come to rely. For their parents' and grandparents' generations, the deal was that if you finished high school, you could expect to find manual work in an industry with pay and benefits that would allow you to support a family. But as we know now, that bargain is a thing of the past for most young people in the United States. The new realities in the world of work suggest that unstable or insecure work will be more and more common. Analyses of work and earnings trends in the United States show that more of the jobs in the "new economy" are contingent (part time, of shorter tenure, with fewer benefits). Since the 1970s family incomes have become more volatile and access to employer-provided health insurance and pensions have fallen for the average worker.[4] Since the job market is less predictable, it also is difficult for younger generations to make educational plans related to careers. Perhaps it is not surprising then that more college undergraduates are hedging their bets with double majors, minors, and certificate programs.

In short, what these families in the industrial heartland of the United States were dealing with was a sign of deeper changes in the terms of the social contract in America. In certain ways, the rules for raising children were changing: there was no guarantee that hard work in school would pay off with steady employment. And while responsibility and loyalty might still be virtues that parents encouraged in their children, there was no promise that employers would repay such loyalties from their workforce by committing to remain in those communities for the long haul.

I didn't feel that there was much that I could do about the economic changes. But I did start to wonder if changes in the nature of work and the amount of control one had over it should cause us to reevaluate the emphasis we place on work as a source of purpose and personal meaning and as the overarching goal of children's education.

People need narratives, stories that they can tell that provide direction and purpose, that help them make sense of their lives. If the rules of the new economy mean that the average person has less control over his or her work, then putting all of one's eggs in that basket and conceiving of schools as mainly a training ground for work seems myopic. What about citizenship as a purpose for living? Just as there are skills associated with different vocations, there are skills that citizens need—such as listening to others' opinions on issues, deliberating with fellow citizens with whom we disagree, and working together to find common ground; learning how to monitor public resources such as water and air quality and how to hold government, industry, and the general public accountable for those resources; working as a team to find creative solutions to problems. Interestingly, these *civic* skills are not in any way at odds with the skills needed in the new world of work. In fact, they are the kinds of competencies that employers list as skills that they seek in prospective employees.[5]

However, we know relatively little about how adolescents think about citizenship or about other political themes. So I considered the changing compact that I was observing, and began to ask questions such as, "How do younger generations develop an understanding of their relationships and bonds with fellow citizens? What, if any, do they believe are the ties that bind us together?"

To address such questions, I conducted several studies beginning in the mid-1990s. Details about the methods and samples are provided in the Appendix. Here I note only that purposive sampling was used in each study in order to capture the political theories of young people from a wide range of social class and racial or ethnic backgrounds. Most of the studies were conducted in the United States, and these are the bases for Chapters 3 through 8.

Chapter 2 is the exception: it is based on a collaborative project that I conducted in the mid-1990s with colleagues from five other nations. Three countries (Bulgaria, the Czech Republic, and Hungary) were grappling with market and political transitions, that is, fundamental changes in their social contracts. We were interested in understanding the implications for younger generations of such fundamental changes in their nation's social contract. The other three countries (Australia, Sweden, and the United States) had in place stable institutional practices that matched their economic and political systems. I use the comparative data to illustrate how adolescents tend to accept as normal those social contracts to which they have become accustomed and to show how mundane practices in mediating settings reinforce the terms of a nation's social contract. At the same time, within the three Central and Eastern European nations, we see how teens' perceptions of the changing social contracts in their societies vary according to the implications of those (especially economic) changes for their group.

## ORGANIZATION OF THE BOOK

In Chapter 1, I discuss the theory and major arguments guiding the project. First, I discuss the social contract as a metaphor for exploring teens' political theories and follow that with a discussion of lay theories in psychology. Next, I discuss concepts that are central to my argument about the development of political theories including mediating institutions and groupways. Mediating institutions are the spaces (schools, community-based groups, etc.) where younger generations spend time, where they have politically relevant experiences including belonging to groups and exercising the rights and responsibilities associated with membership in those groups. "Groupways" is an adaptation from cultural psychology's concept of "self-ways" and emphasizes that teens' political theories depend on the accumulation of opportunities and life experiences that will vary according to the (social class, racial or ethnic, gender) groups to which the teen belongs.

Next I discuss the role of personal and family values in the evolving political identities and views of youth. In the final part of Chapter 1, I briefly summarize research from earlier eras and point to the new framings of "youth" as active political agents in the body of contemporary work on youth civic engagement. This chapter ends with a discussion of the value of considering the perspectives of younger generations as a lens into the future.

Drawing from the comparative data collected from adolescents in six nations, I summarize in Chapter 2 the differences between countries in adolescents' views concerning the role that the state should play in insuring citizens' security by providing entitlement programs as well as differences between countries in adolescents' perceptions of the moral hazards to the formation of good citizens that reliance on such programs implies. Then I draw attention to social class differences within the Central and Eastern European countries in the teens' perceptions of changes in their social orders.

The insights provided by Walzer's essay "What Does It Mean to Be 'an American'?" inspired me to explore in Chapter 3 how teens from different racial or ethnic groups interpret this question. I also ask them to reflect on times when they were aware of their ethnic and cultural roots and times when they were aware of their identities as Americans.

Adolescents' ideas about the personal meaning that democracy holds for them are discussed in Chapter 4. Here I argue that the meaning of democracy held by individual teens is logically consistent with the personal and family values that the teen lives by.

In Chapter 5, I explore youths' understanding of laws meant to protect the public good but that simultaneously restrict individual freedom. Here I argue that between early and late adolescence, there is growth in teens' understanding of the social purpose of laws as well as an increase in their commitments to an individual's right to self-determination.

Then I consider youths' theories about inequality, their explanations for why some people are poor, unemployed, homeless, or wealthy in Chapter 6. As in the chapter on democracy, there is a logical consistency between the teens' personal and family values and the degree to which they hold individuals or society accountable for inequality.

Chapter 7 concerns the developmental underpinnings of social trust, that is, teens' beliefs that people generally are fair and trustworthy. Although social trust tends to decline with age, feelings of student solidarity and pride at school and the teen's report that social responsibility is a core value emphasized at home boost the young person's belief in the trustworthiness of fellow human beings.

The theme of developmental opportunities for building trust is a natural segue to Chapter 8, where I draw from adolescents' reflections on the lessons that they have learned from volunteering in various community-based institutions. When community service is done well, it provides a unique venue for adolescents to get to know fellow citizens whom they would otherwise be unlikely to meet and to reflect on the social compact that binds the teen with these fellow citizens. Throughout the book I draw attention to opportunities in mediating institutions—in families, schools, community-based organizations—whereby young people construct an understanding of the social contract. However, the focus of Chapter 8 is the unique opportunity that community service affords to enable youth to meet fellow citizens who are members of (often stereotyped) groups such as the elderly or the poor. The Coda provides a summary of the lessons learned about political development during adolescence.

I rely heavily on the words of teenagers from different social classes, ethnic and racial groups, genders, and cultures because I believe that these different standpoints provide important perspectives on the terms of the social contract as different teens interpret it. I am grateful to the teens whose voices are summarized in this book for sharing their views.

As a scholar of human development, I am interested in the intersection of the political and the personal. I am also a parent and think that I share with other parents and citizens concerns about the next generation—that is, how our children will navigate an increasingly uncertain landscape and still be guided by the values with which we raised them. I hope that this book will speak to readers in their roles not only as fellow scholars, but as fellow parents and citizens. In addition, I hope that the "youth" lens motivates conversations about the future, the choices we face, and the kind of world our collective choices portend.

In a masterful analysis of the demise of political socialization research in the early 1980s, Timothy E. Cook attributed the loss in vitality of this subdiscipline of political science to "a loss of confidence about what it is we are measuring and then what it all means."[6] It is my hope that the voices of teenagers presented in this book make some strides in addressing the question that Cook asked more than thirty years ago: what it is we are measuring and what it all means.

chapter one

# Adolescents' Theories of the Social Contract

IN 1762, JEAN-JACQUES Rousseau wrote in his treatise on the social contract:

> Each of us puts his person and all his power in common under the supreme direction of the general will, and, in our corporate capacity, we receive each member as an indivisible part of the whole.
>
> At once, in place of the individual personality of each contracting party, this act of association creates a moral and collective body, composed of as many members as the assembly contains votes and receiving from this act its unity, its common identity, its life, and its will. This public person, so formed by the union of all other persons, formerly took the name of *city* and now takes that of Republic or body politic; it is called by its members *State* when passive, *Sovereign* when active, and *Power* when compared with others like itself. Those who are associated in it take collectively the name of *people*, and severally are called *citizens*, and *subjects*, as being under the laws of the State.[1]

The "social contract" refers to the collective decisions of individuals to live together in a society—and in so doing, their decision to give up certain natural rights, elements of their own freedom, in exchange for securing the general welfare and guaranteeing their own liberties. Rousseau claims that by choosing to live together in this way, they create themselves as a people, a citizenry. Because of the title of his treatise, Rousseau is often identified with the theory. But the idea of a social contract has deep historical roots. It appears in the work of Thomas Hobbes and John Locke and, even before them, in the thirteenth century, in *De regimine principum* where Thomas Aquinas writes that government is instituted by the community and may be revoked or limited by the community if it is tyrannical.

Different rationales for a social contract reveal conflicting views about human beings. For Hobbes, governments are necessary to insure that people do not give in to their bestial natures and destroy one another. The price of the common security that governments provide is that individuals must give up their liberty. In Locke's interpretation, individuals (but of course he meant men) retain their liberties. Government, which is instituted by the explicit consent of the governed, exists to insure both justice and individual liberty. Like Thomas Aquinas, Locke held that when governments fail to insure those rights, the citizens have the right, if not the duty, to withdraw their support.[2] I should note that critics of social contract theory argue that those who make the rules of the social order more often garner the benefits, to the disadvantage of racial and ethnic minorities and women.[3] I agree with these criticisms and draw attention throughout the book to adolescents' insights into whether the terms of the social contract apply equally to all groups. However, I believe that the concept of a social contract is a useful one to draw links between the macro level (principles that bind members of a society together) and the micro level (everyday interactions in local institutions and relationships) where the rules of the social order (how to succeed, who is responsible, what are your rights) are enacted and interpreted. Although the structure of a social compact is universal, the specific tenets vary for different societies, that is, the degree to which the government, the market, or individuals are responsible for managing peoples' risks, well-being, and security; the degree to which resources are distributed based on principles of equity, equality, or need; and so on.

Social contracts are not unique to democratic societies. People in every society are bound by some compact, or bargain, in which the citizens agree to live by laws in exchange for the state insuring citizens' security and welfare. As Fyodor Dostoyevsky argues in *The Grand Inquisitor* and Hobbes in

*The Leviathan,* people may opt for greater security at the expense of freedom. But that does not necessarily insure social stability. For example, the changes that took place in 1989 and into the 1990s in the nations of Central and Eastern Europe occurred, in part, because the citizens no longer believed that the state ensured their security and welfare and the price they had paid in freedom had become too great to bear.

The social contract to which people are accustomed (the dominant political and economic arrangements that structure their lives) informs their beliefs about the *right* way for a society to be organized. Societies tend to be stable because people generally believe that the way that their society *is organized* is the way that a society *should be organized*. In other words, societies are not only economic and political systems; they also are thinking systems. Their citizens share a set of ideas and beliefs that explain (even naturalize) the political and economic arrangements of their social order. As psychologist John Jost and his colleagues argue, it takes more mental and emotional effort to question or to challenge the system than to accept it. Thus, consistent with system justification theory, defending the status quo is the default for most people.[4]

So it is not surprising that when adolescents are asked to choose qualities that define a strong democracy, they select qualities consistent with the social contract in their society. According to analyses of the International Association for the Evaluation of Educational Achievement (IEA), when adolescents in the United States were asked to choose from a list the important qualities that define a strong democracy, they chose "protecting human rights" but were less likely than peers in other nations to support a proactive role for government in controlling the economy or distributing income.[5] This view is consistent with the minimal role that the government plays in providing social welfare or oversight of the market in the United States when compared to the more proactive role of government in many other countries. In a similar vein, adolescents from countries that, at the time of the study, had a recent history of socialism and low gross national product (Bulgaria and Russia) were more likely than their peers from free market systems to feel that the government should be responsible for moderating the free market and for overseeing income distribution.[6] In summary, youth tend to endorse as the appropriate, or "correct," role for government the function that the government to which they are accustomed has played in their lives.

In Chapter 2, I compare the views that adolescents from nations with different social contracts hold about the role of the state in providing various safety nets for citizens. Those data were collected when three of the nations (Bulgaria, the Czech Republic, and Hungary) were negotiating economic and political changes from centrally planned to free market economies and from one- to multi-party rule. Differences between these adolescents' views of the social contract and those of their peers from three stable democracies with market economies in place (Australia, United States, and Sweden) reveal that youth tend to endorse those economic and political arrangements to which they are accustomed. As system justification theory suggests, the default for most people is to accept as fair and just the system with which they are familiar.[7]

## SOCIAL CHANGE

In spite of people's tendency to accept the system with which they are familiar, the terms of a nation's social contract are still subject to change. Such changes usually occur over many years; consequently people gradually get used to the new rules. But other changes are more precipitous as is the case when an economy collapses or a government is overthrown. Such historical moments are turning points when the old ways of doing business or organizing life no longer fit the will of the people or the rules of the new order. This was the situation in Central and Eastern Europe after the Soviet Union collapsed in 1989. The implications of such sudden change will vary for different age groups because the settings of development are structured to fit the rules of a particular social contract. The older adolescents, who had been raised under one set of rules and were entering young adulthood under another, had less time than their younger compatriots to adjust to the new contract. Compared to the early adolescents, they had already made choices about the type of secondary school they would attend based on assumptions about how their society worked; specifically, they chose school tracks (vocational, gymnasium) based on assumptions about the jobs that they assumed would "be there" once they completed school. Not surprisingly, they were more cynical and pessimistic about the changes than were their younger compatriots (see Chapter 2).

During periods of stability, we rarely reflect on the terms of the social contract. There is no need to. We act based on assumptions about the effects our actions will have. And those assumptions typically are reinforced. However, during times of rapid change, alternative visions of the way a society could be organized become matters for public discussion. The positions that people take are likely to reflect the implications of the social changes for their group. Adolescents in Central and Eastern Europe had different views about how a society should be organized and about the economic changes that were taking place in their society. These views reflected differences in the youth's social location within the old and new orders: those youth who were more likely to benefit from the shift to a market economy were more likely than their compatriots who stood to lose from the shift to see the new deal, that is, the impending changes in the social contract in a favorable light (see Chapter 2).

Besides the precipitous type of change that occurred in the early 1990s in Central and Eastern Europe, the terms of a nation's social contract also change more gradually over time as different political parties and leaders take office and enact new policies. As the political scientist David Easton pointed out, politics is the "authoritative allocation of values" and different political parties will allocate values through their policy agendas. In the process, they will alter the terms of the social contract that bind citizens with their polity.[8] Political elites are cognizant of the social contract and ways that their proposals shape it. So, for example, President Franklin Delano Roosevelt referred to the "New Deal" to signal the set of policy responses to the Great Depression in the United States that provided a safety net to the unemployed and poor and reined in the financial system to prevent future economic collapses. In the mid-1990s, then Speaker of the House Newt Gingrich again referred to the relationship between policy makers and the people when he vowed that he and fellow Republicans would deliver a "new contract with America." And Dr. Martin Luther King Jr. alluded to a social contract in his classic "I Have a Dream" speech when he noted that the founders of the republic had signed promissory notes in the Constitution and Declaration of Independence but that "America had defaulted on this promissory note insofar as her citizens of color are concerned."

In the United States the terms of the social contract have been undergoing fundamental changes with implications for the safety nets as well as the political theories of younger generations (see Chapters 6 and 7). Over the past three decades, income inequality has grown and the threads of the social safety net are now in tatters. Yet, consistent with system justification theory, few adolescents criticize the system. Instead, by and large they tend to defend the status quo. In fact, youth whose prospects are most imperiled in the new economy are, if anything, more ardent in holding individuals accountable for their economic status. However, these youth also are more likely than their advantaged peers to hear from their parents that they will have to work twice as hard as others if they want to succeed and that they shouldn't depend on society or on other people to help them out.[9] In short, the youth in disadvantaged families learn that the lack of safety nets and the shrinking supply and uncertain nature of remunerative jobs are part of the new deal. The social class lens into adolescents' and their families' interpretations of the social contract suggests that they perceive how the tenets of that contract apply to people "like them" (see Chapter 6).

## NEW IMMIGRANTS AND THE SOCIAL CONTRACT

Historically, waves of immigration have raised thorny debates about the terms of the social contract in the United States—both whether newcomers should enjoy equal protections and benefits from the state and whether they should be expected to relinquish certain cultural customs and identities as part of the "bargain." People on various sides of the current debates have employed the principle of a "social contract" to raise questions about how inclusive our definition of American citizenship and the rights associated with it should be. For example, the Social Contract Press and its journal, *The Social Contract,* raise the specter of massive waves of immigrants threatening the core values and lifestyles of the United States. On the other side of the debate, the phrase also is invoked to raise concerns about a constricted definition of citizenship in the midst of rising income inequality and increasing diversification of the population in the United States.[10]

Adolescents from different ethnic backgrounds and from new immigrant groups define "we the people" from their points of view (see Chapter 3). We see that hyphenated American identities have more salience for some groups than others and that multiple identities and allegiances need not detract from the civic commitments that teens feel for the United States. Furthermore, for teens from ethnic minority backgrounds, awareness of their ethnic identity is positively associated with their civic commitments to contribute to local and national communities and to improve tolerance and understanding between ethnic groups.

## LAY THEORIES

My work on young people's interpretations of the social contract is grounded in the concept of lay, or naïve, theories in social psychology. Just like scientific theories, lay theories are an attempt to explain or to make sense of phenomena. They provide a lens through which we filter our experiences and give them meaning. Lay theories enable us to act: based on assumptions about the outcomes our actions will have, lay theories boost our confidence and reduce uncertainty and the anxiety associated with it.[11]

With respect to political issues, people make sense of the issue by developing a lay theory about its causes and solutions.[12] One example from the program of work, "Adolescents' Theories of the Social Contract," concerns American adolescents' theories about inequality (i.e., their explanations for why some people are poor while others are rich). The teens' explanations are logically consistent with their beliefs about opportunity in their society: those teens who hold individuals accountable for their economic station also are ardent in their commitment to meritocracy and in their belief that there is a level playing field in the United States, that is, that anyone, no matter what their background or challenges, can succeed if they work hard.[13]

Adolescents' political theories are socially mediated: they are generated within a socio-historical context of widespread beliefs in circulation at a particular time in a particular society. Without a long historical lens, it is difficult to illustrate this point. However, I have tried to make this point by capturing the theories of teens in Central and Eastern Europe at a unique moment in their history. Although many studies are conducted at one point in time, it is important to be mindful of the period in which they are conducted. As Nicholas Emler and Julie Dickinson note in their review of the research on children's understanding of social class and social stratification, the lack of historical perspective in studies of societal cognition "leaves developmental psychology vulnerable to mistaking widely held beliefs characteristic of one historical context as if they were universals and rendering invisible the social processes that generated those beliefs."[14]

In line with Emler and Dickinson's observation, I point out how the terms of the social contract and the safety net in the United States have changed over the past three to four decades and how teens' theories about inequality may reflect the new realities of precarious futures that their generation faces (see Chapter 6).[15] I make a similar point about historical context and note that the meaning of terms such as democracy or we the people have evolved over time (see Chapters 3 and 4).

## POLITICS AS A DOMAIN OF EXPERIENCE AND KNOWLEDGE

By focusing on adolescents' lay theories about political phenomena I am treating politics as a domain of experience and knowledge. In contrast to political socialization accounts of the process whereby children become citizens (a largely transmission process passed down from older to younger generations), cognitive approaches emphasize the dynamic interactions and relationships of the young person with other people that are the bases for the systems of meaning that she creates. However, cognitive approaches to the political domain conducted in earlier eras privileged the notion of cognitive structural changes as if they were universals across domains—with relatively little attention to the diverse experiences of children from a wide range of social, racial or ethnic, and cultural backgrounds.

In recent decades, domains of knowledge and children's experiences in those domains have supplanted universal cognitive development theories.[16] I conceive of the political domain as a domain of knowledge, but one that is much broader than the electoral arena or representative government. Politics is not merely the business of government or the president in power, nor can it be reduced to how we vote. Rather, teens' political theories are built up over time as they negotiate power and privilege in their relationships; as they encounter discrimination and wrestle with exclusion; and as they interact with fellow citizens from diverse backgrounds, reflect on the different perspectives they bring to the table, and try to find common ground.

Children are active constructors of meaning in their world but the material with which they work is a fundamental building block for the meanings that they construct. In other words, adolescents' political theories do not materialize out of thin air. Rather, as Lev Vygotsky argues, all of our ideas and beliefs are internalizations of social, collaborative practice.[17] Teenagers' political theories, their concepts of how their society works, and their ideals about how it *should* work are ideas constructed and internalized from their actions with others, a point to which I will return in the discussion of mediating institutions.

## MEDIATING INSTITUTIONS

Compared to their experience in and cognition about the natural world, adolescents' understanding of the government or the economy is indirect—it is interpreted and filtered through the relationships and practices of mediating institutions (schools; extracurricular activities; faith-based, cultural, and other community-based organizations; media). I have referred to these spaces as mini-polities to emphasize the fact that it is through their experiences in these local, proximal contexts that teens formulate ideas about their membership, rights, and obligations as citizens in the broader polity. In other words, adolescents' concepts of themselves as citizens, as members of the body politic, are built up via their memberships in groups and institutions— peer groups, schools, community-based institutions—spaces where they enact what it means to be part of a group, that is, exercise the prerogatives and assume the responsibilities of membership in the group or institution.

The practices of mediating institutions reflect the values and principles of the polity in which those institutions exist. For example, in most societies, schools encourage students' identification with the dominant culture through three common sets of practices: through the ethnocentric biases of curricula, through explicit positive narratives about the nation's history, and through adoption of symbols and practices of civil culture.[18] However, although the processes are similar, the political content that children learn varies in ways that are consistent with national policies. For example, comparisons of middle school students in twenty-seven countries reveal that students are more knowledgeable about international human rights in those countries that mentioned human rights in their reports to United Nations–affiliated groups.[19] In other words, not only do the political positions and policies of nations reflect, borrowing from Easton, an authoritative allocation of values, but those values trickle down into the practices of mediating institutions and become part of the political theories of younger generations.

Political and economic stability is typically maintained across generations because the routine practices of mediating institutions and the rationale for those practices tend to reinforce dominant narratives and beliefs. What do I mean by routine practices? According to cultural psychologists, practices are regular ways of acting that are followed by most of the people in one's group. Because they are both routine and because everyone "like me" does them, these practices tend to reinforce the belief that they are the natural, the proper, and perhaps the *only* way to do things. Concepts and beliefs about the world—about what *does* and what *should* occur—flow from participating with others in these practices.[20]

I argue that the younger generation's participation in the routine practices of mediating settings and the words and symbols that accompany those practices help to stabilize the political and economic system by reinforcing a dominant set of beliefs, (e.g., independent work in school trains character and results in independent success in life; do your own work, don't share your answers with your neighbor; children should be seen and not heard; students have a right to question teachers and other authorities, as long as they are respectful). Through such practices and the rationales that go with them, dominant cultural beliefs gain hegemony and often are adopted even by groups whose interests are marginalized by those views.

It also is through their participation in the routine practices of mediating settings that the dispositions of younger generations develop. Different kinds of societies require different kinds of dispositions in the population. For example, a society might depend on deference to traditional leaders or to a strong sense of collective identity. In a classic article in the *Annual Review of Psychology,* the psychologist John Sullivan and the political scientist John Transue make a case for the importance of certain psychological dispositions as underpinnings for democracy. They argue that laws and institutions alone cannot ensure democratic governance. Rather, democratic societies also rely on large numbers of people who are disposed to participate in civic affairs and who are tolerant of fellow citizens with whom they fundamentally disagree.[21] Democratic dispositions are not inborn; they develop because young people engage in certain kinds of relationships and practices. For example, teens' trust in other people and their willingness to give people they do not know the benefit of the doubt are boosted over time by feelings of solidarity with fellow students at school (see Chapter 7). Teens' commitments to participate in the civic affairs of their society are higher among teens who engage in volunteer work or whose families emphasize social responsibility in their child rearing (see Chapter 8).

## AFFECTIVE FEELINGS FOR THE POLITY

More than four decades ago, theorists of political socialization argued that stable democratic systems depend on "diffuse support" among the people and that in every society, such support for the political system (not for the incumbents in power but for the principles of the system) developed in childhood:

> Every society introduces its members to the political system very early in the life cycle. To the extent that the maturing members absorb and *become attached to the overarching goals of the system and its basic norms and come to approve of its structure of authority as legitimate* [italics added], we can say that they are learning to contribute support to the regime.[22]

Empirical tests of this political socialization thesis were not well grounded in theories of human development. Nonetheless, the notion that diffuse support for a political system develops early in life is compelling. It speaks to the fact that emotional bonds to fellow members of one's community and positive affect for the symbols of a political community precede political knowledge but may well motivate the search for knowledge. Although first graders may have a hard time with the words of the national anthem, singing or humming it in concert with fellow students forms an emotional bond between students, their school, and by extension, their nation. These emotions often precede factual knowledge and inevitably color our understanding of the "facts." As Giyoo Hatano and Keiko Takahashi point out, compared to knowledge of the natural world, societal cognition (knowledge about society, its institutions, laws, cultural and linguistic groups, economic principles, etc.) is "hot" cognition.[23] Our political theories are not objective truths but are entangled with our affections for and allegiance to the groups with which we identify, with our passions about the right way to live, and with our values about what constitutes a just society.

Borrowing the notion of diffuse support from theorists in the political socialization tradition, I expand it to include the emotional attachment and the identification that members of the younger generation develop for local institutions, groups, and fellow citizens. Whereas political socialization theorists studied diffuse support to distal and abstract authorities (the government, the president), I argue that young people experience the power of the state and the principles of the system in proximal settings, that is, in their everyday interactions with fellow citizens and authorities. Furthermore, youths' confidence in the system, their *buy in* to the terms of the social contract in their society, occurs via the accumulated experiences of fair (due) process and responsive interactions with adults (teachers, police, parents) with whom they interact and who have direct power over their lives.

Adolescents who feel that they have been treated fairly by authorities value such treatment and feel that others deserve it as well: they believe that racial minorities deserve fair treatment and are concerned about the injustice of racial exclusion.[24]

Other scholars also have alluded to the significance of youths' relationships with proximate authority figures as the basis for their broader beliefs about political authority. For example, in his critique of the early political socialization research, Timothy Cook argues from a Vygotskian perspective that children's concepts of political authority are constructed from their proximate experiences with adult authorities.[25] Similarly, in his research on efficacy, Albert Bandura contends that "children's beliefs about their capabilities to influence governmental functioning may also be partially generalized from their experiences in trying to influence adults in educational and in other institutional settings with which they must deal."[26]

Theorists in the political socialization tradition held that diffuse support for the political regime developed in children because they observed that authorities of the regime attended to the opinions of their parents. Building on their point, I have argued that children who are members of groups that are marginalized from mainstream power learn that the terms of the social contract may not apply equally to all groups. Research on racial socialization shows that some parents in ethnic minority families report that part of their socialization practices includes preparing their children to deal with discrimination, including discrimination from authorities who wield power over the young person's or their parents' lives (such as teachers, police, or employers; see Chapter 3). At a macro level, political scientists have shown that the interests and needs of more privileged groups in society receive far more attention in policy formation than those of the disadvantaged.[27] Insofar as there are differences in the political attention and respect that different groups enjoy, we can expand our investigation into the mechanisms underlying the development of diffuse support by looking at how different subgroups of young people perceive that authorities pay attention to their parents and others "like them."

## TEENS' EXPERIENCES IN MEDIATING INSTITUTIONS

Families can have an impact on teens' political theories in four ways: through the advantages to civic learning that accrue through parents' education

(Chapters 4 and 6); through family discussions of current events and politics (Chapter 4); through the values that parents emphasize in their child
rearing (Chapters 2, 4, and 6); and through parents' views about the world,
about fellow human beings, and about the trustworthiness of society's institutions (Chapter 7).

Schools figure as a mediating institution in several chapters. For example, we see that adolescents are more likely to appreciate complexities in the
law if they are in classrooms where students are encouraged to discuss issues
and to share different points of view (see Chapter 5). Many adolescents from
different ethnic and immigrant backgrounds report that the civil climate of
inclusion and respect at their school makes them feel that they belong and
that they're a vital part of the community (see Chapter 3). This sense of being part of something larger than oneself also is related to adolescents' social trust (see Chapter 7). In this case, the sense of solidarity with fellow
students that an adolescent feels characterizes the school he or she attends
boosts the teen's trust in his or her fellow human beings. The civil climate
for learning that teachers create (insisting on inclusion and respect for different students' experiences and points of view) also boosts teens' social trust
by enabling more inclusive feelings of student solidarity to thrive.

Adolescents may use their discretionary or out-of-school time in extracurricular activities, community-based organizations, and community service (see Chapter 8). Other mediating institutions such as the media, youth
culture, and religion, also exert important influences on adolescents' political theories.

Mediating institutions are not only settings where the social contract of
a society is reinforced. They also are contexts where younger generations
may question, contest, and reinterpret dominant narratives and, in the process, build the foundations for social change. Teens tell us many ways that
their actions in mediating institutions are contributing to social change.
For example, youth in immigrant families refer to times when they "act
ethnic" and other times when their parents are angry that they are acting
"too American." Others talk about their experiences at school or on a sports
team where they learn that what they do together causes both individuals
and the whole to sink or to swim (see Chapters 3 and 7). Young people provide many different examples of how they changed and their relationships
with others changed through their community service (see Chapter 8). And
finally, different kinds of schools (gymnasium versus vocational) provide dif-

ferent spaces for young people to explore the new rules of their nation's evolving social contracts (see Chapter 2).

## CHANGES IN POLITICAL THEORIES BETWEEN
## EARLY AND LATE ADOLESCENCE

Age differences in teens' political theories should not be construed as evidence for discrete developmental stages. Rather, age is a proxy for the accrual of experience, for increased cognitive capacities in perspective taking and in handling abstractions, and for an enlarged repertoire of ideas that develop over time. Compared to early adolescents, late adolescents typically provide a greater quantity of and more accurate information about political topics.

The increase in knowledge about society does not mean that late adolescents necessarily take different positions on an issue than their younger peers. Rather, they tend to see different perspectives on an issue and realize that political phenomena are complex. Between early and late adolescence, exposure to different ideas increases and the capacity to see issues from different perspectives grows. These age-related changes in capacity and in exposure have implications. As just one example, concerning laws, between early and late adolescence, there is a linear increase in defending an individual's right to self-determination, that is, an individual's right to decide about risks that could pose harm to health. But at the same time, late adolescents are also more aware than their younger peers of the need for the government's enacting of laws to protect the public's health (Chapter 5). Similarly, we see that the older adolescent's theory is more complex, that is, he is more capable of distinguishing and integrating different perspectives on an issue such as inequality (see Chapter 6). These age-related trends are consistent with the increasing ability as adolescents mature to deal with abstract concepts, to reason about social issues, and to understand those issues from different perspectives.[28]

## GROUPWAYS

Cultural psychologists coined the term "selfways" to capture the accumulation of relationships and ways that an individual acts in the world that form the bases for his or her identity. In order to emphasize that collective action is foundational for the civic domain, I have coined the term "groupways" to refer to the accumulation of activities and choices made over time by members of groups, choices shaped in fundamental ways by the position and status of the group in the polity.[29] Adolescents' actions, choices, and the very possibilities they imagine are, borrowing from Erik Erikson, based on "ideological alternatives vitally related to the existing range of alternatives for identity formation."[30] My point is that the *existing range* of alternatives that youth will imagine varies based on the groups to which the young person belongs. An integral part of youth's political formation concerns issues of where people "like me" fit in the social order or how the rules of the social contract (the ties of rights, protections, and obligations between citizens and the state) apply to "our group."

Adolescents' interpretations of the social contract are refracted through lenses of race, ethnicity, social class, gender, nation, and immigrant status. In other words, an important aspect of becoming politically aware is realizing how the terms of the contract apply to different groups—the groups to which the teen belongs or with which she identifies or other groups with whom she comes in contact. For example, I draw attention to the vexed relationship with the American mainstream social contract voiced by several youth from ethnic minority families and to the relationship between adolescents' views about immigrants and how they conceive of their identities as Americans (see Chapter 3). And I explore the potential of community service to enlarge teens' awareness of ways that the terms of the social contract may not apply equally to all groups (see Chapter 8).

## SOCIAL CLASS

Adolescents' social class backgrounds figure regularly in their political theories. At a most basic level, exposure to information about society and politics varies based on the level of education of the teen's parents. For example, discussion of current events is more common in families with higher levels of parental education. In these more advantaged families, teens are more likely to participate in such discussions and to have their opinions on political issues heard. And such discussions increase the likelihood that a teen will understand political topics, for example, what democracy means (Chapter 4). Social class also plays a role in the teens' theories about inequality (Chapter 6): youth from more educated families and those who attend schools in more advantaged communities provide a greater number of explanations for poverty and are more likely to note the structural or systemic bases for inequality. But social class stands in for a host of opportunities for learning. The advantages to learning about society that accrue from growing up in a more privileged family have been noted repeatedly in research on adolescents' understanding of social stratification, occupations, and the economy.[31]

## RACE AND ETHNICITY

In the earlier discussion of the social contract, I noted how new waves of immigrants to a country tend to bring the terms of the social contract into high relief. Their numbers also raise questions about the essence of a people's identity. I take up this point in my discussion of comments by first- or second-generation American adolescents on times that they feel American and times that they feel like a member of their ethnic group (see Chapter 3). Here we also see how ethnic identity is more salient for minority youth who have experienced discrimination. Research on racial socialization is summarized for the political messages I contend are communicated in discussions of discrimination and of inequalities in the social contract. Finally, we see that forms of civic participation vary for teens from different ethnic backgrounds. Specifically, ethnic minority youth are more likely than their majority counterparts to be motivated to improve intergroup understanding and tolerance.

## GENDER

Gender differences have regularly been identified in studies of youth political development. The shorthand conclusion is that males are more interested in politics than are females. However, this finding depends on how the political domain is framed: if politics is framed as a competition between powers, armies, or leaders, men pay more attention. However, if political issues include access to health care, environmental degradation, children's nutrition, or education, women are equally or even more interested.

I have noted gender differences in teens' theories about certain principles of the social contract. A rather consistent picture emerges that females appear to be more attentive to inequities in the terms of the contract and to the implications of eroding safety nets for marginalized groups. In the cross-national comparisons, for example, female teens voice more concerns than do their male compatriots that economic disparities are growing in their country (see Chapter 2). On teens' views of laws meant to protect public health, females are more likely than their male peers to endorse the government's role in enacting laws to protect the public (see Chapter 5). And some gender differences also are revealed in teens' theories of inequality: whereas females tend to attribute unemployment to systemic or structural factors, males are more likely to hold individuals accountable for being unemployed (see Chapter 6).

My identification of gender differences is consistent with patterns identified in research on gender socialization, moral reasoning, and values. According to gender socialization studies, parents are more likely to emphasize values of caring, helping, and attending to others' needs when raising daughters than when raising sons.[32] Research with adults suggests that women, on average, are more likely than men to endorse values of benevolence and universalism, values that transcend self-interest.[33] And, according to a meta-analysis of over one hundred studies, in reasoning about moral issues, consistent,

Figure 1.1. Otro mundo. Banner at the May Day parade, Santiago, Chile, 2009. Translation: "Another world is possible; another economy is possible."

although moderate, gender differences are found, with women more likely than men to use care-oriented, prosocial reasoning to resolve moral issues.[34]

## VALUES AND POLITICS

During his tenure as the first president of the Czech Republic, Vaclav Havel observed that values are an essential foundation for democratic states:

> I am convinced that we will never build a democratic state based on the rule of law if we do not at the same time build a state that is—regardless of how unscientific this may sound to the ears of a political scientist—humane, moral, intellectual and spiritual, and cultural. The best laws and the best-conceived democratic mechanisms will not in themselves guarantee legality or freedom or human rights—anything, in short, for which they were intended—if they are not underpinned by certain human and social values.[35]

Havel's assertion introduces another theme, that is, the relationship between adolescents' personal and family values and their political views. When Easton described politics as the "authoritative allocation of values," he was referring to the competition for and distribution of resources in a society and to disagreements about how to resolve those differences.[36] Values, in this sense, meant tangible things (goods, services) as well as intangibles (beliefs, principles) that most members of a particular society would consider desirable. Politics does raise competing claims on resources as well as contested images of a good society.

In psychology, values also indicate what an individual or a group feels is *desirable*. Values reflect our beliefs about desirable behaviors that transcend specific situations; they guide our selection of behaviors and events, and are ordered by relative importance.[37] In short, our values reveal the principles we believe in and the standards that we use to guide our choices and behaviors. Those standards help us to be true to ourselves, that is, to be the kind of people we want to be. Erikson argued that, for an adolescent, fidelity to his values was the cornerstone of his identity.[38] Our values become so much a part of who we are that they guide our actions automatically—without our having to pause and reflect on where we stand.[39]

Just as values reflect our beliefs about a just life, they also inform our beliefs about a just society. Thus, I argue that values are a basis for our political views and positions on social policies. I draw from Schwartz's universal structure of human values, in particular the higher order dimension that Schwartz calls "self-enhancement versus self-transcendence." In the former (self-enhancement), individuals value goals such as power, status, control over others, achievements that put the self at a competitive advantage over others. In contrast, self-transcendent values include such things as tolerance and concern for the welfare of other human beings whom one may or may not know and for other living things.

Self-enhancing versus self-transcending values, whether emphasized by their families or held by the adolescents themselves, are related to the teens' political theories and civic commitments: those teens who endorse self-transcending values are more likely to refer to the common good, to consider the needs and rights of others, not just themselves, and to be open-minded and inclusive. In the cross-national work, adolescents' civic commitments (serving the nation, helping people in the community, and preserving the earth for future generations) are associated across all countries with the teens' reports that social responsibility and compassion for others are emphasized in their families (see Chapter 2). The values that are most central to an adolescent's identity are concordant with the aspects of democracy she finds most meaningful and with her ideas about what it means to be an American (see Chapters 3 and 4). Likewise, those values that are most important to an adolescent and his family shape the teen's theories about inequality in America (i.e., the degree to which he conceives of inequality as due to individual or systemic factors) (see Chapter 6).

Besides personal and family values, I also explore the core values that have been fundamental to our vision of democracy and to the principles that bind us as Americans. To do so, I draw from the two reigning public philosophies that throughout our nation's history have animated policy debates and defined who we are as Americans. These have sometimes been referred to as "liberal" and "republican" philosophies. The terms do not refer to political parties but do reflect different ideas about liberty. The liberal, or thin, democratic philosophy emphasizes the rights of citizens to live independent lives and to determine *on their own* what they value and how they want to live. In the civic republican, also known as strong democracy vision, citizens obtain and guarantee their liberty by participating in political communities and deliberating with fellow citizens about how, collectively, they want to live.[40] I do not mean to be reductionist or to imply that these interpretations of citizenship are mutually exclusive. In fact, individuals can embrace elements of both. However, I argue, as does Schwartz in his theory of personal values, that there are differences between individuals in the priority, weight, or emphasis placed on these alternative conceptions that figure in the teens' political theories.

## THE EVOLVING FIELD OF YOUTH CIVIC ENGAGEMENT

In the past few decades, the field of youth civic engagement has grown by leaps and bounds, and I have gained valuable insights from the work of fellow travelers in this interdisciplinary field. I also have gained insights from the attention paid in earlier eras to the developmental foundations of political interest and understanding.

Scholarly attention to the developmental precursors of adult civic action has waxed and waned for nearly six decades. Attention tends to increase when there are concerns about generational replacement, specifically whether the younger generation is knowledgeable about politics in general and the democratic process in particular, and is motivated to participate. The focus has at times been on the formation of individuals (their knowledge and dispositions) and at other times on the settings and institutions (particularly families, schools, and community-based organizations) where civic dispositions and skills for action would be nurtured.

Concerns about the political stability of fledgling democracies motivated the political socialization work conducted in the wake of World War II. That work focused on childhood as a critical time when affection for and loyalty to a political system was instantiated and argued for a vertical model in which loyalties were transferred from older to younger generations, thereby insuring system stability. Less attention was paid to the adolescent years, to political change, or to politics as a contestation of views.

A second wave of interest that occurred in the United States in the 1960s was due to the confluence of social movements (civil rights, anti-war, women's) that engaged the hearts and minds of large numbers of the baby-boom generation and also caused them to challenge politics as usual. This work departed from the transmission model of the earlier political socialization work by emphasizing the active decisions of youth in making history. It also pointed to the role of history in shaping generations. According to longitudinal studies begun in those years, the opportunities that historical events presented and choices that young people made predicted their political views and actions well into midlife.[41]

Insofar as late adolescence and young adulthood comprise a time in the life course when political identities take shape, the historical events and ideas circulating when a cohort comes of age help to define the politics of a generation. As one national survey of American adults found, no matter what their age, the events that people nominate as most important in the history of the United States tend to be those events that took place during their late adolescent and early adult years, in other words, in the years when they came of age.[42]

Contemporary research on youth civic engagement has been motivated in part by macro-level political changes. For example, the end of the Cold War and the formation of new democracies in the nations that were formerly members of the Soviet bloc instigated interest in the practices of formative institutions (i.e., community-based organizations such as Scouts which replaced groups such as the Young Pioneers and Komsomol) and their role in developing democratic dispositions and skills in younger generations. Shortly after German reunification, scholars set about comparing how family and school practices and structures in the eastern and western parts of the country affected the formation of the younger generation's attitudes, values, and identities, including their attitudes toward foreigners and new immigrants. Attention to children as active citizens and as agents of their destinies also is the result of the 1989 United Nations Convention on the Rights of the Child and the activities of nongovernmental organizations around educating children about their rights.

In the United States and Western Europe, trends over the past three decades have pointed to declines in conventional forms of political participation such as voting among younger generations. These observations have led to concerns about generational replacement, that is, whether a sufficient number of the younger generation would replace their elders as participants in the body politic.[43] Robert Putnam's landmark publication, *Bowling Alone,* cast a wide net by claiming that there was a broader problem of participation: it wasn't merely that fewer people were voting but that Americans were spending less time in the very community groups and associations where they could get to know fellow members of their communities and the issues that they shared; younger generations contributed disproportionately to those declines.[44]

Interest in youth civic engagement also is a logical extension of new paradigms in the field of youth development that insist on understanding ways that young people are assets rather than risks to their societies. Scholarship on positive youth development, service learning, and youth activism have enlarged the definition of politics beyond representative democracy and voting behavior to include community voluntarism and action. Youth activism, in particular, has revealed the distinctive insights that youth from ethnic minority, economically disadvantaged, and immigrant communities have about the social compact that binds citizens with polities. It also has connected the personal frustrations that many young people feel to larger political issues.

As a form of civic engagement, activism draws from community organizing practices and from what Brazilian educator Paulo Freire terms "praxis," or critical reflection and action. The community psychologist Roderick Watts, and his colleagues, Matt Diemer and Adam Voight, make the case that there should be more attention to the process of critical consciousness in the field of youth civic/political development. Drawing from Freire and other scholars of liberation, they assert that youth who are marginalized by the political system will be more committed to social justice if they participate in practices of critical reflection and collective action through which they gain a sense of collective efficacy.[45]

Youth activism borrows heavily from community organizing, typically involves a critical analysis of social, political, and economic power, often uses participatory action research methods, and emphasizes collective concerns identified by young people to improve their everyday lives. According to Brian Christens and Ben Kirshner, a growing body of work points to the personal benefits to youth (including those labeled "at risk" of dropping out of school) of participating in activist projects. Critical analysis of the system and awareness of systemic inequities does not seem to engender feelings of political disaffection. Rather, it motivates collective action and is positively related to psychosocial well-being and to educational and vocational achievement among ethnic minority and disadvantaged youth.[46]

Taken together, contemporary studies of youth civic engagement point to the following conclusions: First, youth are more likely to be civically active as adults if they have had opportunities in the high school years to work collaboratively with peers and adults on engaging issues and to discuss issues with parents, teachers, and peers. Interest in political issues tends to be generated by controversy, discussion, and the perception that it matters to take a stand.

Second, adolescents' experiences of social incorporation in local institutions and relationships (e.g., through feelings of solidarity with fellow students, identification with community institutions, being respected and heard by adults) is positively related to the likelihood that as adults they will identify with and assume responsibility for improving the quality of life in their communities by engaging in voting and volunteering. These relationships are true for youth from different social class and racial or ethnic backgrounds.

Third, there is a class and racial divide in the civic opportunities available to young people: cumulative disadvantage built up over the kindergarten through twelfth grade (K–12) years depresses civic incorporation and action later in life; events such as school drop out or arrests have an especially negative effect. Studying the early origins of the class and racial divide in adult civic participation led political scientists Sidney Verba, Nancy Burns, and Kay Lehman Schlozman to the conclusion that political participation was "unequal at the starting line."[47]

Fourth, practices of critical analysis, group solidarity, and partnering with adults who respect young people are effective strategies for engaging young people, particularly those from marginalized communities, in civic action.

Fifth, a broader conceptualization of civic engagement is evolving as a wider range of youth groups (new immigrants, racial or ethnic minorities, sexual minority youth, young people from different nations) are included in studies.

## THE "YOUTH" LENS

Why should we pay attention to political development during adolescence? First, adolescence is a time in life when we see gains in the ability to deal with abstract concepts such as democracy, capitalism, or institutional racism. Further, it is during the adolescent years that views about individual rights and responsibilities and the ties that bind individuals with fellow members of their society evolve. Thus, examining adolescents' views provides interesting insights into the development of political theories and the experiences that contribute to those theories.

Second, the period, especially of late adolescence, is a time when one "takes stock"—exploring ideas and possibilities for oneself and directions for one's future. For this reason, Erikson argues that developing an ideology or a set of beliefs and standards to live by is a psychological necessity at this time. Developing beliefs about what constitutes a just world is part of that process. In the course of reflecting on directions for their own lives, young people will inevitably make assessments about their society and where it is headed.

> But in youth the tables of childhood dependence begin slowly to turn: no longer is it merely for the old to teach the young the meaning of life. It is the young who, by their responses and actions, tell the old whether life as represented to them has some vital promise, and it is the young who carry in them the power to confirm those who confirm them, to renew and regenerate, to disavow what is rotten, to reform and rebel.[48]
>
> Adolescence is thus a vital regenerator in the process of social evolution; for youth selectively offers its loyalties and energies to the conservation of that which feels true to them and to the correction or destruction of that which has lost its regenerative significance.[49]

Despite Erikson's claim that social evolution depends on the young telling the old how they feel about the social contract that is their legacy, we rarely ask teenagers to tell us their views. Seldom do we ask how they feel about the economy or race relations or the state of the world. Maybe we think they're too young or disinterested in such topics. Maybe we think that they're too focused on themselves. But the young people whose words appear in this book taught me quite the opposite: they are interested and were even grateful for the chance to reflect on and share their views. Often students would thank our research team for coming to their school, noting that they had never been asked for their ideas or opinions on these topics before. The words of one high school student are illustrative. This particular student had more to say about race relations than she could fit in the allotted space on the survey. So she used the back of the survey to add these final thoughts: "In my book, anyone of any color: black, white, Puerto Rican, etc. any nationality in the world, has a chance to be my friend. I always remember—treat people how you want to be treated because if you act racial or ignoring to someone, you'll only get the same in return. Thank you for coming in and giving us this survey. I learned a lot." Since our research team did nothing but administer the survey that day, apparently she learned a lot simply because the questions posed on the survey caused her to pause and consider where she stood; she learned a lot simply because we invited her to share her views.

Erikson held that each new generation contributes to social change by reinterpreting the social contract that is the legacy of earlier generations. Consequently, examining adolescents' views provides a lens to the future. In any historical period, youth embody the collective anxieties of their society as well as its hopes for the future. More than their elders, youth represent the possibilities of the future rather than the patterns of the past. The voices of the young people in this book reveal the world as they see it and the future as they imagine it. It seems prudent for the rest of us to listen to what they have to say.

chapter two

# Teens from Different Social Orders

DURING THE 1990S, the nations of Central and Eastern Europe (C/E Europe) were negotiating fundamental changes in economic and political structures, from command to market economies and from one- to multi-party rule. In the forty years prior to 1989, when the Soviet empire crumbled, these nations could be described as security societies where risk was socialized, that is where the state secured the basic needs of citizens for such things as health, food, shelter, and employment. In addition, a highly compressed wage structure minimized differences in income, and policies were designed to keep social disparities in check. The Marxist dictum, "from each according to ability, to each according to need" translated into full (mandated) employment and government programs including child care for working parents, health care, retirement insurance, and family leave.

People worked full-time and for their lifetimes in a company or industry. Although they might move up to management, they were unlikely to leave the company. Nor was the industry likely to abandon them. Companies did not have the option to move out of communities in search of cheaper labor. Problems such as unemployment and homelessness did not exist, though the quality of housing was poor and extended families often had to make do, living under one roof. Although income disparities were small, the standard of living of most people was also low, and consumer choices minimal.

For young people the social contracts of these societies could be described as providing clarity and security but at costs in self-determination, freedom, and flexibility. Future occupational paths were delineated by early adolescence when decisions about the type of secondary school a student would attend were made. Partnerships between vocational schools and industries were common, ensuring a smooth transition from school to work. There was scant monetary return to education because jobs that required a college degree typically did not pay more than manual labor jobs. The leisure pursuits of young people were also organized for them. Through membership in the official youth organizations, the Young Pioneers or Komsomol, opportunities were provided, regardless of ability to pay.

Nonetheless, as early as the 1960s and 1970s, alternative youth cultures had developed and were tolerated by those in power as safety valves. These and other more organized forms of dissidence (e.g., challenges to environmental degradation) were contributing factors in the demise of the Soviet bloc. In fact, attention to civil society (the vast array of labor unions, parent associations, environmental and faith-based groups) and its importance as a free space for challenging the state came from the discourse and writings out of C/E Europe in the 1980s and 1990s.

It is tempting to conceive of social change as if it occurs suddenly—at particular moments in history—which typically is the episodic way in which the media portray social change. Consider the way that the Arab Spring of 2011 was framed as if instant messaging and Facebook made it happen, or how the TV cameras at the Berlin Wall in 1989 marked the smashing of the wall as the moment that the Soviet empire crumbled, or even the way that the civil rights movement is treated in many American textbooks as if it just happened because one woman on one day refused to sit in the back of the bus. Clearly, each of these events is symbolic of a much larger historical process. However, what children miss in the episodic interpretation of history is that a coalescence of forces and of people's collective decisions that build over time ultimately makes these events possible. For example, among the factors that contributed to the break up of the Soviet Union were environmental movements in C/E Europe that challenged the state's negligence of natural resources, second economy experiments among families starting small businesses, and the fascination with the West in youth culture.

The 1990s were a decade when the people in these nations were in the throes of what David S. Mason has referred to as an "ideological limbo"— struggling with the historical fact of having rejected the old system, but dealing with the vagaries of a new order, without everyone being clearly committed to its principles.[1] It was at this time that my colleagues and I surveyed adolescents in Bulgaria, the Czech Republic, and Hungary as part of a larger study that also included adolescents from Sweden, Australia, and the United States. A purposive sampling technique was used to obtain groups of adolescents from "high-" and "low-"status backgrounds within each country. In the C/E European nations this was accomplished by sampling in different secondary school types (i.e., vocational, technical, and gymnasium). Between five hundred and one thousand adolescents (twelve to nineteen years old, with a mean age of 15.7 years) from each of the six nations participated. The project was described to students as an international study of young people's opinions about issues in society. Measures were developed after lengthy discussions among the collaborating scholars about the terms of the social contract in their country, the policies that flowed from that contract, and the social changes that were under way.

As the C/E European nations were transitioning to a new set of rules, a psychological and practical shift was imperative. The practices of institutions designed to incorporate younger generations (from school-industry alliances that smoothed the transition from school to work to structured outlets for free time) were no longer a good fit for the rules of the new order that demanded a new set of skills, values, and personalities (that is, more entrepreneurship, self-direction, and personal management of risk). The scaffold of state benefits and institutional guides were disappearing. Suddenly, young people with the help of their families were responsible for finding jobs and for paying for the training and education needed to obtain those jobs.

What did we learn from our study? I begin at the macro-level—comparing how teenagers, accustomed to different types of social contracts, perceived the proper role of the state vis-à-vis its citizens. Adolescents were asked to indicate how strongly they agreed or disagreed that their government had a responsibility to provide citizens with various entitlements (e.g., assistance with housing, health care) or with special protections in times of need (when people lose their jobs) or for certain groups (assistance to those with children). In addition, we asked adolescents their opinions about whether they believed that moral hazards could result from social welfare policies (i.e., how strongly did they agree or disagree that "when the government provides services for free, people tend to get lazy").

Comparisons of adolescents in the security societies (Bulgaria, Czech Republic, Hungary, Sweden) versus those in the opportunity societies (Australia, United States) revealed that, consistent with the principles of their economic order, youth in the security societies endorsed the government's role in providing safety nets for citizens. Compared to their peers in the opportunity societies, youth in the security societies were more likely to endorse the government's role in providing affordable housing, basic services such as health care and legal services free of charge, and compensation for the unemployed until they find new jobs. Overall, youth in the United States were the least likely and Bulgarians were most likely to contend that the state was responsible for providing a safety net of services to citizens, although adolescents' endorsements of specific social entitlements varied based on the policies to which they had become accustomed. For example, in reaction to the country's negative birth rates, Hungarian pro-natalist and family support policies had been in place for decades. Hungarian adolescents were far more likely than any other group to endorse the belief that "Society should give financial help to families who are raising children" and to reject the belief that "If people have children, they should find a way to support them. They shouldn't rely on society for help."

In contrast, youth in the United States and Australia were more likely to endorse beliefs consistent with the individual meritocratic values that shaped social policies in their *opportunity* countries. Not only were these youth less likely to feel that the government or society *should* provide various safety nets for citizens, they also believed that there were moral hazards associated with the government's provision of social entitlements. More than their peers in the security societies, adolescents in Australia and especially in the United States held that "when the government provides services for free, people tend to get lazy and tend to cheat."

Although Sweden was not one of the transitional nations, it is considered *the* prototypical welfare state with a progressive tax system and a broad range of government entitlement programs. Because they are accustomed to the state providing entitlements to citizens, it is not surprising that the Swedish youth were as likely as their peers in the post-communist nations to endorse the government's responsibility for providing such safety nets as unemployment compensation or shelter. Taken together, these contrasts in adolescents' theories about the social contract reinforce the point that societies are not just economic and political systems but also thinking systems. The social contract to which people are accustomed— the political and economic arrangements that have structured their lives and choices—also inform their beliefs about the *right* way for a society to be organized.

## VIEWS OF THE IDEAL SOCIAL CONTRACT AND PERCEPTIONS OF CHANGE IN "THE DEAL"

A second set of items tapped adolescents' views about equality as a characteristics of an ideal society and about inequality in their own society: when asked how much they agreed or disagreed that "It's not right for there to be rich and poor people in society. There should be more equality," teens in the post-communist societies were more likely than those in Australia, Sweden, and especially the United States to endorse this belief. Note that this variable taps an abstract belief about a just society, not a perception about one's own society. To uncover the latter, teens were asked to "think about how things are in your country" and to mark their agreement with the following statements: "Economic changes in our country are making the life of the average person worse, not better" and "A few individuals are getting wealthier but many people are becoming poorer." With the exception of the Czech Republic, youth whose economies were changing rapidly to a market system (Bulgaria, Hungary) were significantly more likely than their peers in Australia, Sweden, and the United States to agree with these items. Note that the material conditions for most people did not change immediately; there were rifts in the social safety net due to economic shock therapy rules introduced at different paces in each of these nations. Perhaps more important to the teens' perceptions that "many people were becoming poorer" was the fact that changes within these nations were front and center in the media and public discourse, and anxieties about what the future might portend were driving perceptions. The loss of psychological moorings—as the old social contract was eroding but no definitive new one was in place—was also obvious in cross-national comparisons of the adolescents' perceptions of social stratification in their country.

As part of the survey, teens were presented with a graphical representation—five diagrams representing social class distributions in different types of societies. These diagrams were adapted from cross-national work by sociologists who argue that people have pictorial representations of social stratification: although they may find it difficult to articulate the class composition of their society, they can visualize how equal or unequal they picture their society to be.[2] The five diagrams with words describing each diagram ranged from an extremely elitist society with a tiny middle class and a great mass of people at the bottom to a top-heavy egalitarian society with more people at the top and only a few near the bottom. Adolescents in Hungary and Bulgaria were far more likely to choose the elitist society diagrams: 71 percent of Hungarians and 79 percent of Bulgarians chose the two most unequal diagrams to indicate "what their society looked like today," whereas 30 percent of Australians, 42 percent of Americans, and only 21 percent of Swedes chose the two most unequal societies as indicative of the composition of their own society. The diagrams had not been included in surveys in the Czech Republic. Very few teens in the transitional nations chose the top-heavy egalitarian diagrams: 14 percent of Hungarians and 13 percent of Bulgarians chose the two types of society at the egalitarian end, whereas 41 percent of Australians, 40 percent of Americans, and 55 percent of Swedes chose the two most egalitarian societies. In the midst of the economic shock therapy that the transitional nations were going through, teens in those nations seemed to feel that the great mass of people were scraping out a living with only a very tiny elite enjoying a measure of financial success.

Although system justification theory holds that people tend to endorse the status quo by default, in times of social change alternative visions of a "good society" circulate in public discourse and provide contrasting images of a social contract from which citizens can choose. As noted, my colleagues and I purposely sampled adolescents in different types of schools in Bulgaria, the Czech Republic, and Hungary. Specifically, we recruited students from three school tracks: gymnasium, or college preparatory; technical; and vocational schools. The levels of parental education reported by adolescents were significantly related to the type of school that the teen attended with students in the gymnasium having the most educated parents.

Additional analyses based on parental education revealed group differences within Bulgaria, the Czech Republic, and Hungary in adolescents' choices about the social contract and social change. Specifically, those whose parents had higher levels of education were less likely than their compatriots whose parents had low levels of education to endorse government provision of social safety nets. Parental education also was inversely related to adolescents' concerns that economic disparities were growing in their country. These differences, which illustrate the concept of "groupways," suggest that adolescents were aware of their group's political interests and the implications of change to a free market system for people "like them."

The concept of groupways also was evident in the gender differences found across countries. Across all six nations, gender was consistently related to adolescents' interpretations of the social contract. Within-country analyses comparing male and female students revealed that females were more likely than males to endorse the protective role of the state in ensuring the welfare of the people and were less concerned about the potential moral hazards of social welfare programs. Females also were more concerned than their male compatriots that disparities between the haves and have-nots had been growing in their country. Although these gender differences were found in all six nations, they were especially marked in the three nations that were grappling with the transition to a market economy.

We also found variation in the teens' perceptions within the three nations in transition (Bulgaria, the Czech Republic, and Hungary) to be related to their ideas about the ideal social contract. That is, there was a logical consistency between the teens' views of the proper relationship between a state and its citizens and their concerns about growing inequality in their country: those youth who endorsed a strong social welfare role for the state in equalizing outcomes between people also were more likely to voice concerns that economic disparities had been increasing in their country. In contrast, their peers who felt that it was natural for a society to have both rich and poor were less worried that disparities were increasing and also believed in the logic of a meritocracy, that is, that anyone could make a good living and get ahead if they worked hard and applied themselves. This latter group was endorsing a belief in the payoff of individual initiative, a belief that was more widely held by youth in the opportunity societies.[3]

## WINNERS AND LOSERS IN THE NEW ORDER

The costs of fundamental changes in the social contract of a society (such as the changes that the citizens of Bulgaria, the Czech Republic, and Hungary were undergoing) are typically not evenly distributed. For example, the impacts of the economic changes were more immediate for the lives of late adolescents as compared to those of early adolescents. Further, in the shift to a market economy, youth with more formal education and English fluency were more able to take advantage of liberalization and better prepared to compete. I turn next to a consideration of group differences within the nations of C/E Europe. These differences suggest that youth are sensitive to ways that the terms of the social contract play out for people "like them." They also point to the agency of people as contributors to social change.

In each of the three C/E European countries, older adolescents (15 years and older) were more cynical about the changes than were their younger (12–14 years, 11 months) compatriots. They felt that economic disparities were increasing and were less likely to believe that anyone willing to work hard could get ahead. The older youth also had more misanthropic views of society in general. Unlike their younger compatriots, they were less likely to say that people in their communities cared about one another or would pull together to help one another.[4]

Comparisons within countries revealed that the youths' views reflected the educational background of their parents and their own evolving social status: youth from the least educated families (who themselves were typically attending vocational schools) were the most favorable toward government supports in housing, health, subsidies to families with children, and unemployment benefits. In contrast, those whose parents were professionals and had the highest levels of education were the least likely to favor these government supports. There were similar contrasts in adolescents' views about the implications of economic liberalization. Those in families with the least education felt that it wasn't right for a society to have rich and poor people; rather, there should be more equality. With respect to growing economic disparities in their own country, teens from the most educated families were the least concerned about a growing gap between the rich and the poor.

Besides these macro-level results, similar patterns were found for youths' views about a mediating institution, the school. It was clear that youth were cognizant of the role that schools had played in their lives and the way that role might be shifting: whereas students attending vocational schools were more likely to say that schools should help students find jobs (as had been the practice during the communist era), those in the gymnasium, or upper tier, were more likely to endorse the role of schools in facilitating the self-determination of individual students. The latter group was more likely to endorse the belief that "encouraging students to disagree with their teachers would help those students to become more independent thinkers" and to believe that "competition in school prepares you for competition in life." At the same time, the youths' views of fellow students in the college prepara-tory schools painted a misanthropic picture: not only did the gymnasium group believe in a competitive ethos at school as good preparation for life, they also felt that most students at their school were untrustworthy, that is, they cared only about their friends and were more inclined to look out for themselves rather than try to help others.[5]

## ROUTINE PRACTICES AND THE SOCIAL CONTRACT

Societies are not only economic and political systems; they also are think-ing systems. Their citizens share a set of ideas and beliefs that explain and justify the political and economic arrangements of their social order. Think-ing systems are not innate but are learned through the formative practices of groups. As cultural psychologists have pointed out, at the most fundamen-tal level, culture and cognition are mutually constitutive. In other words, a culture's traditions and practices shape how people think. Reciprocally, the schema with which people mentally organize their world reinforce those cultural views and traditions. The practices of a cultural group are routine ways of acting that are followed by most of the people in one's group. Because they are both routine and repeated and because everyone "like me" does them, these practices tend to reinforce the belief that they are the natu-ral, proper, perhaps the *only* way to do things. Concepts and beliefs about the world—about *what does and what should occur*—flow from participating with others in these practices.

Across cultures, routine practices may look similar on the surface. The important distinctions in routine practices include the way they are done, by and with whom, how practices are combined, and how they are rational-ized or interpreted. When we engage children in a practice, we assume that they will learn certain habits and will internalize certain values. We rationalize the practice and give meaning to the routine in the way we talk about it.[6]

My colleagues and I used the concept of routine practices to examine the links between chores, allowances or pocket money, and adolescents' concepts about responsibility, wages, and work. Notably, across all of the countries in the study, it was common practice for children to do chores and for parents to give children some pocket money. However, it was not common that the two actions were linked. For example, in Hungary, children might be given spending money but it was unlikely that that pocket money would be tied to doing household chores. In contrast, in the Unites States, the two practices tended to go hand in hand.

With the following set of items, we asked the teens to tell us their views about household chores and allowances. We asked the same set of three items, first, as applied to chores associated with children cleaning up "their own things," and second, as applied to "general household work." Our goal in posing these distinctions was to get at differing concepts about (private and public) responsibility—"for me and my stuff" versus "for the group and things we share in common."

Concerning household chores, teens answered three questions: First, at what age should children be expected to do "general household work like doing dishes, sweeping floors, or other jobs around the house?" Second, what was the major value of having children do household work? (Options were "no value," "helping the parents," "good training for the child in responsibility and self-discipline," and "it helps children learn that they're part of a family and everyone should help the group.") Third, should children earn an allowance or pocket money for doing such household work? (Options were "yes, they should be paid for *each job* they do"; "yes, they should be paid an allowance as a *general payment* for the work they do"; "sometimes, they should be paid only for extra or big jobs"; and "no, they should not be paid for the jobs they do.")

Across countries, teens felt that children should do household chores and that they should begin to do those chores in the early elementary years. However, the rationale for this practice varied according to the dominant principles of economic organization in the societies: youth from nations with a strong social welfare contract (Bulgaria, the Czech Republic, Hungary, and Sweden) felt that doing chores taught children responsibility for the group or what we might call public or social responsibility, that is, the major value for doing chores was that it helped children learn that they're part of a family and that everyone should help the group. In contrast, the major value for doing chores chosen by teens in the United States and Australia was that it was good training for the child in self-discipline and individual responsibility.

Besides differences between nations in the major value nominated by teens, there also were differences in their opinions about whether children should earn an allowance for doing household work. It was only in Australia and the United States that the teens felt that kids should be paid for doing chores. Ten percent of the American youth actually endorsed a piece work principle—that is, they contended that children should be paid an allowance according to *each* job or task that they did at home.[7] In our view this option suggested that the routine practice of linking chores with an allowance was naturalizing the principles of wage work in the minds of those youth. In summary, although doing household work and having pocket money or an allowance were common socialization practices across countries, the particular ways in which these practices were combined and the lessons that were emphasized differed in ways that were consistent with the different principles of the social contracts of the nations.

## THE ROLE OF VALUES IN ADOLESCENTS' THEORIES ABOUT THE SOCIAL CONTRACT

Although our team was interested in comparisons between countries, we also adopted what the sociologist, Melvin Kohn, has referred to as a "nation as context" approach. Thus we looked for similar patterns across nations—in the correlates of adolescents' personal and family values and in the correlates of their engagement in community-based youth groups.[8] I have conceptualized values both as personal standards for behavior and as reflective of youths' views about a just world.

In the cross-national study, we asked adolescents to report on a set of items that tapped the extent to which they held altruistic or self-transcending values (i.e., were willing to sacrifice certain comforts for a higher good such as preserving the earth for future generations) and the extent to which their families emphasized compassion and social responsibility for needy others as principles that the adolescent should live by. Values were consistently related to the adolescent's endorsement of the government's role in providing services and safety nets to citizens, that is, providing affordable housing, basic services such as health care and legal advice, unemployment compensation, and supports to families raising children. Altruism was a significant predictor in all countries, and the family's emphasis on social responsibility was significant in five countries, suggesting a connection between the adolescent's personal willingness to share resources with those in need and his view that the state had a similar obligation. In other words, personal values and political views were consistently and significantly correlated across national contexts. It is as if the teen's personal beliefs about desirable goals or end states, the standards she used to determine how she should live her own life also are the desirable standards by which she believes the social contract of her society should be structured.

Values were not only a standard that informed teens' views about the social contract and the state's role in providing safety nets. Across all of the societies in the study, the family value of social responsibility (the emphasis that families placed on attending to the needs of others and responding especially to the less fortunate) was the most consistent predictor of the importance that the teens attached to civic or public interest goals. The teens were asked, "When you think about your life and your future, how important is it to you personally (a) to contribute to your country and (b) to do something to improve your society?" The most robust result in the study was the consistent and significant effect that a family ethic of social responsibility had on adolescents' civic commitments, although not on the importance that adolescents attached to engaging in electoral politics. Using Kohn's nation as context approach and including variables such as parental education, adolescent's age, and student solidarity at school in the models, this family value was the most consistent and significant predictor across countries of teens' civic commitments.

In addition, in five nations, feelings of peer solidarity with other students at school were positively and significantly related to an adolescent's desire to engage in public service, that is, to the teen's commitments to serve his community and society later in life.[9] The measure of peer solidarity taps the teen's identification with fellow students, her sense that she is part of the group, and her positive perception of fellow students, that is, that they care about one another. It is interesting that this positive affective regard for fellow students and the sense of membership in and identification with the student body were positively associated with broader civic commitments to support one's community and society but not with commitments to electoral politics. I will take up the role that such feelings of solidarity play in the development of social trust or beliefs that people generally are fair and trustworthy (see Chapter 7). The general point is that in the mini-polity of the school, students' experiences of bonding with fellow student-citizens are a foundation for their identification with and loyalty to the broader polity.

## CORRELATES OF TEENS' ENGAGEMENT IN COMMUNITY-BASED GROUPS

Community service or volunteer work is a common practice in some but not all nations. Based on the reports of the teens in our study, volunteering was lowest among Swedes (20 percent) and highest among Hungarians (60 percent). However, across all nations, family values were consistently and significantly related to the teen's participation in volunteer work: in each country, teens who volunteered were more likely than their nonvolunteering compatriots to report that their families emphasized compassion and social responsibility for others as values to live by. This association between values and volunteer work provides some evidence that teens' behaviors were concordant with their values. We can conclude that, in each country, adolescents practiced (by volunteering) what their families preached (social responsibility).

Like community service, there also were differences across countries in the structured opportunities that youth had for their free time. The dearth of youth organizations was especially acute in the C/E European nations: with the demise of the Young Pioneer and Komsomol organizations that had been common outlets for youth during the communist era, fledgling chapters of groups like Scouts or 4-H had begun, but these new organizations had not yet taken hold. According to our study, the youth in the three nations in transition were involved in fewer organizations when compared to their peers in the other countries in the study.

However, when we again employed Kohn's nation as context approach, we found consistent relationships between youths' participation in organizations and other civic outcomes: across countries, those youth who were engaged in community-based youth groups were more likely than their compatriots who were not involved in such groups to be interested in current events and to report a general sense of social trust in fellow members of their local communities. Such nonformal youth groups are important for building democracy, especially in fledgling democracies. It is in the routine practices of these settings of civil society where the dispositions of younger generations—to cooperate, to trust, and to work with fellow citizens—are nurtured. Civil society as a free space for dissident voices had played a role in the challenges to the old order in C/E Europe that ultimately brought an end to that order. After 1989, civil society also provided a space for the reinvention of mediating institutions—schools and community-based organizations to name just two—where the dispositions of younger generations could be shaped.

The study reported in this chapter was conducted at one historical moment, a pivotal one for the youth in the nations of C/E Europe. For those youth in particular, the study provides a snapshot of teens' views of alternative social contracts at a juncture when stark contrasts were before them. Since that time, the liberal market and democratic political practices have replaced the old systems. Youth growing up today have no firsthand experience of the old social order, although their parents would remember it. Yet, as late as 2001, youth in the nations of C/E Europe continued to express ambivalence about the economic changes that had transformed their lives. In national surveys, half preferred a centrally planned to a market economy, and the other half endorsed exactly the opposite.[10]

## CONTEMPORARY LIFE

Education is now coupled with the demands of the market in these nations. Whereas educational attainment had little connection to earnings in the old system, it is the determinant of success in the new. In the vernacular of economists, there are now "returns to education" in the form of better paying jobs. Not only do youth see the inextricable links between educational attainment and market payoffs, many also are accumulating credits and qualifications as the only rational strategy.[11]

Today young people are less likely to work in industry and more likely to be employed in consumer services, tourism, small business enterprises, or as migrant labor in agriculture. Many are cobbling together part-time and seasonal employment, and most have to be entrepreneurial. Some, especially young men, even do business by selling small quantities of cigarettes, alcohol, or clothing. Losing the supports of state benefits exacted a deeper cost on working-class youth in these nations. They shouldered the brunt of unemployment during the transitional years as the seamless connection between vocational schools and industries dissolved. This group was more likely to lose their moorings and feel anxious about the future. For example, in a national study of Hungarian youth, those from working-class backgrounds were more likely than their middle-class peers to feel insecure about their futures and concerned about finding their way in the world.[12]

Today, youth in C/E Europe can expect to spend considerable lengths of time in insecure and marginal employment. And most seem to expect that the shouldering of those risks by individuals and their families is a fait accompli. Surveys conducted across Europe indicate that with the exception of the Nordic countries, young adults considering how to combine paid work with family life expect neither government, nor employers, nor trade unions to provide the necessary measures and benefits. Instead, they expect to rely on their families or their own ingenuity and resources.[13]

As a snapshot of a unique generation at a pivotal turning point in the transformation of their economic and political systems, the data discussed in this chapter point to some conclusions we can draw about adolescents' theories of the social contract. On average, adolescents' normative beliefs about the relationships between states, citizens, and institutions reflect the arrangements of the social contract to which they are accustomed. Nonetheless, within any society there is variation in political opinion. The analyses within the C/E European nations indicated that when faced with opposing social contracts, youth preferred the terms that were more beneficial for people "like them." The results suggest that in these presumably classless societies, an emerging class consciousness was developing for youth in the higher tier schools who ultimately would become members of the professional middle class. But the results also point to the role of mediating institutions (families, schools, community-based organizations) as free spaces—where people make their own choices about the values they hold dear, the practices they embrace, and the kind of society and world they want to inhabit.

chapter three

# We the People

We the People of the United States, in Order to form a more perfect Union, establish Justice, insure domestic Tranquility, provide for the common defence, promote the general Welfare, and secure the Blessings of Liberty to ourselves and our Posterity, do ordain and establish this Constitution for the United States of America.

A FEW YEARS AGO, I reviewed the Preamble to the Constitution of the United States, thanks to my grandson, Stevie, who with his first-grade classmates put the words to music for the school's spring concert. Stevie wasn't all that sure who "we the people" were or what the words meant but that didn't matter. The meaning was in the practice—of performing together—reciting the words, enacting "we the people" at a public event where teachers and parents assembled and celebrated the younger members of their community.[1] It was in that collective public act that the first graders knew, in their hearts, what it felt like to be included in the political identity of "we the people." It was through that practice that they developed feelings of diffuse support for the polity, although they could not put the meaning into words. The first graders were filled with a sense of pride in their collective achievement of performing in public. They felt what it was like to be part of a public, to represent their school, to be applauded by fellow citizens, to belong to a community that was larger than themselves and their individual families (Figure 3.1).

Who is this "we the people" that first graders celebrate in song? What are the ties that bind us, the ideals that unite us as Americans, and in what ways do new generations of Americans contribute to our collective identity? Michael Walzer addresses this question in his essay "What It Means to Be an American":

> There is no country called America. We live in the *United States of America,* and we have appropriated the adjective "American" even though we can claim no exclusive title to it. . . . our sense of ourselves is not captured by the mere fact of our union, however important that is. . . .
>
> The United States isn't a homeland but rather a country of immigrants who have roots elsewhere. The people are American only by virtue of having come together. And whatever identity they had before becoming Americans, they retain (or, better, they are free to retain) afterward.[2]

Following Walzer's allusion to our hyphenated American identities, I asked adolescents to share their ideas about who "we, the American people," are.

Figure 3.1. Viva la escuela publica. Wall mural in a barrio in Buenos Aires, Argentina. Translation: "Long live public education."

This chapter is organized into two parts based on the teens' responses to the following questions that were posed to them:

- Besides being a citizen of the United States, how would you describe what it means to be an American?
- Sometimes a person identifies strongly with their ancestral or cultural group. Other times a person may identify more with being an American. Can you think of times when you felt very much like a member of your ancestral group? How about times when you felt very much like an American?

The aim of the study was to understand how teens from different ethnic backgrounds as well as those whose parents or grandparents were recent immigrants to the United States experienced their identities as Americans and as members of different ethnic groups. As Walzer suggests, I wanted to know what, in their minds, captures the "sense of ourselves."

The chapter is based on the responses of an ethnically and socioeconomically diverse sample of eleven- to eighteen-year-olds who identified as African-, Latino-, Arab-, or European-Americans. Families of the Latino- and Arab-Americans were more likely to be recent immigrants to the United States.

Adolescents could give multiple responses to the two questions; these were coded into discrete categories that preserved as much detail as possible. Here I summarize their first and second responses, which I have organized by references to three broad thematic categories: (1) liberalism and individual rights, (2) civic republicanism and the common good, and (3) patriotism and loyalty. These three categories captured the majority of the responses that were assigned to discrete categories.[3]

The first two categories are based on two public philosophies that have shaped our identities as Americans. Each of these philosophies provides a different perspective on liberty and how it is guaranteed. In the liberal philosophy, also known as a thin version of democracy, individuals are conceived as bearers of rights with minimal emphasis on their civic obligations. In contrast, the republican tradition, also known as a strong version of democracy, goes beyond the simple recognition of others' rights and emphasizes that individual liberty can only be ensured by people's active participation as the sovereign authority, by deliberating together to determine the goals of their community and the terms of the social contract that binds them.[4] I used the third category largely because so many responses reflected the theme of patriotism or loyalty. Responses in this category do not refer to a core philosophy or principle but rather to a general sense that to be an American, one should be loyal to the nation, its principles, and policies.

To complement the adolescents' views, I have interspersed reflections from the *Atlantic Monthly's* 150th anniversary edition (November 2007). According to James Russell Lowell, *Atlantic's* founding editor, the mission of that periodical in 1857 was to "honestly endeavor to be the exponent of what its conductors believe to be the American idea" (p. 13). For this anniversary issue, the editors asked poets, novelists, public servants, and scholars to comment on the future of the American idea. My excerpts illustrate that the question that was posed to the teens about our American identity has been at the heart of our national conversation from the time that the nation was founded and has been a subject of debate and soul searching since then. They also go to the heart of our experiment in democracy and the need to regularly reinvent what we mean by the phrase, "we the people," and what principles we believe hold us together as a people. Finally, they illustrate my fundamental point that teens' theories about what it means to be an American is a political idea—because it reflects their views of the polity of which they are members—and that political ideas and identities are already forming in the teen years. As we shall see, there is considerable overlap between the teens' insights and those of poets, pundits, and public servants.

## WHAT IT MEANS TO BE AN AMERICAN: FREEDOM, EQUALITY, PATRIOTISM

### Individual Freedom and Rights

Freedom of the individual was the most common theme in the adolescents' views about what it means to be an American; 30 percent of the first responses used "freedom."[5] Insofar as only 7 percent of the second responses invoked "freedom," this concept may be the first one that comes to mind. However, since many youth combined references to individual freedom with other views about American identity, the meaning of freedom will vary for different people. In general, references to freedom reflected a liberal interpretation insofar as few teens alluded to a moral community or even to the existence of "others" as fellow members of their world. The image, for the most part, was one of a self-determining individual, unhampered by others' opinions or views.

Several young people juxtaposed the freedom that we enjoy as Americans with its lack in other countries. For them, the freedom that we enjoyed as Americans set us apart from other nations where self-expression was limited: "FREEDOM! Look at what the other countries have to put up with. They're expected to be seen & not heard" or "living with freedoms that most in the world will never experience, can only dream of." A Latina specified freedom "from persecution," whereas an Arab-American said "from prejudice"; a co-ethnic of the latter said that Americans had "more freedom than people in my culture." Consistent with the interpretations in our founding documents, a sixteen-year-old female of European descent cited protection of individual liberties from government intrusion in her response: "Free to do your own thing, without government, army, etc. getting in your way."

References to individual opportunity also were coded in this general category. Although a less common theme, opportunities to determine one's fate were mentioned, primarily by youth in recent immigrant families, and contrasted with its absence in other countries: "It means that I have a lot of opportunity—especially as a female, that a lot of other people don't have in other countries" and "being an American means you have a lot of privileges [sic] and opportunities without someone holding you back (communist countries)." Her allusion to communist countries suggests that, for some, our sense of ourselves is in part shaped by beliefs about "who we are not," that is, defining our identity in contrast to those images that we have come to believe about other nations, cultures, and political systems.

References to civil liberties (freedom of speech, religion) guaranteed in our founding documents comprised 6 percent of the first and 12 percent of the second responses. For this group, "to be an American" meant "to have freedom, total freedom as defined by the Bill of Rights" and "to have the freedom of speech, freedom of religion, and the freedom to do anything." References to these liberties were more common as second responses rather than as first responses (i.e., the first thing that came to mind), which may suggest that they are not the most available idea. Instead, identifying civil liberties as the core of our identity as Americans requires more time and consideration.

Some teens described an individual's freedom as if it were boundless, that is, the freedom to act as you please: "to be free to make your own decision any place you go," "Freedom, you are your own person, do what you want," and "to have the right to do or say anything you please." Others alluded to constraints: "having the freedom to do as you please with some restrictions," "having the freedom to do as I please *as long as I am not breaking any law* [italics added]," and "being true to yourself *without hurting anyone in the process* [italics added]." Only one teen used responsibility and rights in the same sentence, although his statement lacks specificity: "I think it means having the rights and responsibilities to act freely."

Several ethnic minority youth claimed the freedom to embrace and celebrate their cultural roots. One Latino said, "being you, your culture, being American means nothing to me if I can't have my identity." Clearly his identity had a lot to do with his unique cultural roots. Others wanted to break out from their culture and its customs: they distinguished the constraints that they felt from their family's cultural traditions with the freedoms they enjoyed as Americans. For example, an Arab-American female referred to the autonomy her parents granted as a sign that they had become American: "My family isn't strict on what I do, or what I where [sic] so my family is referred to as 'Americanized.'" For many youth from new immigrant families, acting American created tension in their families insofar as older generations felt that it implied a rejection of family and traditional culture. The tensions felt in their hyphenated identities made these new immigrants cognizant of the choices inherent in American identity. Each expressed the view that it was up to the individual to determine who she wanted to be, what she believed, and how she behaved. As captured in this statement by an eighteen-year-old Arab-American male, "there is no average American, we are all different . . . that is what America is all about."

The foregrounding of the individual in these adolescents' views of what it means to be an American is echoed in John Updike's *Atlantic Monthly* essay entitled "The Individual":

> The American idea, as I understand it, is to trust people to know their own minds and to act in their own enlightened self-interest, with a necessary

respect for others. . . . Empowerment of the individual was the idea in 1857, and after a century and a half of travail and misadventure among human societies, there is not a better idea left standing.[6]

Like Updike, many young people embraced the liberal tradition, acclaiming the individual's right to explore and to develop him/herself in the fashion s/he freely chose. That freedom was defended even if it resulted in poor decisions; as one female stated, "To be American means to make your own choices *even though sometimes they may be bad* [italics added]." The liberal ideal of an individual unfettered by responsibilities or loyalties to anyone else was captured in a sixteen-year-old, white male's statement. For him, to be American meant "to get up in the morning and know that you are free to make choices—you can staff a proprietorship and give no money to the gov (except taxes), marry who you want, say what you want, & do what you please!" Aside from this rare reference to taxes, these adolescents' concepts of liberty were not balanced with any references to the obligations of citizenship.

Updike's individual who knows his own mind and acts in enlightened self-interest figured prominently in several teens' beliefs that the essence of being an American inhered in following your dreams, defining your own destiny without inviting others' input: "I believe you should try to be your best, but *for yourself*" or "Being American means *you and you only can make your future* [italics added]." For others, this ardent commitment to the individual alone determining his aspirations, this penchant to "know their own minds," as Updike put it, implied a responsibility for the individual to achieve the goals that he set for himself. One European-American male said, "Being Americans allows us to not only dream but to go after those dreams," and his African-American classmate that "You have certain guaranteed rights. Having freedom to learn and grow etc."

If an individual is truly free, she alone bears responsibility for setting goals and for making the best of her opportunities. In these teens' words, "I think it means to be in a country where the only limit of where your [*sic*] gonna go is yourself" and "that there are jobs and opportunities for everyone if they look hard."

For these youth, there was an aspirational quality to American identity. The sky is the limit, the frontier is endless *unless* a person constrains his imagination or fails to *look hard* for the jobs and opportunities that are out there. (For more on this theme of the self-made individual, see Chapter 6.)

A few young people contrasted their prototype of the self-reliant, hard-working American with their stereotype of the citizen with the character flaw of dependence: "An American is Someone who pays taxes, has a job, and is not on welfare." To be American meant "not being lazy, working for yourself, and *not relying on others* [italics added]." To turn to others for advice and to have needs that you cannot satisfy yourself were identified by these teens as signs of personal weakness that were distinctly un-American.

These adolescents' visions of liberty are a good fit with the liberal framework in which individuals are conceived as independent, free selves who are capable of choosing their own values and ends. Government and fellow citizens, for that matter, should mind their own business. Indeed, engaging in some of the practices consistent with a civic republican philosophy, such as deliberating with fellow citizens or considering others' judgments as better than one's own, could be interpreted as character flaws.

## Civic Republicanism and the Common Good

Not many of the adolescents' responses were an easy fit for the civic republican/common good category. Perhaps this finding is an indication that teens are not often exposed to these themes about American identity. Scholars have observed that over the past forty years, the civic republican tradition has been drowned out in public discourse by the liberal tradition's emphasis on individual rights. Further, content analyses of civic textbooks used in America's secondary schools show that students are far more likely to read and to hear about citizens' rights and far less likely to learn about citizens' responsibilities.[7]

My decision was to code *any* reference to equality, tolerance, respect for others, or standing up for a principle in the interests of the common good in an adolescent's statement *even if* the respondent also mentioned a liberal philosophical interpretation.[8] For example, the following references to individual freedom and equality were coded in the civic republican/common good category: "Being American means being able to be free to do what I want within the law. It means *living as an equal*" or "to be free to have the liberty to walk out your door and know there are opportunities out there for you. *Liberty and justice for all.*" Likewise, the following emphasis on English fluency combined with a commitment to equality was coded in the same category: "to be American, you should at least be able to speak English, but other than that, have hopes & dreams, *to want equality for all people* [italics added, underlining was in original]." These statements were coded in the civic republican category because the adolescent made at least one allusion either to fellow members of society, to equal opportunity, or to respect for the rights of other people. Based on this all-inclusive coding strategy, just over 22 percent of the first and 38 percent of the second discretely coded responses were collapsed into the civic republican/common good category.

References to civic republican themes were more often the second than the first or top-of-the-head response, which may suggest that it takes a bit more time, reflection, and thought for teens to remember these aspects of our identities as Americans. By forming the civic republican category based on these broad parameters, I hope to show that adolescents, for whom any aspect of the common good is a feature of American identity, have significantly different views toward immigrants compared to their peers who are less cognizant of or who may have rejected the civic republican philosophy.

References to equality and civil rights accounted for 3 percent of the first and 5.8 percent of the second responses: "to be *created equal. And to be given the same oppertunities* [sic] *as everyone else* (caps in original)"; "that everyone should have equal rights"; "freedom (rights for *all* people, male and female, gay and straight)"; "to have a fair, just, & equaled [sic] life"; and "I believe that to be an American you must be treated equally among others, don't be stereotypes, and no looked down upon."

There were fewer references to tolerance and respect for the different customs, beliefs, and opinions of others, but there were some such as "An American is a member of a group that includes many different people, ideas, cultures, & beliefs." To be American means "to work with other people and not exclude them"; "accepting all people for who they are not how they look"; "be willing to learn from everyone . . . open mindedness to a great variety of cultures/ethnic groups"; and "trying to be tolerant and understanding of others, and loving our diversity."

The idea of America, according to Walzer, is the incorporation of oneness and manyness in a "new order" that celebrates cultural pluralism. Approximately 3.7 percent of the first and 4.8 percent of the second responses to "what it means to be an American" referred to cultural pluralism. Most of these simply mentioned our cultural diversity, but some also noted that tolerance and respect for that cultural plurality is what defines us as Americans.

"Togetherness. In other countries, it's almost all the same religion. But America is one big mixed—pot of religions"; "I think an American is someone made up of different races"; "Being aware that we are all very different people of different descents living in the same country"; "To be a part of this culturally diverse mess we live in"; "It means all different races are combined to form a new one—the American race." Some teens referred to the hyphenated character of our collective identity: "Being proud of where you came from and where you live now," or as one Latino, echoing Walzer, put it, "America is every one that comes into it."

Based on the fact that a civic republican philosophy implies a sense of belonging to a larger public, a concern for the whole, a moral bond with the community whose fate is at stake, and a formative politics in which people deliberate together,[9] any reference to social responsibility (1.8 percent of first and 4.1 percent of second responses) or to working to improve society (3.2 percent of first and 3.4 percent of second responses) were coded in this category as reflecting commitments to the common good. As Michael J. Sandel describes the republican tradition, liberty depends on self-government and self-government depends on the members of a political community who identify with the role of citizen and acknowledge the obligations that citizenship entails. These youth felt that being American implied such obligations: "to care about people & try to help them"; "helping other countries even when they see us as a snobby country"; and "caring about our country and trying to make a difference."

When people venture out and "try to make a difference," that is, when they get their hands messy by digging into community affairs, they often find that something needs to change. Thus I also included in the civic republican category adolescents' observations that to be American meant to stand up for a principle, even when taking a stand challenged the status quo: "Standing up for what you feel is right; obeying the laws, finding your own way within the guidelines of your society or working to change those guidelines if they don't work"; "Have pride in yourself and in everyone around you. Don't be afraid to speak your mind; to be involved with the things around you if you can change something bad, do it." I felt that such statements belonged in this category because they recognized that there were others "around you," that there was a society with guidelines, that people were responsible for determining the guidelines, and that an individual's opinion was one among many. These phrases suggest that the teens are aware that there are divergent points of view besides those of the individual and also that in a democracy individuals have responsibilities as citizens to wrangle with others in shared governance.

The proclivity to challenge the status quo, reflected in the views of these youth, is what Azar Nafisi, author of the best seller, *Reading Lolita in Tehran,* considers "the American Idea." She calls that idea "a slight subversion, an instinctive urge to do the right thing, which, in the eyes of the 'correct' world, might seem to be exactly the wrong thing. The idea that I want to believe America was founded on also depended on challenging the world as it is and, by standing up to civilized society, redefining it."[10]

## Patriotism and Loyalty

References to loyalty and patriotism were the second highest discrete category after "freedom" in the teens' responses to what it means to be an American. They accounted for nearly 22 percent of the first and 15 percent of the second discretely coded responses.[11] These included references to feeling a sense of pride and faith in the nation and its history: "To have pride in America, and to believe in what the country thinks is right"; "having pride in the country and faith in it as well"; "It means take pride in your country and be proud to be a free individual."

Patriotism should not be equated with nationalism. According to social psychologists, items tapping each of these sentiments factor into two separate scales: whereas patriotism captures feelings of pride, emotional attachment, and respect for the nation and its symbols, nationalist sentiments reflect beliefs that one's nation is better to or superior over others.[12] For the most part, the teens' responses fit in the patriotism grouping. Very few were nationalistic in tone, for example references to being part of the "greatest," "most powerful," or "strongest" nation or "the best country on earth where truth and liberty reign supreme." National chauvinism also was obvious in a few responses indicating that American identity meant "to be free and #1" or "following the American superior way of life." As Americans, one youth asserted, we had "the responsibility to lead the world as the last super power."

The patriotism/loyalty category included references to our history as a nation such as "to be able to understand and appreciate what our forefathers went through to get our freedom" as well as references to those who died in the service of the nation. "Being an American is a blessing and privilege. If it weren't for those who died for America it wouldn't be the same." Finally, there were many references to loyalty to the nation, its symbols, and principles with some youth asserting that it was un-American and unpatriotic to challenge national policy: "to be American I think that you must love & respect your country in all means"; "that you stand tall and not be ashamed in being a American"; "to support the country (even) if you don't agree with it"; or "when things are not going well"; and "to love and respect our country, not destroy it and become a leach [sic]."

Compared to the few challenges to the status quo coded in the civic republican category (i.e., standing for your beliefs, even when they challenge mainstream views), these responses coded in this category reflected the view that to be an American meant *not* to raise any challenges to the status quo, not even to harbor a healthy skepticism about policies or laws in place. For these youth, being American means that one has to defend the nation 'as it is.' This differs radically from Nafisi's more aspirational definition, that is, that the idea America was founded on was "challenging the world as it is." One has to wonder whether the Civil Rights Movement that overturned the laws of segregation, a movement that challenged the world as it was, would have seemed un-American in the minds of these adolescents.

In contrast to this view that being American implied a lack of dissent, in *Civility and Civic Virtue*, Michael Walzer writes that wrangling with one another over what is in our common interest is implied in our American identity, that out of *E pluribus unum* no oneness can come but that "there is a kind of sharing that is possible even with conflict and perhaps only with it. . . . Citizens learn to ask, in addition to their private questions, what the common good really is."[13]

In another essay, Walzer observes that "the conflict between the one and the many is a pervasive feature of American life. Those Americans who attach great value to the oneness of citizenship and the centrality of political allegiance must seek to constrain the influence of cultural manyness; those who value the many must disparage the one."[14] Some teens did feel that the *one* (white and Anglo) was privileged over the many: references to being born within the United States or to speaking English accounted for nearly 5 percent of the first and 3 percent of the second responses to what it means to be American. These were *not* coded in the loyalty/patriotism category but are noted here simply to show that some teens were committed to the one identity (and typically an Anglo and white one) over the many. Such *ascriptive Americanism* persists in definitions of who is an American, despite the fact that citizenship in the United States is based on being law-abiding and supportive of the Constitution regardless of one's particular race, gender, religion, ethnicity or original nationality, culture, or language.[15]

For these teens, to be American meant "to be born in America" or "to live in America and speak English. Cause some Whites don't know Spanish" or "To have ancestors who came from England, nowhere else." Notably, it was not only youth from European ancestry who endorsed these views. For example, an African-American male said, "knowing how to speak English, doing things the 'American' way." Similarly, several teens whose families were relatively recent immigrants to the United States felt that it was important to be born and raised in the United States in order to be American. An Arab-American male felt that to be an American, "you have to have roots

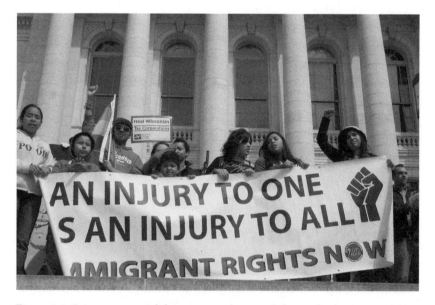

Figure 3.2. Injury to one. Adolescents marching in defense of immigrants' rights, May Day, 2011, Madison, Wisconsin.

from here." And a Latina said, "An American is someone born and raised in the U.S."

Assimilation was invoked by a few teens who rejected the concept of hyphenated identities: "To be American is forgetting about your ethnic background and become an American." These references to the one over the many are what the social psychologist Kay Deaux, in her research on immigration and American identity, has called zero-sum thinking about identity, thinking that is out of sync with empirical evidence. Deaux refers to the "zone of the hyphen" as "territory rich in meaning and dynamic in process, belying efforts to impose simple categorical systems."[16] Citing an impressive and growing literature on bicultural identity, she shows that people draw from their different identity resources as situations dictate or allow.

## Attitudes toward Immigrants

What relevance does an adolescent's sense of what it means to be an American have for the body politic? I tackle this issue by showing that there is a strong relationship between the defining features of American identity that are salient to an adolescent and her attitudes toward immigrants.

Throughout our history, the political discourse on immigration has raised fundamental questions about what it means to be an American and the ties that bind us as a people. Some have agreed with Walzer's assertion that the United States is a "country of immigrants who have roots elsewhere" and "whatever identity they had before becoming Americans, they retain (or better, they are free to retain) afterward." Others assert that there is an "Anglo-Protestant American" identity and that other cultural, religious, and ethnic traditions will at best contaminate and at worst obliterate it. Entangled in these discussions are thorny issues—of who "we" and "they" are and of what "*we*" fear we may lose by embracing "*them*."

Historically, immigration has brought the terms of the social contract into high relief—both with respect to whether newcomers should be entitled to the same rights and protections that other citizens enjoy and whether they should maintain or relinquish their culture and customs as part of the bargain. Although the United States is a nation of immigrants, the issue of immigrant incorporation has been contested throughout our history. In the late 1770s, Benjamin Franklin dabbled in demography and raised concerns about the increasing proportion of Germans in the population of

Pennsylvania: "Why should Pennsylvania, founded by the English, become a colony of aliens, who will shortly be so numerous as to Germanize us, instead of us Anglifying them?" Over the years, even presidents of the republic have raised concerns about the loyalties of those who held on to their ethnic roots. Theodore Roosevelt said that a hyphenated American was incompatible with being a good American, and Woodrow Wilson that the hyphen posed a threat to the republic. Today, immigration is assailed for supposedly threatening America's Anglo-Protestant culture. Celebrating one's ethnic roots and maintaining the left side of the hyphen is vilified because, as the argument goes, embracing the left side of the hyphen undermines feelings of loyalty to the United States.[17]

On the contrary, empirical work shows that there is a positive correlation between feelings of pride in one's cultural and ethnic roots and loyalty to the receiving nation, associations that are even stronger among ethnic minorities who feel that their cultural group is valued by others.[18] Furthermore, immigrants' cultural and religious values are strong motivators of their commitment to engage in civic affairs in local communities in the United States (see Figure 3.2). According to the developmental psychologist Lene Arnett Jensen, cultural reasons (references to their culture of origin and self-identification as a person from another country) were the main motivators of civic engagement for the Asian Indian and Salvadoran adolescents and parents in her study who were new immigrants to the United States.[19] Likewise, in their studies of immigrant high school students, developmental psychologists Kimber Bogard and Lonnie Sherrod found that commitments to (their immigrant) family were strongly and positively correlated with adolescents' civic orientation (helping the needy, engaging in community service, and staying informed on current events).[20] Although young adult immigrants may be less likely to vote when compared to their native-born peers, they are very likely to be active in service to their local communities and extended families, functioning as mediators between and translators of the social contract in the United States for older and younger members of their cultural group.[21]

To check for relationships between adolescents' ideas about our American identity and their attitudes toward immigrants, I first collapsed the detailed coding of their open-ended statements into the three thematic categories: the first, defined by an emphasis on liberalism and individual freedom and rights (any references to individual freedom, self-determination, opportunity, achievement, power); the second, by an emphasis on civic republicanism (references to equality, tolerance and defense of the rights of fellow citizens, and the common good); and the third, by an emphasis on patriotism and loyalty to the nation and its policies.

As noted, two responses were coded and the combinations are important to keep in mind. Teens who mention *only* freedom of the individual or combine freedom with references to patriotism or loyalty to the nation conceive of the essence of American identity in a qualitatively different way from their peers who combine references to freedom with references to equality and the common good. When I combined the teens' first and second responses, typically they fell into the following categories: the first combined references to an individual's freedom and rights with references to the common good or others' rights; the second combined references to individual freedom with references to patriotism. There were no combinations of patriotism with civic republican themes. The first combination was assigned to the civic republican grouping, and the second combination was assigned to the individual freedom category.[22] Of the 539 cases that were assigned based on this coding combination, 48.2 percent were assigned to the liberalism/individual rights group, 35.3 percent to the civic republican/common good group, and 16.5 percent to the patriotism/loyalty group.

There were some ethnic differences in the meaning that adolescents attached to being American. Although individual freedom and the liberal tradition was the most common category invoked by youth, this category was more often mentioned by adolescents from European- and Arab-American backgrounds. Latinos were less likely than others to mention it and were more likely than all other groups to make references to equality and loyalty. Both African-American and Latino youth tended to combine references to freedom with references to equality or the common good. An awareness of the common good may be more salient for these groups because of cultural values and traditions. For example, responsibility to one's extended family is known to be highly valued among Latinos. Among Mexicans, a child's *educación* refers to the family's responsibility to inculcate *social responsibility* not only for learning but for applying what one learns for the benefit of the collective. This standard appears to be a factor contributing to the civic engagement of Mexican immigrants to the United States.[23] Alternatively, African-American and Latino adolescents may simply be more cognizant of the challenges of realizing equality and full civil rights. Although cynical responses about what it means to be an American (e.g., "being American means that you're rich and care only about yourself") accounted for less than 1 percent of the responses and were not included when discrete codes were collapsed into the three major categories, African-American youth were more likely than others to give such responses.

Next, I ran analyses to compare the attitudes that the three "American identity" groups (liberalism, civic republican, and patriotism) held about immigrants. The survey that these adolescents completed also included eight items tapping attitudes about immigrants and using a 1–5 (strongly disagree to strongly agree) response format. The eight items factored into three 'attitudes towards immigrants' scales, each composed of several items. The first reflected a belief that immigrants should assimilate—by adopting English and mainstream customs; the second, that immigrants tended to bring crime into the country and posed dangers to Americans' jobs and way of life; and the third that immigrants enriched "American" culture and should be encouraged to maintain their unique cultural heritage and customs (see the Appendix for items). In the graph below, these three 'attitudes towards immigrants' scales are truncated in the legend as *assimilate, danger, and enrich.*

Figure 3.3 summarizes the results of analyses of covariance for three groups with the adolescent's age, gender, parents' educational level, and racial or ethnic background as covariates. Reading from left to right on the x-axis, the three groups were as follows: Youth for whom the essence of our American identity emphasized liberalism and individual rights (48.2 percent based on the combined first and second responses); those who alluded to civic republican/common good values (35.3 percent); and those for whom patriotism and unquestioning loyalty to the nation figured prominently as the essence of our American identity (16.5 percent). The y-axis displays the mean scores on the three attitudes toward immigrants' scales. As the figure illustrates, there were significant differences in the attitudes toward immigrants of the three groups. I note again that the civic republican group includes individuals who made *any* reference to equality, diversity, others' rights or the common good *even if* those individuals *also* mentioned elements that could be coded in the individual freedom category. I repeat this point to emphasize that the adolescents in the civic republican/common good group should not be dismissed as altruists, oblivious to their own self-interest: they are attentive to the common good but not at the expense of individual liberty.

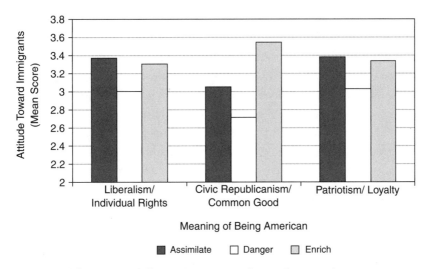

Figure 3.3. The meaning of being American and attitudes toward immigrants. The scales are based on the mean score for items in each scale. See the Appendix for Chapter 3 for a description of the study and for the wording of items in the scales.

As Figure 3.3 illustrates, the views about immigrants expressed by the civic republican/common good group differed from the other two. This group was more likely to feel that immigrants enriched the culture of the United States and should be encouraged to maintain their customs rather than give them up and assimilate to the mainstream language and culture. This group was the least likely to think that immigrants posed a threat to the jobs and way of life that citizens of the United States have long enjoyed. Many in this group embraced both the liberal and civic republican traditions. However, in light of the "crowding out" of the republican or common good tradition that Sandel and Bellah and others contend has occurred over the past four decades, this group remembers that our identities as Americans also include moral bonds with a broader community of others.[24] Perhaps it is not surprising then that their perceptions of immigrants—a group that in public debates is often stereotyped as "other" or "outsider" is more open and welcoming.[25]

In contrast, those adolescents who conceive of the essence of our American identity as either privileging the rights of individuals with less regard for their bonds to others or pledging loyalty to symbols of our unity and implying that challenges to the status quo are unpatriotic are more likely to believe that immigrants pose a potential threat to our jobs and way of life in the United States. However, across all three groups, teens were least likely to endorse this most negative of the attitudes toward immigrants scales. Views on how immigrants should incorporate into the American polity, that is, whether they should assimilate or maintain their cultural traditions differed according to adolescents' dominant views of what it means to be an American: adolescents who endorsed a civic republican/common good view of the essence of our American identity were far less likely than the other two groups to feel that immigrants should assimilate and far more likely to hold that they should maintain their language and customs because these diverse cultures enriched "American" culture.

Teens' theories about what it means to be an American is a political idea—because it reflects their views of the polity—the community, the state, and the nation of which they are a member. Here we see that the idea of America that is most meaningful or salient to a teen, the elements that, according to the teen, are most essential to our identity, are correlated in logically consistent ways with his attitudes toward immigrants. Those teens who conceive of American identity as connected more strongly with a public "we the people" tend to give "others" (in this case, immigrants) the benefit of the doubt. In other words, those teens who at least mention an ideal consistent with a civic republican philosophy (equal opportunity, open-mindedness, tolerance, diversity, social responsibility, civil rights) are more prepared to invite "them" to be one of "us." In contrast, those teens who feel that the essence of our American identity inheres in the freedom and independence of individuals (their autonomy, power, achievements) unencumbered by civic ties and those teens for whom being American connoted blind loyalty to the nation preferred that immigrants assimilate to the dominant mainstream culture.

## E PLURIBUS UNUM

Next I turn to a discussion of the teens' responses to times they are keenly aware of their ethnic identity and times when they feel most like an American. The most common response to the item, "Tell us some times when you feel like an American" was "always." It was mentioned in nearly 26 percent of the first responses. Another 11 percent said that they had never thought about it. And some were taken aback by the question: "What do you mean American? I don't know how else I would ever feel. I was born in the U.S. & speak the English lang. I feel like an American everyday."

Several adolescents felt that over generations they had become "American" by shedding their ethnic roots. For example, one European-American female felt American "everyday, because there are no real strong ties between me and my heritage"; another said that "I almost always feel like an American because my family has been here for so long we don't do a lot of *cultural* things [italics added]." The identification of ethnic roots with culture has been noted in the work of developmental psychologist Jean Phinney, who observes that cultural roots are less salient for youth from European-American backgrounds, many of whom actually conflate "culture" with "ethnicity."[26]

For many of the European-American adolescents in my study, identifying times when they feel American seems like a strange question: they simply *are* American. According to their lay theory, their right to claim that identity is uncontested. Although they are aware that at one point their family emigrated to these shores from another homeland, they rarely experience or are reminded about those connections anymore. "Most of the time I don't ever feel European or Australian or anything"; "I don't know what Americans are supposed to feel like but I don't feel like I belong back in Germany where my family came from." Even when adolescents are aware of their family's cultural background, the melting pot over generations has, for many, obliterated the left side of the hyphen. As a sixteen-year-old female said, "my dad's grandparents came from four different countries, and my mom's family has been in America too long to know what nationalities might be there, so I just consider myself an American most of the time." The question for these teens is "what else would I feel?" It points to the absence of hyphenation in their experiences and the potential difficulties they would have with understanding the hyphenated experiences of others. The ascriptive definition of American identity that dominates cultural images is a good fit for their experience.

In contrast, for youth in recent immigrant families, the question of "times they felt American" was very meaningful. Their families had made conscious decisions to move to these shores, which provided a basis for them to compare times when they felt American or more ethnic. For some, the fact that their families were recent immigrants to the United States also meant that they could not assume that they would be treated as Americans. A seventeen-year-old Latino said that he felt American "when my father tells me why he came to this country. And why it is so much better than Mexico." Some recent immigrants seemed to have a metric with American at one end and their ethnic group at the other. The choices that they made were measured along this yardstick of identity. For example, a sixteen-year-old female of Arab descent felt American, "When I rather would do things the American way than the Arabian way." Another female co-ethnic said, "I feel like I'm American when I am communicating with my parents or other immigrants to this country." The ethnic versus American metric also was used in social comparisons with peers. Several teens observed that they felt American when they were in the company of their comparatively less assimilated co-ethnics: as an eighteen-year-old Arab-American put it, "I go out more than most arab girls do."

Other teens who were not recent immigrants also applied a "more or less American" metric in their responses with "American" defined racially, culturally, or linguistically. For example, an eighteen-year-old white male said he felt American when he met someone that is "'less American' than me. Example: doesn't speak English as well." There were a few teens who used an "us-them" or "ours-theirs" distinction with "us" white Americans in the superior position. One fifteen-year-old white male said that he felt American "when immigrants from other countries try to move into the U.S. and take the American land away," and a sixteen-year-old white female said she felt American "when I'm around all White people because the color of my skin."

The hegemony of "white" and "Anglo" as defining features of American identity were not lost on youth from ethnic minority backgrounds, some of whom referred to the vexed relationship they felt with this identity. According to one Latina, "I may feel like an American when it comes to citizenship. But that's as far as it goes." And an Arab-American female stated, "since I'm a U.S. citizen, in this country I'm considered an American, but I will continue to follow my culture, and only act by which my culture is."

Some teens made an interesting distinction between being "American" in public and "ethnic" in their private lives, as these quotes from Arab-Americans reflect: "Just when I'm out in public and everything is American";

"Any place outside of my home because when in America, do as the Americans do." The public nature of our shared identity and the private (typically more homogeneous) sense of ethnic identity was expressed, respectively, by an Arab-American female and an African-American male: the former felt American, "When I'm at school or shopping or around friends. I don't categorize myself as Arab at those times because there is no need to," and the latter said, "when I'm out, at school, the mall, movies, practically anywhere besides church and home."

So, among familiars at church or in the privacy of one's home, there is no need to reflect on one's identity—because it surrounds and envelops you. This experience in private is similar to the uncontested identity that we heard from the white youth whose families had been settled in the United States for several generations. Surrounded in public spaces with the Anglo identity that has become hegemonic in mainstream American culture, they don't categorize themselves as anything but American because, as the teen above stated, "there is no need to." These teens seemed to have an intuitive understanding of the distinction between the public and private realms that the philosopher Hannah Arendt discusses in *The Human Condition.* For Arendt, the public realm is defined by the fact that the things that we do in public are seen and heard by everybody present, including ourselves.

In contrast to the previously quoted African-American teen who did not feel American at church, other adolescents specifically mentioned exercising their religious freedoms as a time they felt American: "I feel American when I am practicing my worship to God, because the religious freedom given here was not allowed in Syria, so I feel American because of freedom to be a Jehovah's Witness."

Youth who were first- or second-generation Americans echoed the liberal tradition of individual freedom as they contrasted the "new" ways in America with the "old" traditions of their ethnic group. As a sixteen-year-old female of Arab descent said, "I don't follow things from the 'old' country, I use new ideas and am very willing to change. I feel American when I feel that women have more of a chance than ever before to succeed." Her co-ethnic peer felt American "When I go out with guys of *their* races [italics added]."

Generational tensions around the theme of acting "too American" were raised by several young people. For example, a fifteen-year-old Latina related that times when she felt American were "when I go out with friends, disagree with my parents about how things should be done. The only times I feel like an American is when my parents say that I am too Americanized. They say my beliefs are very different from theirs." Another Latina said, "the way I act or my beliefs and morals differ. Communication for me at times can be difficult, especially with elders, which makes me feel very American." A seventeen-year-old Arab-American female said, "I feel like an American when I have or share the same opinions on issues *that my culture doesn't agree to* [italics added]." The intergenerational tensions and greater similarity of young immigrants' values to those of their nonimmigrant peers to which these adolescents allude, have been identified by other scholars as drivers of social change.[27]

But even adolescents of European descent whose families had lived in the United States for many generations identified self-determination as an American trait. They felt very American when they asserted opinions that were distinct from those that their parents held and considered such independence of thought a distinguishing American trait. For example, a seventeen-year-old female of European descent said, "I feel like an American when I am discussing different issues with my parents and we have different ideas." The freedom to think for yourself echoes the empowerment of the individual captured in John Updike's interpretation of the American idea as well as the proclivity to challenge the world that Azar Nafisi described as a defining feature of American character.

The ability to speak their own mind and to hold their own opinions was nominated by several teens as a time when they felt American: "Free speech—stand for my opinion" or "I feel like an American when people let me say what I want to." Closely linked to free expression were references to individual achievement. For example, several teens said that they felt American at times when they exercised their freedom to accomplish something: "Freedom—self determination to make something of myself"; "freedom and the opportunity to make of yourself whatever you put your mind to." A fifteen-year-old African-American male said that he felt like an American "Everyday when I wake up and know I have the freedom to do what I want with my life. You have freedom, the ability to go and do things in the future."

Whether their families were recent immigrants or not, ethnic minorities had unique insights into the relationship between ethnic and American identity. Although there were relatively few teens who said that they "never" felt like an American (less than 1 percent), those who did were disproportionately ethnic minorities. A fifteen-year-old African-American male was adamant: "I don't feel like a American!!!!!!!" and a fourteen-year-old female said, "really I don't know, I never really felt like an American (maybe African-American)." These youth echoed what Clarence Page, the Pulitzer Prize–winning journalist, referred to in his book, *Showing My Color: Impolite Essays on Race and Identity,* as "the ancestral desire of my ethnic people to be 'just American'" and the "rudeness of race" intruding on that dream.[28]

But African-Americans were not the only ethnic minority to allude to their hyphenated identities. A fifteen-year-old girl felt "more so as an Asian-American almost always." Others expressed a more vexed relationship with the right side of the hyphen: "I've never felt like an American because my parents are hispanic, and I have to learn my ethnic background I'm really not interested in America, because of *their* prejudice [italics added]." Finally, a rather savvy thirteen-year-old Latina said that she never felt like an American "because I am proud of being Puerto Rican and I'm just fine the way I am."

When such feelings were invoked, they were stated with as much passion as one could put into words. For example, one Latina reflected, "I have never felt like an American in my life. I will never fit that picture"; and an Arab-American male was very cynical about the only time that he felt American: "I have once and that was when I was with an American friend and it was one of the worst moments of my life." Similarly, his female co-ethnic said, "To me, it does not mean much, because many times I have experienced prejudice. The title of 'American' does not protect you from anything." These young people already had a palpable sense of the contradictory narratives about American citizenship that, as Rogers M. Smith has noted, privilege categories of native-born, WASP, and male, despite the more inclusive definitions.[29]

These quotes illustrate my point that teens interpret the social contract from the standpoint of their group—and make decisions about their identity and membership in the polity based on whether they believe people "like them" are included in that polity and protected under the terms of its social contract. Importantly, perceptions of the respect accorded to their ethnic group by fellow Americans is critical to their sense of inclusion in the body politic. As Alejandro Portes and Rubén G. Rumbaut found in their study of second-generation American teens, experiences of discrimination can cause a *reactive identification,* that is, an intensification of teens' identification with their ethnic group and with their parents' sending country.[30] Thus, it is not the act of embracing one's ethnic roots that poses a threat to their allegiance to the United States. Rather, feeling excluded from the terms of the American social contract, feeling that one's claims to citizenship are conditional, that, as Clarence Page puts it, you can never be accepted as "just an American," causes individuals to choose a form of ethnic identification that is a reactive identity against an exclusionary one that privileges some groups over others.

Both political theorists and scholars of adolescent development have noted that a common element of the ethnic minority experience is a vexed relationship with the Eurocentric culture that dominates American economic and political life (i.e., a sense that full membership in American society is contested and that the principles of the social contract do not apply equally to all groups).

For adolescents from ethnic minority backgrounds, personal experiences of discrimination may carry political overtones because it is in adolescence when youth are able to connect the dots. In part their assessments are due to the teen's increased social cognitive capacities and ability to understand social groups and categories. In addition, adolescence is a time when individuals begin to understand that the larger social system is constructed from the opinions and perspectives of its members,[31] that societies reflect the biases of their members, and that social institutions and systems can be discriminatory.[32] Compared with younger children, adolescents are more capable of seeing the links between personal experiences of prejudice, membership in a particular racial or ethnic group, and the status of that group in the larger society. Sensitivity to the status of their ethnic group in society at large may increase as they mature. According to one longitudinal study that followed ethnic-minority and ethnic-majority students from high school into college, perceptions of personal discrimination decreased as individuals matured; however, perceptions of society's devaluation of their group increased, and that awareness had negative consequences for the mental health of the ethnic-minority students.[33]

Besides the growth in cognitive capacities that occurs during the teen years, adolescence also is a period in life when society begins to send clear signals to ethnic-minority youth that they belong to a particular minority group. Beverly Daniel Tatum, psychologist and president of Spelman College, describes the shift in feedback and self-perceptions that occurs as African-Americans, and especially males, enter adolescence: "the environmental cues change and the world begins to reflect (one's) blackness back to (her or him) more clearly."[34]

Personal experiences of discrimination and exclusion are likely to be implicated in the adolescent's encounter with what it means to be a member of her ethnic group as well as in her theories about how the tenets of the mainstream social contract apply to "my group." For example, one seventeen-year-old African-American was reminded of her membership in an ethnic-minority group when, despite her good grades, teachers did not recommend her for advanced classes. She was aware of her ethnic identity "when in a group with only 1 ethnic group besides myself (e.g., in a class with all white children)." She goes on to explain that her exclusion from advanced classes was an act of discrimination, an exclusion that she believes would likely happen to other students based on their race and social class: "Where I live, children are discouraged from taking higher levels of classes when they should be able to just because their parents aren't rich or hold status in the community or they are minorities. While I earn A's & B's in my classes, I am not always recommended to take the next level of honors classes the next year. While white students with rich parents who don't do as well are." Her political awareness in this statement is palpable, although she might not refer to her insights as political.

Experiences of discrimination are a common denominator even for the most highly achieved minorities. As a result, middle-class ethnic-minority parents are more likely than their counterparts from lower socioeconomic status (SES) backgrounds to prepare their children for bias,[35] in part because they are more likely to move in mixed ethnic circles and have regular encounters with the ethnic-majority culture. According to racial socialization research, instilling a strong sense of cultural pride and awareness is a common practice reported by ethnic-minority parents, and many studies have documented the positive effects of such practices on adolescents' mental health, academic self-efficacy, and engagement.[36]

Less is known about the impact of racial or ethnic socialization on adolescents' perceptions of barriers to opportunity. When ethnic-minority parents alert their children to the existence of prejudice, it is very likely that they also are warning them that such barriers are not abstractions; rather they are telling their children to be prepared because such barriers are likely to have personal implications in the teen's life. Parents' own encounters with discrimination and blocked opportunities are often a motivator for such discussions. For example, African-American parents are more likely to tell their children that they should be prepared to deal with bias *if* the parents have experienced incidents of prejudice at work.[37] Adolescents' direct experiences with prejudice also motivates such family discussions. For example, adolescents who report experiences of discrimination also report that their parents engage in more frequent ethnic socialization practices. Thus, some act of exclusion—from people who wield power over the child or the parent—often is the factor that triggers conversations about how discrimination operates in excluding people "like us" from being fully accepted into American society.

These are political messages insofar as discrimination is defined as an act of prejudice leveled against someone because of their membership in a group.[38] Thus, youths' awareness of discrimination points to a political consciousness and a skepticism about the terms of the social contract. Adolescents' experiences of discrimination and parents' own experiences of discrimination are teachable moments. Very likely, these hurtful instances provide occasions for political discussions in families and, as Vygotsky argues, those experiences and discussions are fodder for teens' evolving beliefs about their ethnic identity, their society, and the position of their group in society.

Developmental scientists have referred to such parenting practices as "prearming," that is, teaching children defensive strategies for sticking up for themselves and disregarding the negative influences of others.[39] Such prearming alerts youth to the group stereotypes circulating in society, and there are potential benefits as well as costs associated with this knowledge. On the positive side, one study found that in response to hypothetical dilemmas involving discrimination, adolescents whose parents had alerted them to bias were more likely to come up with proactive (and often collective) strategies such as seeking support and problem solving to deal with it.[40]

At the same time, such prearming practices that enable young people to label instances of prejudice also may sensitize them to the negative judgments that are "out there" about people "like them." For example, African-American and Latino children whose parents report racial socialization practices are more aware of the racial stereotypes that "others" hold and also are more likely to interpret hypothetical negative interracial encounters as discriminatory.[41] Likewise, according to longitudinal work, when African-American adolescents believe that various daily life experiences (being ignored, excluded, treated with disrespect, accused of something, having your ideas ignored, called a name, being followed in public, or stared at by strangers) happens "because you are black" six months later, those youth are even more likely to believe that the public holds negative stereotypes of their racial group.[42] Discrimination also carries a heavy psychological burden. As the developmental psychologist Diane Hughes and her colleagues have shown, family discussions of bias are associated with higher levels of depression and antisocial behavior and lower academic achievement in adolescents.[43]

Although group discrimination historically has been a basis for political organizing and action, we have few developmental studies of how personal experiences of discrimination might affect adolescents' political views and commitments. In the growing body of work on ethnic socialization and the role of discrimination in that socialization, little attention has been paid to whether teens from different ethnic groups believe that the terms of the social contract in the United States apply equally to all groups. And, if they are skeptical that the terms are equal, whether that skepticism has any impact on their political commitments or actions.

A few exceptions to this general rule are noteworthy for what they reveal about teens' evolving political theories. First, among Latino, African-American, Chinese-American, and white families, adolescents are more likely to believe that the public in general has negative regard for their racial or ethnic group *if* their parents have prepared them for bias in society. This "prearming" affects teens' beliefs about the negative regard that the public holds about their group, even after controlling for the effect that interpersonal discrimination has on these beliefs. Similar relationships are noted in a study of Latino college students: according to the psychologist Deborah Rivas-Drake, students were more likely to feel that their instructors held negative views about the potential for Latinos to succeed academically *if* their families had discussed discrimination. The students' political views also were affected insofar as family discussions about discrimination were positively related to the students' beliefs that non-native English speakers as well as families who lack economic resources encounter more barriers to educational and economic mobility in the United States.[44]

One other interesting study uncovered racial differences in adolescents' beliefs about whether the terms of the social contract in the United States apply to their group. Phinney and her colleagues measured the extent to which adolescents and young adults believed that the ideals and opportunities that define American society apply to them and their ethnic group. Items tapping these American ideals included "A democratic country in which the laws protect *my interests*"; "a land of economic opportunity *for me*"; "a society that is accepting and tolerant of *my cultural background or ethnic group*"; "a society that is concerned about the welfare of *my cultural group* [italics added]." Phinney and others found that African-American youth were more likely to identify with their ethnic group but were less likely to believe that the ideals that define American society applied to their group, whereas European-American youth showed the opposite pattern.[45] The racial differences revealed in the work of Phinney and colleagues suggest that some youth may believe that the social contract in America—the land of equal opportunity, of tolerance, and of inclusion—is a contract that preferences groups from European backgrounds and excludes groups from other ethnic and cultural backgrounds. These results suggest, as Rogers M. Smith has argued about ascriptive narratives of American identity, that one has to be a certain kind of American in order to enjoy the fruits of full membership as a citizen.[46]

Convergent information is provided by scholars who have shown that although marginalized groups may believe in the promise of the American dream as a general principle (i.e., that it is an equal opportunity society where anyone can succeed), they may be less convinced that the principles of the American social contract apply in real life to people *like them*. For example, sociologist Roz Mickelson has shown that while African-American students endorse an abstract belief in the American ethos that hard work and education pay off in success, they also endorse a more concrete belief that education has not paid off for members of their own families.[47]

Experiences with discrimination leave some youth with diminished social and political trust but that does not necessarily mean that they give up. Experiences of group discrimination may spur political action. A good example is provided by Latino youth mobilizing against anti-immigrant legislation and lobbying for the DREAM (Development, Relief, and Education for Alien Minors) Act. Although the undocumented are the stated targets of anti-immigrant legislation, in practice profiling the undocumented targets their co-ethnics of legal status along with them. Discrimination against their ethnic group, against people who look like them or talk like them, has been a unifying force for political action. Attaining the American dream via access to education has become the political cause uniting documented and undocumented Latinos, and for many, lobbying for DREAM legislation has resulted in their becoming political leaders, symbols for younger and older co-ethnics.[48]

My colleagues and I also have documented relationships between adolescents' experiences of discrimination, their ethnic awareness, and the forms of civic action they endorse. As part of the project on ethnic and American identities that is the basis for this chapter, adolescents were asked about their personal experiences of discrimination. African-American and Arab-American adolescents reported a greater number of personal instances of discrimination than did their Latino-American or European-American peers. But among all ethnic minorities, teen's awareness of their membership in an ethnic-minority group was stronger *if* they reported some personal experiences of discrimination. And, consistent with racial socialization research, those who reported an experience of discrimination also reported that their parents had warned them that prejudice is likely to pose a barrier in their lives.

Not surprisingly, experiences of discrimination played a role in adolescents' beliefs about the social contract in the United States and in their civic commitments: those youth who reported that they or someone close to them had been a target of discrimination were less likely to believe that America is an equal opportunity society where anyone can succeed if s/he is willing to work hard. In addition, African-Americans were least likely to believe that the government was responsive to the average person. But this critical analysis of the system did not mean that ethnic-minority youth had given up on the ideal of an equal and inclusive democratic society. On the contrary, they were as committed as their ethnic-majority peers to serving their country and community and were even more committed than their majority peers to promoting tolerance, improving race relations, and advocating for their ethnic group.[49] These results (that teens' critique of the system can motivate actions to improve it) resonate with research by counseling psychologist, Matt Diemer who has found that critical reflection on inequality can motivate teens who are disadvantaged by the system to overcome structural barriers to their success in school and work.[50] Although their experiences may teach them that ours is not a perfect union, that the principles of equality and inalienable rights codified in our founding documents remain unrealized ideals, at some level these adolescents also appreciate that if ever those ideals will be realized, it will take the collective work of people *like them.*

Whereas instances of discrimination and exclusion were related to awareness of their ethnic identity, instances of inclusion also were nominated by teens from ethnic-minority backgrounds as times when they felt like an American. Times nominated by two Latinas were "when I'm around people that treat me like anybody else" and "I felt I was in the picture—it felt good." Personal experiences of being included in the community also were meaningful to one African-American thirteen-year-old whose family had recently moved to a new community. He felt American when "the community invited us to the cook out." These statements suggest how simple acts of invitation, of reaching out to welcome newcomers to a community, contribute to a sense of belonging, to the sense of the public captured in the phrase "we the people."

Robert Pinsky, who served three terms as poet laureate of the United States, refers to the work yet to be done if we are to realize the American idea made explicit in our Constitution:

> The United States itself can be considered a partly realized idea. A nation not defined by blood or religion must cohere by the force of ideas, or not at all. Sovereignty of the people is an example. So too is equality. Such ideas are made explicit in our governing documents precisely because they are unrealized.[51]

In 1974, the partly realized idea of "we the people" was articulated in remarks by Barbara Jordan, who, as a representative from Houston, Texas, was the first African-American congresswoman elected from the southern United States. Serving on the House Judiciary Committee during its hearings into the impeachment of President Nixon, Jordan said the following in a speech on the floor of Congress:

> Earlier today we heard the beginning of the Preamble to the Constitution of the United States, *we the people.* It is a very eloquent beginning. But when

that document was completed, on the seventeenth of September in 1787, I was not included in that *we the people*. I felt somehow for many years that George Washington and Alexander Hamilton just left me out by mistake. But through the process of amendment, interpretation, and court decision I have finally been included in *we the people*.[52]

## How "We the People" Takes Shape

The meaning of "we the people" has been reinterpreted throughout our history through laws and amendments to the Constitution. It also is reconstructed in our interactions in public spaces as we grapple with the ties that connect us to fellow citizens and imagine the kind of political community we want to share.

The language of the Preamble to the Constitution is aspirational in tone: "In order to form a more perfect union." But, as the philosopher of pragmatism John Dewey insisted, we have to wrangle with what we mean by that "more perfect union" in concrete communities of real people. Democracy itself and the ideals of liberty and equality are utopian—abstract and meaningless—until people give them definition through the commitments they form on the ground:

> Only when we start from a community as a fact, grasp the fact in thought so as to clarify and enhance its constituent elements, can we reach an idea of democracy which is not utopian. The conceptions and shibboleths which are traditionally associated with the idea of democracy take on a veridical and directive meaning only when they are construed as marks and traits of an association which realizes the defining characteristics of a community. Fraternity, liberty, and equality isolated from communal life are hopeless abstractions.[53]

Teens in this study provided insights into the concrete human relationships and associations in which their identities as Americans were forged. Particularly noteworthy themes in their reflections on "times when they felt American" concerned feelings of bonding and acceptance and references to finding common ground that surmounted differences. As one thirteen-year-old Latina put it, "I felt happy because in America I have friends that respect me as *who I am—not who they want me to be* [italics added]."

The importance of diverse interactions and friendships for forging their American identities was noted by several youth. For example, a seventeen-year-old African-American female felt American "when being able to interact with people from different backgrounds and from different ethnic groups as well as some from my own and being able to share commonalities in our lives"; and a fourteen-year-old Latina felt American "when I'm treated like everyone, which is most of the time."

In the *Nicomachean Ethics*, Aristotle describes the role of friendship in the polity.[54] He asserts that the most complete form of friendship, superior to all others, is that in which friends are concerned with the good of one another rather than with the personal advantages gained through the relationship. In other words, the "political" in friendship is found when individuals cooperate in pursuit of a common goal or, as several teens in this study commented, when they find common ground with peers from different backgrounds.

The political significance of friendship was articulated by two European-American teens who said, "When I am with my friends we all are different cultures. That's American" and "when I'm with my friends. It doesn't matter what color we are we all love each other." A young Latina said she felt American at times "*That we all stick for each other* [italics added]." This "sticking for each other" captures the sense of belonging to something larger than oneself—an identity that transcends individual uniqueness—that is at the heart of the republican, or strong democracy, tradition.

Not surprisingly, holidays that celebrated our unity as a nation were mentioned by 12 percent of the young people, but the theme of friendship also figured in that unity. One teen noted that a time she was very aware of her American identity was "when we went to NYC for 4th of July, we were all 'friends' at the moment watching the fireworks."

Friendships and peer solidarity also were described in the context of school, as these teens observed: "When I am in school. I have friends of many colors and in school, everybody is American"; "When I am at school, and there are so many different kinds of people, and most of the time everyone still gets along." A fifteen-year-old European-American female referred to the civic community at school and the way fellow citizens *ought* to treat one another. She felt like an American "in school, because *you can't and shouldn't feel prejudice in school.* I have all kinds of friends (Not just rights)."

Her principle that "you can't and shouldn't feel prejudice in school" alludes to the standards of a civil climate for learning that public schools need to ensure. Schools are public spaces where members of the public, especially younger members, gather. As such, public schools need to stand for and to enact those principles that bind members of the larger polity together. Specifically, schools in the United States need to practice principles of equal opportunity, of tolerance, and of respect for differences of opinion, beliefs, and cultural practices.

Such inclusive school contexts do not happen by default: as the adult authorities within classrooms, teachers are instrumental in ensuring civil climates for learning. When they create such climates, teachers convey messages about social inclusion, about who belongs and whose opinions count, and they model how members of a society should treat one another. Furthermore, when teachers insist on such climates for learning, their actions are instrumental in shaping the democratic dispositions and civic commitments of their students.

In another part of the questionnaire, students completed scales reporting on their teachers' behaviors and the climate for learning they experienced at school. Aspects of a civil climate for learning included the student's perception that his teachers held the same high standards for all students, listened to and considered students' ideas even if those ideas opposed the teacher's own views, insisted that students respect one another's ideas, and actively intervened to put a stop to any acts of bullying or intolerance. Regardless of their age, social class, or gender, when teens reported these kinds of practices at their school, they were more likely to endorse beliefs that America was a just society where all people are given a fair chance and an equal opportunity to get ahead. I interpret this as a mechanism whereby diffuse support for the polity develops in younger generations. Experiencing civil climates at school where fellow citizens learned to listen to and to respect differences of opinion informed the teens' beliefs that this mini-polity (the school) that they were part of must be a microcosm of a larger polity (the United States of America) that was similarly fair and inclusive.

The teen's reports of civil climates for learning at school also shaped their civic identities and commitments: those teens who reported that inclusion and respect for diverse perspectives were common practices at their school were more likely to be personally committed to patriotic goals and to building intergroup tolerance and understanding. These associations were true for all teens but were especially strong among ethnic minorities.[55] Results like this support my claim that it is through their experiences of membership in mini-polities such as schools that teens develop their beliefs about, affection for, and commitments to the larger polity.

Other scholars also have documented the value of open class discussions in which students learn to listen to and to consider different perspectives for nurturing students' civic understanding and commitments. For example, open classroom climates, which the developmental psychologist Judith Torney-Purta defines as one in which "students experience their classrooms as places to investigate issues and explore their opinions and those of their peers," are positively related to such democratic skills as perspective taking, tolerance, and trust, and are correlated with students' knowledge about international affairs, their abilities to think critically about civic issues and to tolerate dissenting opinions, and their commitment to voting in the future.[56]

School reminded some teens of their American identities because of routine practices or rituals such as that described by a thirteen-year-old who felt American "every morning when we say the Aplegaledence [*sic*]." Likewise, sports events sometimes served as reminders because the national anthem was played before a game. But participating in sports also was described by some youth as a context in which they played as a team with peers from different backgrounds. A seventeen-year-old white male felt American "when I'm on a team, like a football team, we all go out there together. Working w/ each other knowing *if one fails we all fail* [italics added]."

The teamwork and the need for others in order to succeed ourselves that was noted by this young man also is at the heart of civic republican ideals about democracy. In his 2005 book, *Democratic Faith,* the political scientist Patrick Deneen draws attention to an argument Plato makes in his *Republic* for why we need to band together in a "city of utmost necessity" to fulfill our common needs. Each of us has unique talents to contribute but no one of us can meet all of our needs; as Deneen says, "each of us isn't self-sufficient but is in need of much."[57]

Teens' recognition of others who are in need of much and their response to those needs were expressed by a few in very republican terms: "I feel like an American most of the time because I'm interested in the welfare of the whole nation." A fourteen-year-old African-American male said he felt like an American "when I got to help the elderly and when I got to fix buildings."

Two Latinas whose parents had not made it to high school said they felt American "when I do something good for this country" and "when I do something for my community."

These teenagers experience their American identities when they engage as members of the public. Dewey provided a more sophisticated description of the process in *The Public and its Problems*, where he observes, "association in the sense of connection and combination is a 'law' of everything known to exist." He distinguishes human forms of association from other forms because the participants observe their connections and because their conjoint action takes on a new value when it is observed:

> Each acts, insofar as the connection is known, in view of the connection. Individuals still do the thinking, desiring and purposing, but *what* they think of is the consequences of their behavior upon that of others and those of others upon themselves.[58]

The younger generation becomes part of that democratic community through participation in traditions and by sharing conjoint activities and communication. As Arendt argues, the essence of the public realm is the reality imposed on our actions when those actions are observed by ourselves and by fellow participants in the public realm. It is when the consequences of their combined actions are perceived, understood, esteemed, desired, that the identity of "we the people" takes on added meaning. The first graders who sang the Preamble to the Constitution in public at the opening of this chapter were enacting at that moment what it means to be "we the people." Their public performance was observed and made real. Borrowing from Dewey, we see that in recognizing the consequences of their behavior upon that of others and of others upon themselves, these young people developed an affection for the community, the polity to which they belonged.

In 2008, the Civilian Conservation Corps (CCC) celebrated its seventy-fifth anniversary. To mark the event, the National Park Service, which runs a Junior Ranger program throughout the national parks, organized a special CCC Junior Ranger program at the Grand Canyon National Park in Arizona. One of the activities for children, eager to earn their Junior Ranger badges, was to walk the Grand Canyon Rim Trail and look for a heart-shaped rock implanted by a CCC crew member in the wall that the Corps

> TO say a pldge.
>
> To believe in
>
> each other.

Figure 3.4. "To say a pledge. To believe in each other." Statement of Stevie MacGregor about what a crew member of the Civilian Conservation Corps meant by implanting a heart-shaped rock in the Grand Canyon rim walk wall that his crew had constructed.

crew had constructed more than seven decades ago. Having found the rock, the junior ranger's assignment was to answer the question, "Why would a CCC crew member use such an unusual rock?" Here's what Stevie, my first-grade grandson, thought that the crew member was saying when he put that rock in the wall (see Figure 3.4):

The Constitution of the United States was established "to form a more perfect Union . . . [and to] promote the general welfare," but as Walzer observes, our sense of ourselves is not captured by the mere fact of our union. Rather, "we the people" is a kind of pledge, as Stevie put it, to believe in each other. It is an identity that is redefined and reconstructed over time through countless acts of working together to create a more perfect union.

chapter four

# Democracy

WINSTON CHURCHILL REFERRED to democracy as "the worst form of government except for all those other forms that have been tried from time to
time,"[1] and Abraham Lincoln considered democracy the "last, best hope of
earth."[2] However, as Robert Post, a Dean and Professor of Law at Yale Law
School, points out, democracy is an elastic synonym for good government,
stretching to include whatever is desirable in a state.[3] Thus, although it is
highly valued, the meaning of democracy tends to get lost in a "cacophony
of competing interpretations."[4] In this chapter, I summarize the definitions
of democracy provided by a group of adolescents from the United States
and relate the meaning it holds for individual adolescents to the personal and
family values they consider important. In short, I want to demonstrate that
there is a pattern in the "cacophony" of individual meanings for democracy
that young people espouse.

At its root, the word "democracy" is derived from the Greek δῆμος
(*dêmos*), meaning "people," and κράτος (*Kratos*), meaning "power." Although the textbook definition emphasizes popular sovereignty and majority rule, the mere manifestation of "people power" does not guarantee that

its exercise will be democratic. Popular sovereignty can also be expressed through fascism if the leader enjoys the approval of the vast majority of the people. According to Post, it is wrong to conflate democracy with particular decision-making procedures and to fail to place at its center the core values (equality and freedom) that this form of government seeks to instantiate. Popular sovereignty is not the key because self-government does not concern the making of decisions but the *authorship* of decisions. The real question is who gets to decide. If the authorship of decisions is what matters, then equal treatment of persons is a core democratic value insofar as those persons are autonomous agents participating in the process of self-government.

Democracy in America offers different ideological traditions from which youth can choose. In this chapter, I explore the deeper personal meanings, that is, those aspects that democracy holds as an ideal for individual teens. As Erikson argues, it is in adolescence when youth try to find a concordance between their own ideals and identities and the ideals of a group.[5] Thus I explore Erikson's assertion by looking for a concordance between the ideological tradition an adolescent chooses when discussing what democracy means to her and the personal and family values that reflect the teen's own ideals and identity.

Adolescents' definitions of democracy were obtained via an open-ended question, "People have different ideas about what it means for a society to be a democracy. In your own words, what does democracy mean to you?" A total of three responses (including incorrect definitions) were coded so that the breadth of students' responses could be captured. Next, I discuss correct and incorrect definitions and the factors related to the likelihood that teens would provide at least one correct definition. Following that, I concentrate only on the group with correct definitions and examine the factors associated with the different meanings that young people attach to democracy.[6]

## CORRECT DEFINITIONS OF DEMOCRACY

The decision about correct definitions was based both on political theory and on those definitions of democracy considered acceptable in two congressionally mandated surveys of educational achievement conducted by the National Assessment of Educational Progress (NAEP). Incorrect responses in the current study included simple statements such as "I don't know" or those that were too vague to code meaningfully (i.e., "democracy is how the government tries to run things"; "democracy is very valuable and should be everywhere") or simply incorrect definitions (e.g., "democracy means the rich get richer"). For example, a thirteen-year-old white female whose parents both had post-baccalaureate degrees responded, "I don't know. It doesn't linger in my mind much," and a fifteen-year-old black male said that democracy meant "having a government."

Overall, just half of the respondents gave a correct answer. Before discussing the correlates of teens' correct answers, let us look more closely at one incorrect response—because it illustrates, in my view, the processes through which political understandings take shape. I use this example from a seventeen-year-old Puerto Rican female who answered, "I really don't know what it [democracy] means" to illustrate Vygotsky's premise that people's concepts, ideas, beliefs (on the mental plane) are internalizations of the experiences they have with other people (on the social plane).

Although this young woman feels that she does not know what democracy is, she does articulate relevant personal experiences about what it has been like for her to live in a democratic society. For example, when asked to describe a time when she felt like an American, this same young woman said, "when I'm around people that treat me like anybody else," and when asked to report the most important values emphasized in her own family, she stated, "stand up for your rights/dont [sic] prejudice, do good in life." She had trouble articulating its meaning in words; yet she was learning its meaning through the values emphasized in her family and, presumably, enacted in her life: she was learning the meaning of democracy by standing up for her rights and, at the same time, remaining open-minded rather than dismissive of or prejudiced toward other people, signaled in her family's value, "dont prejudice."

She was reticent to put the meaning of democracy into words. Nonetheless, she knew that there were times when she had experienced being a member of this democracy in the United States, when she was treated as an equal of others, and when she was included "like anybody else." The fact that she did not feel ready to define democracy in words but had an affective sense of belonging to a democratic society and an emotional bond to its principles illustrates the concept of diffuse support for the polity, that is, that positive affective regard for the principles of a political system precede and make possible knowledge about the system. Likewise, as Vygotsky argues, her ideas about democracy were taking shape in her experiences and encounters with others on the social plane.[7]

Three factors distinguished teens who could give a correct answer from those who could not. First, older adolescents were more likely to give a correct definition. The adolescent's age is a proxy for many unmeasured experiences as well as an indicator of increased cognitive and linguistic capabilities. Between early and late adolescence, there is an increasing capacity to deal with abstract concepts, to reason about social issues, and to understand those issues from different perspectives.[8]

Second, a family's socioeconomic status, in this case measured by parental education, is a proxy for many unmeasured opportunities for learning. As other studies have found, many of the experiences that matter for learning about democracy accrue to children whose parents are well educated. Within the home, there are likely to be more resources such as books, computers, Internet access, and adults who engage the teen in conversations about current events. Advantages of parental education extend beyond the confines of the home through the after-school and community-based organizations, lessons, and contacts to which families have access. Further, as is widely known, the quality of public schooling differs across communities because property tax base funding streams for public education vary. Besides schooling, more advantaged families enjoy greater access to social and political capital, greater likelihood of incorporation in political networks with clout, as well as greater attention from elected officials to their concerns.[9]

Third, as reflected in this study, parental education also was positively associated with the likelihood that a family would discuss current events and politics with their teen, a practice that served to distinguish those teens who could correctly define democracy from their peers who could not. Thus, in addition to the finding that teens whose parents had more formal education were more likely to correctly define democracy, a third factor distinguishing those who could define democracy from those who could not was whether the teen discussed politics and current events at home—and this practice was more common in families with more formal education.

## FAMILY DISCUSSIONS OF CURRENT EVENTS

Families are the earliest and possibly the most enduring context in which adolescents' political theories are formulated. When families discuss politics and current events and the teen actively participates in those discussions, that teen, regardless of age or other demographic factors, is able to provide some correct definition of democracy. Why? Several interpretations come to mind: First, such discussions could be driven by teens who are already interested in politics and current events and who therefore initiate discussions with their parents. Second, some families are likely to be more politically attuned than others, and thus current events discussions would more naturally occur in those settings. In this regard, compelling evidence is provided in analyses of data collected from more than three thousand parents and their adolescent children as part of the U.S. Department of Education's National Household Education Survey (NHES). Hugh McIntosh and his colleagues found that adolescents who discussed politics more frequently with their parents also reported higher levels of national news monitoring, political knowledge, public communication skills, and engagement in community service. Furthermore, with respect to knowledge about democracy, McIntosh and colleagues found that adolescents' political knowledge was most likely to be affected by political discussions in homes where parents themselves knew a lot about politics.[10] In other words, parental education would have a multiplicative effect on a child's political knowledge. In summary, there are multiplicative advantages to growing up in a well-educated family—exposure to and inclusion in political discussions, discussions that are informed by factual knowledge and very likely different perspectives, to say nothing of the ripple effects, for example, of being in classrooms with peers who come from families that engage in similar discussion practices.

Considerable evidence from cross-sectional, longitudinal, and retrospective studies shows that family discussions of current events are both correlated with and highly predictive of civic actions such as voting, volunteering, raising money for charity, participating in community meetings, petitioning, and boycotting.[11] In families that discuss current events or controversial issues and that encourage teens to hold their own opinions about those issues, youth are more knowledgeable about and interested in civic issues, better able to see and to tolerate the perspectives of others.[12] Of course, discussions of current events in families tend to correlate with other parent behaviors. Not surprisingly, parents in such families also are likely to be engaged in the civic affairs of their communities and thus provide models of civic action for their offspring. Furthermore, at least one study identified adolescents' participation in discussions of current events with parents as *the* most important factor predicting youths' volunteering and voting.[13]

Consider the civic lessons and habits developed through the family practice of engaging the adolescent in conversations about politics and current events. First, we can assume that this practice teaches a civic value, that is, staying informed on social issues, hearing different perspectives, and voicing one's opinion are important goals. Such discussions in families may convey a message to the teen that political issues are worthy of attention. They matter.

Second, interest in political issues tends to be generated by controversy, that is, by the recognition that political issues are contested. Not only do family discussions of politics increase the likelihood that a young person will vote when s/he comes of age; competitive election climates also increase youth voter turnout.[14] The common denominator is the fact that political issues can be seen from different perspectives and resolved in different ways. When adolescents are aware that reasonable people disagree on issues but that everybody is affected by how the issues are resolved, they may pay more attention. Controversy itself makes issues more salient and may motivate teens to reflect on where they stand. According to Robert Post, without debate, there is no democracy, a point he makes by quoting Hans Kelsen: "The will of the community, in a democracy, is always created through a running discussion between majority and minority, through free consideration of arguments for and against a certain regulation of a subject matter. . . . A democracy without public opinion is a contradiction in terms—in other words, democracy implies that debate is a good thing."[15]

Third, family discussions of current events and politics may predict teens' knowledge about democracy because those discussions play a role in the process of civic identity formation. By participating with their parents in those conversations, teens are constructing an understanding of themselves as citizens, that is, self-determining persons who have their own opinions and who can wrangle with fellow citizens (in this case, parents) over issues of common concern. Some of the items in our measure of family discussions of current events are based on the teen's reports that they and their parents sometimes have different viewpoints but that their parents listen to and consider their views on issues. This suggests that such family discussions can be an occasion for teens to crystallize their positions—argue and defend them with fellow citizens. Through this practice, teens also learn about the authorship of decisions at the heart of democracy. In a democracy, Robert Post argues, government should be experienced as authored by oneself, not by a powerful other.

By listening to and considering the adolescent's views, parents show, despite the difference in age, that the young person's opinions are worthy of respect and that adults ought to listen to what young people have to say. In addition, the parent-child exchange models how members of a civil society should treat one another, that is, with mutual respect. Participating in such discussions might also teach teens that having different perspectives is a way that citizens can resolve shared public problems. Studies of moral development have referred to parent-adolescent communications that are characterized by mutual respect, open communication, and challenging moral discussions as democratic parenting.[16] Emotional bonds between parents and their children are strengthened by such communication, leading to the likelihood that children will want to emulate their parents and adopt their values.[17] Such practices also may motivate an ethic of civic participation: according to one longitudinal study, maternal attentiveness and responsiveness to kindergarten-age children actually predicted the likelihood in their young adult years that those children would be politically active in the social movements of the 1960s.[18] In summary, we can think of families as mini-polities where the civic dispositions and identities of younger generations are being formed. When parents and adolescents engage in discussions of current events and politics, the teen learns the skills of dealing with controversial and contested issues in a civil fashion. The teen learns how to listen and to respect different perspectives and the citizens who hold them. And s/he learns that participation in civic affairs matters, that it's important to take a stand, and that s/he and fellow citizens are the authors of decisions that affect them.

## OPPORTUNITIES FOR CIVIC PRACTICE IN COMMUNITY-BASED ORGANIZATIONS

Besides families, opportunities for various forms of civic practice in schools and community-based organizations (CBOs) matter for the development of civic knowledge and commitments in younger generations.

Several longitudinal studies have shown that voting and volunteering in young adulthood is higher if individuals, regardless of their social background, have opportunities for civic practice during the elementary and high school years. In particular, involvement in extracurricular activities in adolescence that engage students in debate, public speaking, performance, and community service predict civic engagement in early adulthood.[19] The common element in this set of activities is that each engages young people in some form of acting in public. (For more on civic learning through community service, see Chapter 8.)

Civic engagement is public work. It is accomplished by members of the public working together. In each of the extracurricular activities mentioned above, the students are standing in front of or with other members of the public—in debate or public speaking, they are articulating their views, and in performance and community service, they are interacting with fellow citizens to accomplish some common goal. As Arendt points out, two things constitute action in the public realm: First, the term "public" signifies that things that appear in that realm can be seen and heard by everybody. Second, in contrast to mass society that has lost its power to gather people together in a meaningful way, the public realm is the common world that gathers us together.

Practice in the public realm occurs for children and adolescents through their membership in institutions such as schools, extracurricular activities, and community-, cultural-, and faith-based organizations. Historically, the United States has prided itself in being a society of equal opportunity where public schools and community organizations help to level the playing field. Yet, not only are there significant disparities in civic opportunities between schools in different communities, there also are ethnic and social class differences within the same high schools: students from ethnic-minority or working-class backgrounds are less likely than those from ethnic-majority and middle-class backgrounds to be in classes that offer a host of opportunities for civic practice (e.g., debates, mock trials, studying the Constitution, volunteer work).[20]

Besides formal schooling, nonformal opportunities for civic practice, for example, through community organizations or service projects, are less common in disadvantaged communities due to child saturation (i.e., the higher ratio of children to adults) in those neighborhoods. As Robert Atkins and Daniel Hart show, community organizations rely on adult volunteers, and poor communities have fewer adults available for the number of children who could benefit from participating in an organization. Consequently, compared to their peers in suburban communities, children in high-poverty urban neighborhoods have fewer opportunities for nonformal civic practice through community-based organizations that are guided by adults. Youth in affluent communities have more informal opportunities to practice democracy in groups that are guided or coached by adults. Consequently, they have more civic knowledge and are more politically tolerant compared to those growing up in communities of concentrated poverty where there is a much lower adult to child ratio.[21] Taken together, social class and ethnic differences in opportunities for civic practice and political incorporation mean that the civic participation of younger generations is, as the political scientists Sidney Verba, Nancy Burns, and Kay Lehman Schlozman put it, "uneven at the starting line."[22]

## PERSONAL MEANING OF DEMOCRACY:
## CLUSTERING TEENS' RESPONSES

Identifying the correlates of political knowledge helps us predict which adolescents would be more likely to give a correct definition of democracy. However, it tells us nothing about those aspects of democracy that are salient to particular adolescents.

To provide structure to the "cacophony of competing interpretations," I have framed the discussion of the teens' definitions into three major categories. The first category includes references to individual freedom, rights, and self-determination; the second includes references to majority rule or representative government; and the third contains any reference to civic equality, to equal opportunity for all groups, or to the common good. The latter two categories broadly reflect the two previously defined public philosophies of liberalism and republicanism.[23]

The statements that were assigned to the first category (individual rights and freedoms) included references to specific freedoms (e.g., of speech); to statements of "my freedom"; to freedom of information; and, for many, to just the term "freedom." This category captured the liberal conception of an individual who is a bearer of rights unencumbered by responsibilities to a larger whole. The statements assigned to the second category (representative government and majority rule) included those referring to voting, majority rule, electing representatives, and rule by the people. Statements assigned to the third category (civic equality) included references to equal opportunities for participation, the rights of different groups to freely associate and express opinions, and equal protection under the law. This category captured the republican conception of liberty realized in a web of relationships with others. Here the role of citizen, concerned with the whole and the need to defend the rights of all, is salient.

### References to Freedom and Rights of the Individual

An eighth-grade white male said, "Democracy means a place where people are free to decide what they want as long as they aren't hurting other people." A twelfth-grade white female felt that democracy was "not being under control. Free to a point." Each of these statements indicates the teen's awareness that the freedom that an individual enjoys cannot be exercised *at the expense* of others' similar freedoms, that is, that a citizen in a democracy has to respect others' rights. Yet, these adolescents do not refer to any interactions or deliberations with others that would determine what might be "hurting other people" or how one would know the boundaries of "free to a point," although discussions facilitated by adults could encourage teens to consider how those issues would be determined. The teens whose responses were assigned to this category allude to the fact that there are other human beings besides the self and that one should respect them. Such respect for the autonomy of other free human beings but without reference to their relationships or roles in a community is consistent with a liberal philosophy of tolerance for the rights of other individuals to hold their own views but with no necessary exchange of perspectives or attempt to bridge differences.

A white sixteen-year-old from a well-educated family felt cynical about the contrast between the promise and the reality of democracy as practiced in the United States: "To me, true democracy is freedom with the exception of laws to protect others. I don't think our so called 'democracy' is going to survive much longer by the way things are going." On the other hand, the meaning that democracy held for several first-generation Americans whose families were from the Middle East was a contrast to the lack of freedom that their parents had known in their sending countries. For example, one female twelfth grader said, "A democracy means that I am free. Unlike other countries where the people are punished for stupid things or where there is not enough food to survive. For some of my Yemeni friends, girls will get married and not get educated." Her example captures the liberal notion of freedom from social roles that bind the self to traditions that, in her estimation, can suffocate self-determination and free expression. Her statement also alludes to the concept of capabilities laid out in the work of Martha Nussbaum and Amartya Sen, who challenge the idea that autonomy is simply a matter of free choice.[24] Despite her lack of knowledge about food insecurity in the United States, this teen seems to realize that *freedoms to* exercise self-determination depend on certain *freedoms from*—that the satisfaction of basic needs is a necessary foundation in order to be capable of political participation. Although Nussbaum and Sen list capabilities that all human beings should be free to choose, they also believe that democratic processes in communities should be the basis by which people determine how they want to develop the capabilities of their own members.

Additional insights into adolescents' ideas about democracy can be derived by combining their response to the question, "What does it mean to be an American?" (discussed in Chapter 3) with their views on the meaning of democracy. For example, a thirteen-year-old Native-American male said that to be American meant "to be free" and that democracy is "people who think of themselves." Freedom of the individual informs both definitions. We can also consider the responses of a fifteen-year-old girl whose insights were informed by her family's moves to different communities, first from Puerto Rico to New York City and then to a rural and largely white community a hundred miles from New York City. She defined democracy as a society "where everyone can state their own opinions." On its face, the emphasis is on the free speech of individuals, that is, their rights to hold and to speak their own minds. However, if we also consider her responses to what it means to be an American, about times when she felt like an American, and times when she was reminded of her ethnic identity, we see that there are layers of meaning that underlie references to freedom. Consistent with her definition of democracy, she felt that to be American meant "to be able to do or think or even speak out what you feel." But when she relates times when she was reminded of her ethnic and American identities, she states, "When I lived in New York I felt very close to my ethnic & cultural group. Now that I'm here I don't get very many chances to experience them any more. But I feel American when I am actually treated equally." In New York City, her cultural identity was reinforced through relationships with fellow members of her ethnic group. By contrast, in the rural community where her family moved, she is aware of her ethnic-minority identity because she attends schools with a predominantly white majority group. Yet she identifies her experience of being treated equally, the ability to think or even speak what she feels as practices that reinforce her sense of inclusion in the American identity.

In summary, teens' statements that were assigned to the category of individual freedom and rights refer in one way or another to self-determination and to the notion of self-authorship of decisions that Robert Post argues is a central feature of democracy. Some of the teens' statements also pick up on the individual determining when and how and with whom s/he experiences and participates in democracy. However, statements in this category reflect an image of individual liberty that is unencumbered with civic obligations or with responsibilities to the community of which one is a part. The only allusion to responsibility is that an individual is *not* free to infringe on the rights of other individuals.

## References to Majority Rule and Representative Government

This category captured references to representative democracy, that is, to elected officials who base their decisions on the consent of the governed. The words of three Arab-American high school students captured this sentiment: "to be able to vote for your president and to have somewhat of a say in politics"; "a country ruled by the government but by people's consent"; and "majority rule, people's opinions are often given and rightfully so." The voice of the people in the government was salient for one fifteen-year-old African-American female who said democracy is "a form of govt where everybody has a say in the govt." She added that to be American means "to have freedom and know I'm just as good as anybody else." Her addition of the final phrase, "knowing I'm just as good as anybody else" resonates with the equal treatment that the previously discussed Puerto Rican teen mentioned when referring to her experiences of feeling like an American.

A fifteen-year-old white female from a working-class family said, "A democracy is a type of government run by the people for the people. The citizens choose who they want to represent them." A fourteen-year-old white male of German descent who identified his experiences in ROTC (Reserve Officers' Training Corps) as the time when he felt most like an American, said, "To me democracy means the people decide and I like that because unlike a monarchy the leader of our country is not passed down by a family who gets to choose who would be the best for our country." A seventeen-year-old Latino whose parents had not finished high school took the voice of the people a step further, noting that elections were not the be-all and end-all of rule by the people. For him democracy means, "I have a vote on what happens in government. And if I choose I can form protestion [sic] against the government." His sentiments resonate with the theory of a social contract proposed in the works of John Locke and of Thomas Aquinas before him, that citizens have the right to withdraw support from the government if the government fails to be responsive to or protect citizens' rights.

## References to Civic Equality

To be coded in this category, a response had to include some indication that *all* people have the right to an equal voice or that everyone, regardless of their social status, identity, or ethnic background, is entitled to equal treatment under the law or to equal opportunity for political participation. For example, a fifteen-year-old white male felt that "A democracy means to me that everyone has equal say in how something's run. No matter who they are or where they stand." A thirteen-year-old African-American male felt democracy meant "having equal opportunities, equal chances to speak," and a thirteen-year-old white female from a working-class family said, "Democracy is a government where we try to understand one another and not care about the color of your skin." For all her tender years, civic republican sentiments are quite palpable in her choice of words. "A government where we try to understand one another" references the republican view of citizens deliberating together in order to govern themselves. We can dig a bit more deeply into ways that her personal experiences may have contributed to her political views. In response to whether she had ever experienced an instance of prejudice or discrimination, she refers to exclusions based on her gender: "when you can't do things because you're a girl." Based on her own experiences of exclusion, of being told "you can't do that because you're a girl," it would seem that she also has become aware of exclusions that other groups (in this case racial groups based on skin color) might experience and that intergroup understanding and a system that transcends racial divisions are salient features of the democracy to which she aspires. Finally, one Arab-American whose parents had not finished high school felt that the equality standard was an ideal to which the people could hold government accountable. For her, democracy meant "equality. Until we can all be treated equally, then the American government has no right to claim that it is a democracy."

Her observation that we may not have attained the American ideal echoes Walt Whitman's sentiments in his essay *Democratic Vistas,* where he insists that the promise of democracy should be realized in universal suffrage, a notion that many in his day challenged:

> We endow *the masses with the suffrage* for their own sake; then perhaps still more, for community's sake. We try often, though we fall back often. . . . The democratic formula is the only safe and preservative one for coming times. . . . Far, far, indeed, stretch, in distance, our Vistas! How much is still to be disentangled, freed! How long it takes to make this American world see that it is, in itself, the final authority, and reliance!
>
> Did you, too, O friend, suppose democracy was only for elections, for politics, and for a party name? I say democracy is only of use there that it may pass on and come to its flower and fruits in manners, in the highest forms of interaction between men, and their beliefs.[25]

According to Whitman, it is incorrect to reduce democracy to elections, and it is wrong to consider democracy merely as a political system or form of government. Rather, democracy in his view is a training school where people have to practice and learn. By acting, by practice, people will develop certain kinds of dispositions. By their actions as the sovereign authority, the people will develop habits that they will pass on to posterity. Democracy, in Whitman's estimation, is only worthwhile, only useful, if it affects the way people interact, if it shapes what they believe.

Indeed, the full promise of democracy cannot be realized through laws, elections, or institutions but only through the collective will of people committed to its ideals. And that collective will depends on the nurturing of democratic dispositions in people. In a classic paper co-authored by John Sullivan, a psychologist and John Transue, a political scientist, two traits are defined as essential for democracy in America to thrive: First is tolerance, based on open-mindedness to the opinions of others, but also commitment

to the defense of others' rights to voice opinions with which we fundamentally disagree. Second is a commitment to participate in the joint
decision-making process that defines democratic governance. Without
broad participation by the people as the sovereign authority, there can be
no democracy.[26]

Many of the adolescents wrote more than one meaning for democracy
and up to three were coded.

## INDIVIDUAL FREEDOM OR RIGHTS AND MAJORITY RULE

A fifteen-year-old white female from a highly educated family said, "Democracy means being a part of the government you live under. It is the
right to express your feelings and ideas especially in a vote," and another
high schooler from a working-class family said, "having the right to express
your opinions & going w/ the majority of opinion." A seventeen-year-old
white female from a working-class family was adamant that her voice be
heard by a government that she worried might pay attention to more powerful constituents, "Being able to have my part in a gov't that is often ruled
by one group of people, my vote—my opinion—my choice—my country."

## MAJORITY RULE OR REPRESENTATIVE DEMOCRACY
## AND CIVIC EQUALITY

A fourteen-year-old white female whose parents were both well educated said
that democracy meant that "all people are treated fairly no matter what sur-
comstance [sic] or background. People choose how the government is to be
run." A seventeen-year-old white male from a well-educated family, attending
a special summer school based on academic merit, said, "A place where everyone has equal opportunity and gets to make group decisions for our country."
And a fourteen-year-old Arab-American female said, "It means getting a fair
and equal chance at everything. And having a voice in the government."

## CIVIC EQUALITY AND INDIVIDUAL RIGHTS OR FREEDOM

A fifteen-year-old white girl from a single-parent household who attended a
school in a working-class community said, "freedom of speech, freedom of

choice, and just about every one can have some kind of rights." And another girl, "To me democracy means equal rights for all. It means freedom of speech and opinion."

## Democratic Themes: Cluster Analyses

As already discussed, democracy has different meanings and an individual teenager could have mentioned more than one meaning in her statements. However, in order to bring structure to the cacophony of competing views, it is important to form groups based on the salience of particular themes. To do so, I used cluster analytic techniques to form groups based on the patterns of youths' responses. Remember that a total of three responses were coded for each individual. A teen could have referred to majority rule or representative government all three times or could have referred to an individual's freedom once and majority rule once.

The cluster analysis was based on assigning each teen a score on three variables: $A$, the number of times that s/he mentioned individual rights/ freedom; $B$, the number of times that s/e mentioned some aspect of majority rule or representative government; and $C$, the number of times she referred to some aspect of civic equality. Thematic salience was based on the pattern of an individual's response. If a respondent never mentioned a theme (e.g., individual rights), s/he would have a score of 0 on that variable and could not be assigned to that cluster. In instances where respondents mentioned multiple categories, their assignment to a cluster was based on the proportion and order of themes mentioned.

Figure 4.1 presents the mean scores for each cluster on the three variables. The first cluster consists of 108 respondents for whom freedom and the rights of individuals were most salient; the second of 112 cases for whom civic equality was most meaningful; and the third of 148 cases in which the main emphasis was on majority rule or representative government. As the figure shows, some respondents in each cluster mentioned more than one theme, but their assignment to a particular cluster was based on the salience of one theme over others, that is, the fact that they had mentioned a particular category more than others.

Based on chi-square tests of independence, membership in a cluster was unrelated to the teen's race or ethnicity or to their parents' level of education, In other words, the meaning of democracy that was salient to a teen

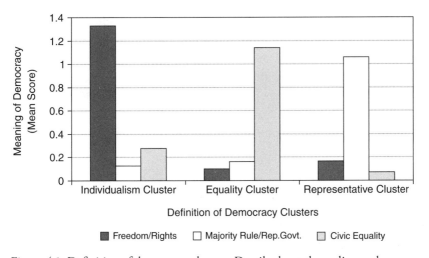

Figure 4.1. Definition of democracy clusters. Details about the coding and construction of clusters and scales are provided in the Appendix in the discussion of Chapters 3 and 4.

(whether representative rule or individual freedom or equality) did not depend on whether his parents had finished college or had less than a high school education. Nor did the words that the teen used to describe democracy depend on whether s/he identified as African-, Arab-, Latino-, or European-American. However, there were significant differences between clusters in the pattern of values that the adolescents endorsed.

## Values and the Meaning of Democracy

Why would we expect values and personal meanings of democracy to be related? The disciplines of political science and psychology provide complementary answers to this question. With respect to the former, Easton refers to politics as the "authoritative allocation of values." In Easton's famous phrase, values refer both to intangibles (goals, principles, ideas) and to tangibles (services, benefits) that large numbers of people within a political community consider desirable. Politics also refers to the policies and practices by which the government distributes goods, services, or benefits across different segments of society.[27]

Psychology provides an alternative argument for the connection between values and political views, one that is rooted in adolescent development.

Adolescence is considered a time in life when an individual explores who s/he is and what s/he stands for. Erikson[28] describes identity as involving a sense of one's uniqueness but also a striving for continuity or inner harmony and for solidarity with a group's ideals. For him, an ideological perspective, a "system of ideas that provides a convincing world image," is a source of identity strength, enabling the young person to simplify the world by finding a correspondence between "the inner world of ideals and the social world with its goals."

In the process of identity exploration, teens will search for ideologies, meaningful philosophies, and images of the world to which they can commit. They will choose values that express the goals that they desire and that reflect the kind of people they want to be. Values are derived from and also influence ideologies; in other words, our values lead us to certain belief systems and those belief systems either reinforce our values or cause us to reflect on and rethink them. In order to be authentic or true to himself, an adolescent also seeks a concordance, an internal harmony in his values and ideals.[29] Drawing from Erikson, I am arguing that the values that guide adolescents' personal lives are concordant with their ideals and their political theories, in this case, the personal meaning that democracy holds for them. In other words, the kinds of choices youth make about their own lives are likely to be associated with the kind of society that has meaning for them. As the developmental psychologists James Youniss and Miranda Yates suggest, as youth consolidate their identities, they also are constituting their society.[30]

In this study, the choice of values was guided by Shalom H. Schwartz's theory about the structure of human values.[31] In studies conducted across many countries, Schwartz has found evidence for a universal structure of human values, which reflects two bipolar dimensions: the first he refers to as conformity to tradition versus openness to new experience, and the second he calls self-transcendence versus self-enhancement. I focus on the latter dimension since it is more relevant to the liberal and civic republican philosophies that have shaped public discourse on the meaning of democracy in the United Sates. According to Schwartz, values reflect our priorities, that is, the importance that a person attaches to one type of goal over others: for example, when personal achievement is a high priority, a goal that an individual desires, she invests time in and attention to her own success and spends less time attending to the needs of others. In Schwartz's model, by investing in self-enhancement she disinvests in self-transcendent values.

In my survey of adolescents, values were tapped in two ways: first, by asking adolescents to rate the personal importance that they attached to a set of future goals; second, by asking them to indicate the extent to which their families emphasized particular ways of treating other people. With respect to the latter, I have conceived of family values as ways that parents frame or interpret the world and relationships with other people in the world for their children: What image of the world, what attitudes toward fellow human beings, do teens hear at home? Is the world a place where you need to look out for yourself lest others get an upper hand, or is the world a place we inhabit with other people, where empathy for fellow human beings and responsibility for the world we share is called for?

Adolescents indicated their agreement with a set of items that tapped the adolescent's personal values as well as the values and practices emphasized in their families. A full set of the items and scales is provided in the Appendix. Here a representative item for each scale is provided. The personal values included scales measuring "altruism," or the young person's reported willingness to renounce certain privileges in order for a benefit to accrue to needy others, and "materialism," or the importance the teen attached to earning a lot of money and having possessions. For family values, the "social responsibility" scale tapped adolescents' perceptions that their parents modeled and inculcated an ethic of responsibility for fellow human beings and the "social vigilance" scale tapped the teens' reports that their parents cautioned them that they should be wary about people in the world who might take advantage of them. Two family practices were also tapped: the first, "environmental responsibility," measured the extent to which a family recycled, and the second, the degree to which they "discussed current events and politics."

Note that adolescents' reports of the values they *hear* in families and not parents' reports of the values they teach are used. This decision is based on value socialization theory, which indicates that children have to first perceive and then choose to follow parents' values if those values are going to be internalized. The decision to use the teens' reports also is consistent with empirical work showing that increases over time in adolescents' sense of social responsibility are predicted by the compassion for others that they *hear* in their family and not by the compassion that their mothers say they emphasize.[32]

Social responsibility, altruism, and environmentalism were conceptualized as occupying the self-transcending end of Schwartz's continuum, and social vigilance and materialism were conceived as reflecting the self-enhancing end. Empirical studies have shown that other-oriented values such as social responsibility are positively related to a wide range of helping behaviors and civic actions in adolescence including volunteering and community service and pro-environmental behaviors.[33] Current events discussions, while not conceived as a value, should be relevant to knowledge about democracy, as reported in an earlier part of this chapter. However, there is no reason to assume that such discussions orient adolescents to particular ideals about democracy. In contrast, personal and family values reflect normative goals, standards about how one should live, act, and relate to fellow human beings. Views about others and about the common world we inhabit are embedded in these values. As such, personal and family values should be associated in consistent ways with the visions of democracy that come to mind when teens are asked about the personal meaning that democracy holds for them.

## SOCIAL CLASS DIFFERENCES IN ADOLESCENTS' REPORTS OF VALUES

There were social class differences in adolescents' reports of their own and their family's values and practices. Specifically, compared to their peers whose parents had lower levels of education, youth in better educated families were less likely to endorse materialist values and more likely to report that their families emphasized social and environmental responsibility. The inverse relationship between social class and materialist values suggests that material goals are more important for groups who have attained less measure of the American dream. This interpretation is consistent with Abraham H. Maslow's hierarchy of needs and their fulfillment. Likewise, it is a good fit with Ronald Inglehart and his colleague's argument about the bases for generational shifts toward post-materialist values, specifically, that people can prioritize values of humanism, self-determination, and environmentalism once they attain a certain degree of freedom from want.[34]

The inverse relationship between social class and materialism has been found in other work on family socialization and youth's values.[35] But it should come as no surprise that if young people are constantly surrounded with messages that material gain is the uncontested mark of success in life and they and their families have attained remarkably little of it, the youth would focus on attaining that goal. Values are functional and, to the extent that individuals do not enjoy the basics that enable them to exercise their rights and responsibilities as citizens, they will yearn for some measure of that aspect of the American dream.

## Values and the Meaning of Democracy

After controlling for any social class differences in values, I next compared the values and practices endorsed by adolescents in the three democracy clusters. These results are shown in Figure 4.2. At the bottom of the figure—starting on the left along the x-axis, two family values are listed (social responsibility and social vigilance) and two family practices (environmentalism

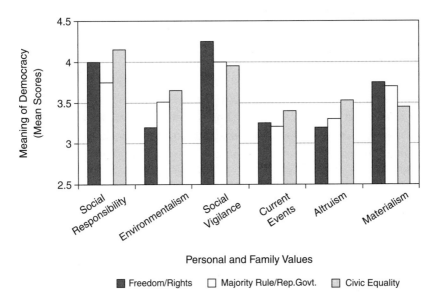

Figure 4.2. Personal and family values. Scales were based on the mean of items in the scale. The precise wording for all items is provided in the Appendix in the section on Chapter 4.

and discussions of current events). On the right of the *x*-axis, two personal values endorsed by adolescents are listed (altruism and materialism).

First, observe that across the three clusters, family values of social responsibility and social vigilance are highly endorsed by all groups. According to the teens' reports, most families engage in these two forms of communication—about fellow human beings and how one should interact with them—reaching out and helping others in need and being discerning about others who might take advantage. In contrast, adolescents are less likely to report that they engage in discussions of current events with their parents. With respect to teens' personal values, materialist values tend to be more highly endorsed, on average, than are altruist goals.

Now let us consider how the three democracy clusters differed in their endorsements of family and personal values and practices. Looking across the constructs listed on the *x*-axis, we can see that the civic equality cluster differs from the other two but especially from the freedom and rights cluster. In terms of personal goals, the civic equality group was less likely to endorse materialism when compared to peers in both of the other clusters. Compared to their peers in the freedom and rights cluster, those in the civic equality cluster said that their families placed more emphasis on environmentalism and less on social vigilance toward other people. Endorsement of social vigilance was also higher for the freedom and rights cluster than for the majority rule cluster.

In other words, no matter what their parents' level of education, those teens who had a liberal interpretation of democracy (emphasizing a free individual unfettered by roles or responsibilities) were more likely than peers for whom democracy meant majority rule or civic equality to hear their parents emphasize guardedness and caution about other people, lest those others take undue advantage. This finding does not mean that one causes the other. It does, however, point to a logical consistency between a liberal interpretation of democracy that favors the rights of an individual, unfettered by having to deal with or accommodate others, with the values an adolescent was urged to follow by his family, values that reflected a particular view of the world and attitude toward others in that world, that is, to treat others with guardedness, protecting oneself from the possibilities that those others may get an upper hand.

Adolescents in the three clusters also differed in reports of social responsibility, with those in the civic equality group more likely than peers in the majority rule cluster to note that their families emphasized social responsibility as a value to live by. In other words, when adolescents heard values of caring for others in their homes and witnessed their parents' anger in the face of injustice, those teens were more inclined to conceive of democracy in civic republican terms.

In summary, there was a significant and consistent pattern of relationships, a concordance between the democratic themes that resonate with adolescents and the values that they and their families endorse. Social vigilance and materialism were more prominent goals for youth whose views of democracy reflected a liberal tradition (emphasizing individual rights and freedom with little accountability to the whole), whereas responsibility for the environment and for people in need were the family values reported by youth for whom a civic republican theme (attending to the larger political community and concern for the whole) was salient.

Particularly noteworthy were the images of other people and of responsibility for the society one shared with them: environmental and altruistic goals (measures of self-transcendent values insofar as they tapped a teen's willingness to do her part in preserving natural resources or in foregoing or relinquishing privileges in order to balance the unequal resources of others) were more likely to be endorsed by the group of young people who defined democracy in civic republican terms. In contrast, the group who endorsed the liberal tradition, emphasizing individual freedom unencumbered by responsibilities of citizenship, also felt the need to safeguard themselves and to defend their advantages lest other people get an upper hand. If Schwartz is correct that our values reflect the setting of priorities (i.e., that when we invest in one type of value we do so at the expense of investing in others), these results suggest that the priority that we give to certain kinds of values in our lives (and in our child rearing) also is associated with the priority we give to certain features of a democratic society in which we live.

In *Habits of the Heart,* Robert Bellah and his colleagues raise concerns that a preoccupation with individual rights has eclipsed attention to the common good in the priorities of Americans today. Echoing Alexis de Tocqueville, they worry that if republican habits (of deliberating with others to find common ground) lose out to rabid individualism, we will no longer have narratives that help us make sense of our lives.[36] In contrast to the concerns raised by Bellah and others, there were roughly equal number of adolescents in the freedom and rights cluster and civic equality cluster.

Furthermore, regardless of their cluster membership, all youth endorsed social responsibility and social vigilance as values emphasized in their families. Thus, with respect to the personal meaning that democracy held for a sizable percentage of the adolescents in this study, some version of civic republicanism appears to be alive and well. With respect to ways that families frame relationships with others in the world, both social responsibility and, even more so, social vigilance were highly endorsed. The high endorsement of social vigilance, that is, warning youth to be wary about other people who might take advantage and get an upper hand—is consistent with the misanthropic image of people that has been ascendant in the past few decades. (For more on this issue, see Chapter 7.)

With respect to the family values reported by adolescents in this chapter, we can infer that most adolescents heard a balanced view concerning how one should treat other people. The teens said that their families told them to treat others with empathy and to be responsive to others' needs, especially those who are less fortunate. These admonitions to reach out and help others were balanced with a more cautious attitude toward people, that is, adolescents also reported that their parents told them that *sometimes* people may take advantage and that caution should moderate the spirit of kindness. Nonetheless, a clear concordance, echoing Erikson, exists between a teen's ideology or the meaning that democracy held for her and the personal and family values she espoused.

What sense can we make of the cacophony of competing interpretations of democracy? Answers can be found in the formative cultures of families and in adolescents' search for values that give their lives meaning. It is in the practices of mediating institutions, in which assumptions about citizenship and liberty inform our public life, that the habits and dispositions of the next generation of American citizens are being formed. Here I have focused on families as a mediating institution. In the next chapters, schools and friendships will figure as mediating institutions.

In the history of the United States, we have known no other form of government than democracy. But there is a danger in taking it for granted: democracy does not survive without constant vigilance and involvement of the people. In his history of American civic life, Michael Schudson traces how the definition of a good citizen has evolved through that history. Today, according to Schudson, we cannot expect individuals to be fully informed citizens because there is simply too much knowledge needed to make informed political decisions. Instead, the good citizen today should be one who is attentive to what the government is doing or failing to do and who is ready for action when action is called for.[37]

In one of the most defining moments in U.S. history, Abraham Lincoln debated Senator Stephen A. Douglas of Illinois in a contest for the U.S. senate seat. Douglas, the Democrat, held that democracy fundamentally boiled down to a question of majority rule (with the majority in 1828 who were eligible to vote composed of white men). In contrast, Lincoln based his interpretation of democracy on concepts of equal dignity as embodied in the Declaration of Independence. The essence of his argument was that popular suffrage alone could not legitimate a sovereign power if it did not respect the inherent dignity of all human beings. Nearly two hundred years have passed since those debates. Yet the story of democracy in the United States continues as a narrative that evolves with the collective values and decisions of her people. As new generations of young people take their place in the body politic, the values that they hold and the identities that give their lives a sense of purpose will determine the kinds of choices they will make. Ultimately, those choices will shape the character of democracy that will be our future.

As Walt Whitman reflected in *Democratic Vistas:*

> I submit, therefore, that the fruition of democracy, on aught like a grand scale, resides altogether in the future. . . .
>
> We have frequently printed the word Democracy. Yet I cannot too often repeat that it is a word the real gist of which still sleeps, quite unawaken'd, notwithstanding the resonance and the many angry tempests out of which its syllables have come, from pen or tongue. It is a great word, whose history, I suppose, remains unwritten, because that history has yet to be enacted.[38]

chapter five

# Laws and Public Health

ADOLESCENCE IS A period of heightened risk taking with potential consequences to the health and safety of the individual and to others in society. What then are teen views about the individual's "right" to take risks, and the role of the state in regulating and protecting the public? In the extensive literature on prevention, a science that focuses largely on averting behaviors that might compromise health, there is scant research on adolescents' views about such issues. In contrast, notions of rights and responsibilities are ubiquitous in public discourse on smoking and alcohol use. For example, in the tobacco litigations of the state attorneys general, arguments about freedom of speech and the rights and liabilities of individuals were pitted against those focusing on the costs to the public and the state's role in protecting youth from the health risks of smoking. Similar themes of individual rights and public accountability are echoed in discussions of binge drinking on college campuses and in debates about health care reform.

Understanding adolescents' views about laws meant to protect public health is important because like other political issues, the role of the state in enacting laws can be considered contested ground. Opponents argue that the consequences of actions such as substance use or extreme sports fall primarily on the individual and that restrictions constitute unacceptable limitations on choice. In contrast, those who favor regulation argue that some individual choices have implications for others' welfare and may result in increased costs and burdens to society; thus the state is justified in enacting laws or taxes to curb individuals from engaging in potential risks to their own and the public's health. The metaphor of a "social contract" is apt insofar as it implies responsibilities of the state to enact laws and policies in the interests of a common good and the willingness on the part of citizens to forgo some freedoms in order to be part of a society with such protections. In the case of a democratic society where authority is vested in the people, it is the people who give the state the authority to enact laws and taxes in order to secure the general welfare. Those laws or taxes may penalize or curb some individual behaviors, but the general public should benefit. The mandate for individuals to buy health insurance that was enacted as part of the health care reform bill of 2010 is an example of a recent policy based on this premise.

In this chapter, I draw from two data sets that focus on adolescents' perceptions of laws related to public health and their reflections on the rights of individuals to engage in risky behaviors. The focus is on laws and taxes, both actions on the part of the government that are meant to protect public health and welfare but that restrict individual freedom. One data set is a large longitudinal (three-year) survey study charting age differences in adolescents' endorsements of individual rights to engage in health risks and the government's right to enact laws that constrain individual choices. The other data set, which is the main focus of this chapter, is based on the open-ended responses of just under two hundred early and late adolescents to a set of hypothetical vignettes. The samples for both studies are socioeconomically and ethnically diverse; they include approximately equal numbers of males and females, and early through late adolescents.[1]

THE VIGNETTES

Adolescents responded to the following three hypothetical vignettes that involved smoking, driving under the influence (DUI) of alcohol, and wearing motorcycle helmets:

- Suppose there's a country where the government pays for health care for all of the people. A law is discussed which says that people who smoke must pay a special smoking tax to the government. The lawmakers say that smoking is bad for people's health and the government shouldn't have to pay for people's bad habits.

- Drunken driving accidents have become a big problem. A law is being discussed that says a person's license could be taken away for a year if his or her test showed that she or he was legally drunk.
- Studies show that if people wear helmets when they ride motorcycles, they won't get killed or have serious brain injury if they're in an accident. So a law is discussed that would make it illegal to ride a motorcycle without a helmet.[2]

For each of these questions, the respondent was asked, "What do you think *would* happen?" and "What do you think *should* happen?" Note that the public implications of individual health risks and the government's argument for why the particular law was justified were made salient in each of the vignettes.

## Responses to the Vignettes

The teens' written responses were coded using an "open-coding" content-analytic procedure with careful attention to subtle differences in the reasoning underlying the words. The seven major categories that resulted from this process are summarized below with verbatim responses included for each category. The discussion of categories is organized in a sequence with the defense of the laws and the state's authority in protecting public welfare discussed first, and the rights of individuals and the law's prejudicial infringement on individual choice discussed last. Thus in the first four categories, respondents tend to defend the state's actions (whether enacting laws, enforcing penalties or taxes), whereas in the last three categories, respondents either defend the individual (arguing for his rights or against the discriminatory potential of laws) or contend that the laws will be ineffective, largely because of the agency and challenges brought by individuals or groups.

### Achieving a Societal Goal: The Common Good of All

Responses coded in this category referred to the importance of laws in achieving a societal goal, one that would benefit the general public. For example, one young person argued that the smoking tax is sensible as a health cost strategy because "the people who smoke would have to go to the doctor more because they are more unhealthy; the government would save a lot of money this way." Concerning the DUI law, another youth contended that "drunk driving is very serious and it costs a lot of people their lives; no punishment is too harsh." The theme of preventing teenage deaths also was commonly invoked to defend the DUI law, as in the following: "it is a good plan to deter drunk driving and lesson [*sic*] teenage death."

The notion that some "hypothetical" country might pay for universal health care was noted by another teen who saw this protection provided by the state as implying a reciprocal responsibility on the part of citizens: "if there were a country like this (i.e., that provided universal health care) it would be great and those who try to cause more sickness to themselves and others should suffer by paying taxes." The youth also argues what, in his view, is a logical extension of such a social contract, i.e., it would be legitimate for such a state that is paying for the people's health care to set some parameters on the risky behaviors of those whom the state insures, even if it means some (who, as this teen argues, cause sickness) will suffer. But others who did not mention the entitlement provided by the state, still felt that individuals, not society, should bear the responsibilities for their own choices: "why should government pay for a persons [*sic*] habits? It is their choice to smoke; it is not like it is a sickness," or "The government should not have to pay for all the smokers' hospital bills when they have to be rolled in for emphazema [*sic*]," and "if more people wear helmets less will be hurt and the less the insurance will have to pay." References to teenagers driving while intoxicated were common despite the fact that teenagers were not mentioned in the DUI vignette. Further, despite the helmet vignette's focus on the benefits to individuals rather than on the costs or benefits of the law to society, teens were more likely to use common good arguments for the helmet law than for either of the other vignettes.

*Protecting Innocent Others: Social Concern*

Closely related to an overarching public goal as a rationale for the law were references to the more specific negative implications of risks taken by individuals on innocent others or on bystanders. The latter was the heart of arguments in this category. Note that none of the vignettes make salient the specific costs of the protagonist's behaviors to innocent others. Nonetheless, the DUI law was defended on grounds that "no one should drink and drive because it is endangering others"; "if they are careless their license should be taken away because someone else's life is in danger; and "if they aren't responsible enough to know when they have too much to drink they are not responsible enough to drive because often times the people killed in these accidents are innocents." Other teens also felt that the DUI law would be likely to pass because "people are tired of getting killed for another person's mistake"; "we want our society to be clean from drunk drivers; they cause danger for the innocent"; and "it is not ethical to have drunken drivers in the streets; they contribute to most teenagers' deaths."

This category was not invoked for the helmet law but was used for roughly 20 percent of the responses for the smoking tax and DUI vignettes. One teen observed the following: "let's say a kid was sitting by an adult smoking the kid would be breathing into the smoke and then they will start to smoke if they like the smoke." Others contended that "passive smoking causes health problems not only for the people doing it but also for the people around them" and "it is proven that smokers are at greater risk for lung cancer and heart disease when smoking around others they put them at risk their health is not as good as nonsmokers. There is no reason that government should support their bad habit." Another adolescent used a bit more sophisticated language to make the same point: "the law should be passed because I am not responsible for someone else's moral hazard; they should pay a tax for their addiction because the non-smokers are at risk." Concerning DUI, this same individual observed that "people who are prone to drive drunk seem to be worried only about themselves; they trust their own abilities and judgment; they do not consider that they are putting others at risk by involving the type of penalty as set forth by the law."

*Protecting Individuals from Their Own Bad Choices*

Like the societal goal category, responses in this cluster point to achieving a goal, but in this case the state's role as protective parent is emphasized. Further, adolescents whose responses were assigned to this category argue that passing the law will benefit the individual protagonist. The tone is paternalistic (i.e., like a good parent, the state has to enact the law to protect these individuals from their own poor or immature judgment): "It is for the cyclist's own good and a lot of lives would be saved"; "The law is for the bikers' own good; the law wants to protect the citizens"; "the law is doing something good for the people mainly for the cyclists." Similarly, for the DUI law, "if you're not responsible enough to not get drunk then you should not have a license."

Responses in this category also alluded to the need for individuals to learn that their choices have consequences. For example, one youth said "people need to learn that drunk driving is illegal and the only way they are going to learn that is by being punished." For smoking, "I hope it will stop people from smoking; it is a terrible habit and I wish they would stop making them"; "the smoker makes the choice to smoke and he should be able to pay for the consequences of that which is his bad health." The value of penalties and punishments is emphasized in making people stop their unhealthy ways. However, the potential of the penalty to cause an individual to reflect and freely choose to change her ways is not mentioned.

*Individual Change*

Adolescents whose responses were coded in this category viewed the law as necessary to enforce healthy and appropriate behavior but in a less paternalistic manner than the (last) individual protection category. Whereas the protecting individuals category emphasizes the immaturity and cluelessness of the protagonist, the distinguishing aspect of the individual change category is the respondent's belief that the protagonist would reflect on and very likely change his behavior in response to the law or tax policy. Note that the vignettes do not suggest that the intent of the law or policy is to get individuals to think twice or to reflect on their actions. Therefore, teens themselves are concluding that, when the rules of the social contract mean that individuals will face serious consequences for their actions, those individuals will be likely to reflect on their actions and change their ways. Another adolescent made a similar argument that the smoking tax "would encourage people to think about their own health as well as others plus you cannot overlook the fact that money talks and if those people knew they had to pay to smoke and possibly lose free healthcare I think they would reconsider." Others made similar arguments about DUI legislation: "A law like this will make people seriously think before driving or even better before drinking"; "the DUI law should pass—it would make people think 2ce before picking up a drink at a party. There is a selfish side in people—sometimes a possibility of hurting others is not a great enough consequence and themselves being hurt is not reality."

Youth whose responses were coded in this category seem to conceive of individuals as having insights and making informed choices. Teens use words such as these: "It would encourage people to think, to reconsider, to think twice." We might assume that they see the laws as being effective in accomplishing the goal of shaping individuals but not in a simple paternalistic fashion (i.e., people will follow the rules). Rather, youth who invoke individual change allude to the individual's self-determination: people can choose to change, and certain laws and taxes will make that more likely. At the same time, unlike the individual rights category discussed in the next section, self-determination is implied rather than overt, and there is no recognition that individuals might object. Youth whose responses were coded in the individual change category did not challenge laws based on arguments that those laws abrogated individuals' rights; rather teens in the individual change category felt that individuals would be likely to change their minds and their behaviors once they were faced with stiff penalties for their choices. This category captured a large percentage of the defenses of the smoking tax and the penalty for DUI, whereas only a small number of the responses to the helmet law fit in this category. In the next two categories, the adolescent took the perspective of and defended the rights to self-determination of the individual protagonist.

*Individual Rights and Freedom from Government Intrusion*

In this case, the youth's major concern was with individuals' rights to do whatever they wanted with their own bodies without government interference. Examples included the following responses: "it is the people's decision of how they want to live so if they get sick because of smoking they get sick" and "this is a free country and people have freedom to do such things like smoke." The individual's right to take risks were sometimes defended with arguments based on the premise that what one does with her body is no one else's business: "If people are dumb enough to ride a motorcycle without having a helmet on then they might as well become a vegetable."

Other adolescents invoked (perhaps unbeknownst to them) specific amendments to the U.S. Constitution in their defense of an individual's right to smoke or to ride a motorcycle without a helmet: "It would be unconstitutional to have people be punished for smoking when it is a free country and they can do as they please" or "powerful tobacco companies along with civil liberty groups pressure government on these grounds of unconstitutionality." References to the potential dangers of creeping government intrusion (i.e., to the state intruding into the private lives of citizens or to the government overstepping its authority) were captured in this category. Concerning the helmet law, one teen said "government officials are determined to take any choices away from the citizens. By protecting these riders they clear their conscience." Another youth felt that "the smoking tax *would not* [italics added] pass because the people would probably believe that the government should not have that much control" but also used an individual rights argument to assert that the tax *should not* pass: "I do not like smoking or smokers but they have the right to kill themselves if they want to."

*Laws and Taxes Are Discriminatory, Unfair, Extreme*

Responses that were coded in this category reflected criticisms of laws for being discriminatory (either because the policies targeted certain individuals or because the laws would be enforced in a discriminatory manner) or because they were too strict (i.e., the punishment did not fit the crime). This category is relevant for understanding why people in general and adolescents in particular might comply with the law. According to legal socialization studies, adults as well as adolescents are more likely to follow the law and even accept a personal fine or judge's verdict against them *if* they believe that the law is legitimate and that the authorities have treated them fairly. Fair treatment (e.g., by police or judges) communicates to those in legal interactions (and vicariously to people in contact with those in legal interactions) that laws are both legitimate and moral.[3] Understanding the democratic process that underlies law making is probably a developmental achievement. According to one Canadian study, children as young as six might consider it unfair for some laws to restrict people's freedom, but by age 11, they are less ardent in their opposition to such laws if the laws were passed by democratic rather than nondemocratic governments.[4]

Perceptions of the law as discriminatory were raised by teens such as the following: "it is really being prejudicial to single out smokers for their bad habits there are many other people who have habits just as threatening as smoking who would not be paying a special tax." That young man went on to argue another perspective, a case for the (lack of) effectiveness of such a law (i.e., that the smoking tax could not be enforced): "how would you regulate who smoked at home and how much and then tax it?" He also felt that the DUI law would likely be enforced in a discriminatory manner: "how can you set a definite number on being legally drunk, alcohol affects people in different ways because of size." Despite his concern that these laws were prejudicial, this young man also raised another (individual change) perspective (i.e., that the intent of the law might be realized because the punishment would cause people to reflect and change their behavior): "if people knew their license would be suspended for a year they would be more conscious about the amounts of alcohol they consumed."

A related line of argument assigned to this category was that by allowing the government to target one group, society would be opening the floodgates of discrimination: One teen argued that taxing other stereotyped groups for their "unhealthy" habits would be a logical next step in government policy. "People would say that it (smoking tax) is discriminations [sic]. It won't pass because once they enact a law like this they will start enacting laws similar to this, for example obese people should pay a tax because being obese is bad for your health and the government should not have to pay for a person's bad health." Discrimination was also invoked by a second teen who felt that "it is going too far, next people would be saying people who drink should pay taxes then people who eat too much it is against their rights and people would feel labeled as a smoker."

Even if an individual teen did not see the discriminatory nature of the tax, s/he might discuss the potential ripple effects, "even though it is a neat idea it is not feasible; are you going to tax those who have high fat and cholesterol diets because that leads to heart disease?" Others argued that the law would likely be enforced in a discriminatory way and that this would violate the spirit of the law: "The law would pass for Americans but it would not with the politicians or rich. A law should pass and be enforced for everyone."

The second subgroup in this category included youths' observations that the behavior did not fit the crime. It did not warrant such an extreme form of punishment, and in most cases, youth suggested an alternative or lighter sentence. For example, one teen invoked the eighth amendment to the U.S. Constitution, arguing that this was cruel and unusual punishment. She said that the helmet law would not pass because it was "too harsh but some accounting is needed. A person cannot be arrested for endangering his or her life; a ticket perhaps as with the seatbelt law but arrest is extreme and unusual punishment." Concerning helmets, another youth felt that "the rider should wear one automatically, but I do not think they should get arrested. The only thing wrong is they should not get arrested they should get a ticket but not arrested." And a third teen felt that fines and prevention education were better methods than arrests: "I do not think that legislatures are to worry about this. To be arrested is extreme, maybe a fine, but anyway some is flat out ignorant if they do not wear their helmet. Make it known the dangers of riding without a helmet; people usually are smart enough to realize it would be smart to wear one."

A third line of reasoning about the discriminatory nature of the laws took the perspective of the protagonist in the vignette and argued that the individual would be judged based on insufficient information. In other words, there might be mitigating circumstances and people deserved the benefit of the doubt: "I do agree with the lawmakers. The people smoking should help pay for their bad habits though there is a catch if a person is really poor and cannot afford medical expenses the government should help them." Another warned that people should be considered innocent until proven guilty and that hard evidence was essential: "They should make sure that it is pure alcohol, not cough syrup because cough syrup makes people drowsy and an accident can occur." This category was used more often in discussions of the smoking than of the other two vignettes.

*Effectiveness*

The last category captured opinions about the likelihood of the laws passing or being enforced. Unlike the discriminatory category, cynicism in this category does not reflect a belief that the law would be enforced in a discriminatory way but rather that enforcement would be ineffective. With respect to the likelihood of the law passing, some youth (maybe future lawyers) invoked precedent, claiming, for example, that the helmet law would pass both because "it already is on the books in some states and because it is similar to the seat belt laws that are already enforced"; "most states already have the helmet law"; "it makes sense that a helmet should be worn to keep people safe and this law has already been passed in some places"; or "when you are in your car you wear a seatbelt, so a helmet is not different." One teen felt that the DUI law was effective, and therefore, it both *would* pass, "due to the fact that most people and representatives have had in some way been affected by a drunk driver and they would prefer to keep them off the road" and *should* pass "due to the fact that drunk drivers are a threat to everybody on the road and taking their license away may not keep them all off the road but it will keep some."

Others felt that it would pass because various political advocacy and pressure groups would get behind it. For example, one teen said "organized groups like MADD [Mothers Against Drunk Driving] and SADD [Students Against Drunk Driving] can really help push the type of bills through. Also with the high accident numbers many people want protection." Another put it this way: "Many organizations have been formed that would support such a law. The seriousness of accidents caused by drunk driving is common knowledge. Many people would agree with and support such a law." However, just as many teens mentioned pressures *against* the proposed laws. One teen felt the DUI law would not pass because "it would inhibit the sale of alcohol which is a multimillion dollar industry that would hurt the community's economy which is what the federal government watches and reacts to." Likewise, the power of big tobacco was mentioned as a challenge to passing a smoking tax: "it would not pass because tobacco companies are the ones with the money; money is power in government." A third adolescent felt that the smoking tax was unrealistic because "the voters who are smokers will go crazy; also tobacco products are all ready taxed like crazy." A few youth argued that the law would be ineffective because it would have negative repercussions, such as the DUI law that "would cause unemployment to rise due to the lack of transportation plus crime goes up."

Finally, some teens felt that the proposed policies would have little effect on people's behavior in part because people would figure out ways to skirt the tax or the law: concerning the DUI law, "taking their license away does not do a lot because they still have their car; they could always get a counterfeit license." Concerning the helmet law, "I do not think a lot of people would wear it cause it messes their hair," or the smoking tax, "the law would not pass because there would be no control over who smoked." In short, these youth were skeptical about the enforceability of the laws. Lack of enforcement also was attributed to the police who "would give second chances. Many cops would not give out tickets either because they know the license would be taken." This same adolescent felt that "people should not have second chances. If you kill someone there is no second chance, so the drunk driver should not have one."

The method of posing two questions to adolescents—what they thought *would happen* versus what they thought *should happen*—was effective in revealing contrasts between the ideal and the real. The effectiveness category picked up many of these contradictions. For example, one teen argued that the DUI law *would not* pass because "some people might think that that punishment is too severe and some of the people who were in charge of the law might drink and they would realize that maybe they would get caught drunk driving someday." She also felt that *it should* pass because "drunk driving is very serious and it costs a lot of people their lives. No punishment is too harsh." A second argued that the smoking tax *would not* pass based on pressures from smokers: "there are too many citizens in the US that smoke and this law would never pass" but that it *should* pass, a position she defended with a moral hazard argument, "smoking is one of the worst habits in north America and why should I pay for someone's bad habit?" A third felt that the helmet law *would not* pass because "people do not want to take that much responsibility for other people's problems" but that it *should* because of the magnitude of the problem, "this is becoming a big problem and something has to be done to stop it."

## Comparisons of Categories across the Vignettes

Adolescents' reasoning varied across the three vignettes. In general, they defended rather than contested the laws, although the basis for those defenses varied. Even the same respondent tended to see the three policies from different perspectives. For example, the following youth invoked a realist perspective based on effectiveness for the drunk driving vignette, contending that it *would not* pass because "the support would not be there in government for such a stiff penalty" and argued against passage of the DUI law (arguing that it *should not* pass) based on his belief that the punishment was too extreme for the crime, "1 year is too long a time for a first time offender." However, his reaction to the helmet law was that government would be stepping on individual rights: "people in government like to think they can better tell what is good for you than you can" and "government should not be able to tell a person how they have to act or behave." Thus he felt that the helmet law *would not* and *should not* pass. Finally, he believed that the smoking tax *would not* pass due to the effectiveness of political interest groups, "the tobacco lobby is too strong," but *should* because individuals should be responsible for their own health risks, "the burden of people's actions should be their own."

Helmet laws were most often defended based on paternalistic arguments (i.e., that the state needed to protect individuals from their own bad choices) and also based on the greater good of society. In contrast, helmet laws were more likely to be challenged on the basis of individual rights (i.e., arguments that individuals have a right to take risks with their own health, what I have called a "my body, my business" perspective). The DUI and smoking penalties were defended largely based on arguments that they would cause individuals to reflect on their behaviors and change. In addition, common good and innocent others were invoked for both vignettes; however, in those categories, statements reflecting how big the problem is and how innocent others could get hurt were mentioned less often. Both the DUI penalty and the smoking tax, but especially the latter, were challenged based on arguments that they discriminated against a stereotyped group or would be enforced in a prejudicial manner. Effectiveness arguments also were used for the DUI penalty (i.e., that the penalty would not work in achieving the goal).

## Age Differences in Adolescents' Theories about Laws

The responses for each category were aggregated across the three vignettes such that each respondent received a score ranging from 0 (did not have a response in this category for any of the three vignettes) to 3 (responses to all three vignettes were assigned to this category). Respondents were divided into either a younger (grades 7, 8 and 9) or an older (grades 10, 11, and 12) age group. There were age differences in two of the codes: older adolescents were more likely than their younger peers to invoke the need for laws to protect innocent others from an individual's risky choices. In contrast, younger adolescents were more likely to conceive of laws in a paternalistic way (i.e., they were necessary to protect individuals from their own poor judgment). There was also a nonsignificant trend with older adolescents defending an individual's right to self-determination: even if s/he were making bad choices, an individual had a right to make mistakes with her own body and her own health.

These age-related trends are consistent with early cognitive developmental work on changes in teens' attitudes toward the balance between the state's authority and the individual's right to self-determination. Joseph Adelson and Robert P. O'Neil found that views of government shifted from the early adolescent's willingness to allow the government limitless authority to the late adolescent's tendency to question the power of leaders, especially concerning issues of individual freedom and rights.[5]

## CLUSTERING RESPONDENTS

The scores for each of the seven categories were next analyzed by means of cluster analysis to identify groups who had responded in a similar manner to the three scenarios. Ultimately, four clusters emerged: The first cluster, to which fifty-five of the respondents were assigned, is distinguished by its relatively high scores on the "common good or societal goal" code, and relatively low scores on the remaining codes. This was labeled the "social engineering" cluster, since the major function of laws, according to this group, appeared to be the "engineering" of a better society in the interests of the common good of all. In this case, the emphasis in interpreting a social contract privileges the role of the government or state (and its policies) in ensuring the well-being of the general public. In this framing of the social contract, it is perfectly reasonable to require individuals to constrain some of their wants, choices, or preferences in the interests of the broader benefits of living in a presumably healthier society.

The second cluster, comprising forty-eight respondents, was distinguished by high scores on the "individual change" code and by low scores on the "individual rights," "discriminatory," and "effectiveness" codes. Consequently, this cluster was labeled "molding individuals" because respondents in this grouping emphasized the potential of laws to shape individual behavior by getting individuals to reflect on what they were doing and to decide to change their ways. At the same time, the low scores on individual rights, discrimination, and effectiveness suggest that this group was less cognizant of individuals' willingness to obey the law and the potential challenges they might raise. Here the notion of a social contract between states and citizens and the processes whereby the terms of the social contract achieve intended goals is rather similar to a behavioral contingencies or modification approach that some families might employ to shape children's behaviors. Through restrictions, time-outs, or denial of privileges, parents attempt to get children to reconsider their actions, to reflect on the consequences of their behavior, and to change their ways.

In contrast, the third cluster, which was labeled "individual rights," consisted of forty-nine respondents and was characterized precisely by such concerns (i.e., with the rights of the individual and with doubts that people would obey the law). This third group also tended to score higher on concerns that the proposed policies, that is, the laws or the taxes, might be too harsh and that those policies potentially could discriminate against some individuals or groups. So they saw the laws from the point of view of the individual and his rights. Rights was the lens through which this group interpreted the social contract, and thus they worried over the potential overreach of government to abrogate individuals' rights.

The fourth cluster, which was labeled "social welfare" and which consisted of thirty-nine respondents, was distinguished by high scores on the "protecting innocent others" and "individual protection" codes. Both of these codes emphasize the role of the state and of policies in protecting the people, and in this regard, there is a paternalistic tone. The extension of protection, not only to the individual who may be engaging in the risky behavior but to the innocent others in society who might be affected by the individual's behavior, points to this cluster's emphasis on the social welfare of all people.

Each of the verbatim responses also was coded for its level of integrative complexity. Integrative complexity refers to the way individuals process information and reconcile different dimensions or perspectives. Those who view an issue in a unidimensional manner are given lower scores, while those who understand that there may be different perspectives on an issue and who seek to integrate these different perspectives in some manner, are given higher scores.[6] Note that coding responses for integrative complexity is different from coding them for content. A response can reflect more than one perspective on an issue but still be coded within a single content category. At the same time, responses that invoke different content categories would be more likely to also reflect different perspectives and thus would have higher "integrative complexity" scores.

Analysis of the complexity scores of the four clusters revealed that respondents in the molding individuals cluster were significantly less complex in their thinking about the three laws when compared to respondents in the other three clusters. So, although their responses point to the potential of social policies for causing individuals to reflect on and change their behaviors, adolescents in this cluster mention only this dimension of the social contract and discuss it in a unidimensional (this and only this) fashion. The social welfare cluster, by contrast, mentions the role of policies in protecting both individuals engaging in risky behaviors and fellow citizens, innocent others who may be affected by those individuals' choices. In other words, respondents in this cluster mention more than one perspective. Likewise, respondents in the individual rights cluster tended to see more than one perspective. This group was the least paternalistic in its interpretation of the social contract, taking rather the point of view of the individual and the challenges she could raise (discrimination, cruel and unusual punishment) about the proposed laws and taxes. Finally, although the social engineering cluster had high scores only on one category (namely, achieving a societal goal of the common good), responses in this cluster had higher complexity scores than the molding individuals group. Responses in the social engineering cluster included more than one perspective when discussing a societal goal (e.g., the financial costs, the social costs, the gravity of the social issue, the goal of the policy) and thus their complexity scores were higher.

Consistent with Vygotsky's perspective that our ideas are internalizations of social collaborative experience, adolescents' social experiences were associated with their complexity scores. Not surprisingly, opportunities to practice perspective taking were associated with higher integrative complexity scores. Specifically, complexity scores were significantly higher among those adolescents who reported that they had taken civics or social studies courses at school in which *students had many points of view*. In other words, such perspective-taking opportunities help teens to move out of their egocentric biases, to realize that they coexist in a society with others who may not share their same perspectives. (For more on my findings related to perspective taking and teens' political theories, see Chapters 3, 4, and 6.)

Age differences were apparent both in the content and complexity of responses. Early adolescents were more likely to focus on the need for laws to constrain individuals from making bad choices but tended not to discuss either individual rights or the effectiveness of laws. In contrast, late adolescents were more concerned that individual rights should not be abrogated by the law but also were more likely to discuss the consequences that risky choices posed for *others* and the function of laws in protecting the public welfare.

## Convergent Findings

As already noted, the public implications of health risks were made salient in the vignettes. However, the second (survey) study yielded similar age trends, despite the fact that a different sample, design, and set of measures were used. This larger study included more than fifteen hundred adolescents, evenly divided among early, middle, and late adolescent age groups. Youth were asked how strongly they agreed or disagreed with a set of items that tapped beliefs about the rights of individuals to engage in various behaviors that might compromise health. One set of items tapped beliefs such as "individuals have a right to smoke or drink because they are the only ones harmed" or "it's no one else's business what an individual does with his/her body." These items factored into a scale dubbed "health as an individual right."

A second set of items tapped adolescents' endorsements of "public health" beliefs. Those with high scores on this scale endorse beliefs that individual health behaviors (smoking and driving while drunk) have implications beyond the individual and thus the government should be proactive in enacting laws to protect society and to curb individuals from engaging in those behaviors (see the Appendix). Among the teens in this second study, there was a relatively high level of endorsing public health beliefs and a comparatively low level of endorsement of health as an individual right. This gap in attitudes was smaller among older respondents due to two age trends as shown in Figure 5.1.

Adolescents' age is shown on the x-axis, and the average score for their health beliefs (their endorsements of public health and individual rights) is shown on the y-axis. As the figure shows, endorsements of individual rights increased dramatically between early and middle adolescence (between age 12 and 14). That commitment continued into late adolescence. The age-related increase in the defense of individual rights is consistent with research on legal socialization that finds an increasing cynicism about the normative bases of laws across the adolescent years. Whereas preteens tend to respect the law "because it's the law," by middle and late adolescence,

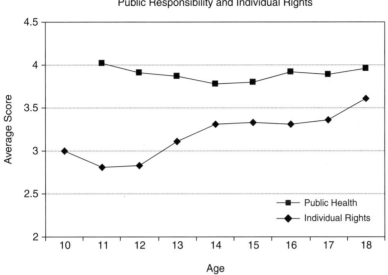

Figure 5.1. Health beliefs: Public responsibility and individual rights. Data were derived from the longitudinal study on Social Responsibility and Adolescents. Scales were based on the mean of items in each scale. The precise wording for all items is provided in the Appendix in the discussion of Chapter 5.

teens are more skeptical. The fact that a law is on the books does not, in itself, mean that the law is right or just.[7]

Somewhat less dramatic, but nonetheless statistically significant, was the second age-related trend shown in Figure 5.1: teens' endorsements of public health beliefs showed a curvilinear trend with middle adolescents less likely than early or late adolescents to endorse the government's right to constrain individual choices, which parallels developmental patterns in moral reasoning about prosocial behavior identified in other work. Whereas prosocial reasoning declines between early and middle adolescence, it shows some increase by late adolescence.[8]

According to Figure 5.1, between early and late adolescence, there appear to be two simultaneous trends vis-à-vis teens' conceptualization of laws to protect public health. Between early and especially middle adolescence, youth are increasingly likely to defend an individual's right to make her own decisions about health and risk. At the same time, this ardent commitment is tempered in late adolescence with a defense of the government's right to constrain individual behaviors in the interests of the public's health. Analyses of the vignettes further confirm that whereas early adolescents are more likely to accept a paternalistic role for government, late adolescents have a more sophisticated or nuanced understanding of laws. They balance a commitment to individual rights with an awareness of the implications to society of individual decisions and with a recognition of the responsibilities of the government for public health. In short, between early and late adolescence, there was a growing appreciation of the purpose of a social contract between states and citizens.

The increase between early and middle adolescence in teens' endorsements of an individual's right to make his own decisions concerning health risks is consistent with work documenting age-related increases in teens' defense of an individual's right to self-determination. According to this body of work, well before adolescence, the notion that children have a right to expect adequate care and protection from the adult authorities in their lives is well in place. Preadolescents endorse the right of children to be cared for and nurtured. Adolescents also maintain this belief in the fundamental right of a dependent child. However, as they get older, youth also defend the individual's right to make decisions on her own, the right to self-determination.[9]

This framing of rights implies a social contract, that is, a relationship between parties (parents and children or states and citizens) and the expectations and mutual obligations that bind them. This framework also is consistent with the way children's rights were framed in the United Nations Convention on the Rights of the Child—within two broad categories— rights to protection and care and rights to self-determination. The implied social contract is that dependents (who cannot care for themselves) deserve the right to care and protection from those who wield power over their lives. Further, as those dependents mature, they will take their place in the body politic and participate in decision making concerning the social contract of their society. Thus, they need practice in making decisions; they need to exercise their right to self-determination in mundane matters because it is through that practice that adolescents improve their capabilities to exercise their civic duties. Because the people are sovereign in a democracy, the people have to practice the arts of democracy, and self-determination in decision making is one of those arts. Other developmental psychologists have found that adolescents' endorsements of individuals' rights (both to protection, or fulfillment of their needs, and to autonomy, or self-determination) are positively correlated with the adolescents' beliefs that citizens also have civic-oriented responsibilities (to be tolerant of differences and to assist fellow members of their community). At the same time, the teen's commitments to individual rights in that study were unrelated to their beliefs that individuals had responsibilities to vote.[10]

Taken together, the data from the two studies discussed in this chapter point to consistent age differences in adolescents' perceptions about laws concerning health issues. Just as late adolescents are more likely than early adolescents to appreciate that there may be more than one side to a social or political issue, in these two studies they also demonstrated greater capacities than younger adolescents in seeing both the individual rights or self-determination issues that laws constrained as well as the consequences to public health or the common good of an individual's risky choices. These age-related patterns are consistent with those found in research on young people's interpretations of individual rights: although even young children appreciate that individuals have rights to free speech and religion, older adolescents and especially college students are more nuanced, considering age and context in their assessments of the appropriate exercise of individual rights.[11]

Besides age, there also were gender differences in beliefs about rights associated with health risks. Females were less likely than males to endorse individual rights and more likely to endorse public health, although these gender differences disappeared by late adolescence. The longitudinal study also revealed links between adolescents' social responsibility for friends' health-related behaviors and their beliefs about the role of the government vis-à-vis individual health choices: across all age groups, adolescents' convictions that they had a responsibility to dissuade their friends from engaging in behaviors that might compromise the friend's health (smoking, drinking and driving, using drugs) were positively predicted by their endorsements of laws to protect the public's health and negatively predicted by their beliefs that individuals have the right to do what they want with their bodies.[12] In other words, to the extent that teens endorsed the government's role in enacting laws meant to protect the public's health, those teens also said that they would be proactive in preventing their friends from engaging in risky behaviors that might compromise the friends' health. In this sense, they endorsed the value of social responsibility—as an ethic they lived by and as an appropriate role for the government—in order to protect the health of the people.

Health risk behaviors are one of the major foci of research in the field of adolescent development. However, the dominant paradigm in that body of research is a rational choice model (i.e., if provided with the facts about the potential harm of experimentation with alcohol, tobacco, or other substances, an adolescent will make decisions that are in his own best interest). The (perhaps unexamined) assumption is that health and risk are choices that individuals make on their own with the potential harm of such choices a burden that they alone bear. This paradigm leaves underexplored a question relevant to adolescents and health, that is, to what extent they are cognizant of the public consequences of individual decisions and behaviors concerning health and risk. Furthermore, the paradigm tends to consider only the negative influence of peer pressure and, by implication, underestimates the potential of friendship and loyalty to exert positive pressure. Although there are few studies, there is some evidence that awareness of the public implications of substance use is inversely related to one's use of alcohol: college freshmen who endorsed the belief that drinking can negatively affect other people reported drinking less per week.[13] In the longitudinal study reported in this chapter we also found that adolescents who endorse public health beliefs and those who endorse social responsibility values were less likely to smoke or to drink and were more likely to say that they would discourage peers from smoking or drinking. Furthermore, we have found positive social contagion effects of social responsibility. Specifically, adolescents are more prepared or inclined to dissuade friends from smoking or drinking if they are in classes at school where social responsibility (treating everyone equally and caring for those in need) is a family value shared by the members of their class.

The social representation of health as a private choice may be a peculiarly American one insofar as the government in many other nations provides health care as a fundamental right of its citizens. Despite the dominant social representation of health as a private rather than a public good, the adolescents who shared their insights in the studies summarized in this chapter did appreciate the state's role in constraining individual choices in the interests of public health. And the open-ended responses suggested that campaigns concerning the dangers of passive smoking and DUI for innocent others had already been incorporated in the teens' schema about the public health implications of these risky behaviors. Perhaps it is time to appeal more in our health promotion and risk prevention programs to teens' social conscience and sense of social responsibility, that is, to make more salient the consequences to others and to society in general of an individual's risky choices.

# chapter six

# Inequality

ADOLESCENTS' UNDERSTANDING OF economic phenomena has been a rare topic in developmental research, despite the considerable implications of the economy for the quality of their lives. A notable exception was a study in the 1970s by Robert Leahy who asked six- to eighteen-year-olds to explain "why some people are rich and others are poor." That study followed on the heels of a decade and a half of social programs that were part of America's War on Poverty.[1] Social policy has done an about-face since that time.

Over the past three-plus decades, structural economic change combined with massive shifts in welfare and tax policies have widened the gap between the haves and have-nots. Starting in the 1980s and continuing today, policies including regressive taxes, cutbacks in social spending, and declining investments in low-income housing have resulted in the transfer of money to the wealthy and a shrinking middle class. During the 1990s, welfare policy was reformulated from Aid to Families with Dependent Children (AFDC) to Temporary Aid to Needy Families (TANF), which emphasized the provisional and temporary character of the new "safety net."

Figure 6.1. Por pan y trabajo. Mural in a barrio in Buenos Aires, Argentina.
Translation: "For bread and work."

Besides social policies, structural economic changes have shrunk the
pool of industrial jobs that, in past generations, paid a family wage to workers
who had not gone on to college. More of the jobs in today's "new economy"
are part-time, contract work with fewer health and retirement benefits. And
most of these jobs require education beyond high school.[2] In addition to
these structural changes in the nature of jobs, regressive tax policies[3] and
declines in the share of the workforce organized in unions have contributed
to a growth in income inequality between poor and affluent Americans over
the past forty years, one that is wider than at any period since the Great
Depression.

These inequalities increased over three decades, continued into the new
millennium, and predated the market crash of 2008 and the stubbornly
high rates of unemployment that followed. The economists Emmanuel Saez
and Thomas Piketty estimate that, from 2002 to 2008, income for the top
1 percent of Americans rose by $261,930, or 30 percent, while the bottom
90 percent saw their incomes drop by $1,170, or 4 percent, on an inflation
adjusted basis.[4] In September 2011, the census revealed the numbers of
Americans in poverty based on its 2010 census—46.2 million, a 15.1 percent

rate, the largest number since the census started tracking in 1959, and one that rose faster in three years than during any other three-year period since the 1980s. That report got scant attention in the national TV or print media, even less than the few weeks of media attention devoted to poverty in the wake of Hurricane Katrina. In light of these changes, it seems timely to revisit Leahy's results from the 1970s and to ask again how young people interpret why some people are rich while others are poor.

In this chapter, I summarize the theories of adolescents who were asked in surveys administered in their social studies classes in the mid-1990s to "Imagine that someone from another country were visiting the United States and they asked you to explain some things to them. Suppose they asked you to explain why some people in the United State are poor, what would you say?" The same open-ended format was used to solicit the adolescents' thoughts about why some people in the United States are rich, unemployed, or homeless.

The nearly eight hundred young people who shared their views were living in communities in the industrial heartland of the United States where jobs in the auto industry had been a legacy passed down for generations.[5] But industrial downsizing meant that expectations of steady jobs with incomes and benefits that could support families were no longer a sure thing. The teens participating in the study came from schools that represented a wide range of household incomes. Some youth in this study had parents who were doctors, lawyers, or executives in the auto industry. Others had parents who were online workers in factories, domestics, or were unemployed. The sample also was ethnically diverse with 21 percent of the youth identifying as African-American, 13 percent Arab-American, 6 percent Asian-American, 5 percent Native American, 3 percent Latino, and 52 percent Caucasian.

The adolescents' open-ended responses were coded for content and complexity. Concerning the latter, an integrative complexity coding system was used. In this scoring system, commonly used to code the speeches of politicians or of adults' resolution of political, moral, or social dilemmas, complexity refers to the degree to which a response reflects different perspectives on an issue and the degree to which contrasting views are integrated.[6]

Concerning content, I have organized responses into three major categories commonly used in studies with adults to distinguish their attributions for inequality: individualistic (holding individuals accountable), systemic or structural (explaining the structural, institutional, political, economic causes), and uncontrollable factors (good or bad luck, illness).[7] These three major categories captured 70 percent or more of the discrete codes for each of the questions. The major codes that were not captured by these three categories included definitions (homeless people don't have homes; rich people have money, poor people do not; unemployed don't have jobs) and general references to education with no indication about whether the respondent meant the quality of schools (a structural attribution) or the efforts of individuals studying in school (an individual attribution).

Adolescents could give more than one response. My summary focuses on the first two responses because few young people gave more than two and because psychologists often consider as most meaningful or salient those ideas that first come to mind. Note that these are three large categories into which more discrete responses were collapsed. The percentages that follow refer to the subcategories to which the more discrete responses that maintained detail were assigned. Considering only the first and second responses, individual attributions were invoked in 35 percent of the responses for wealth, 38 percent for unemployment, 23 percent for poverty, and 21 percent for homelessness; structural or systemic attributions were invoked in 32 percent of the responses for wealth, 36 percent for unemployment, 38 percent for poverty, and 27 percent for homelessness; uncontrollable factors were invoked in 12 percent of the responses for wealth, 7.5 percent for unemployment, 15 percent for poverty, and 9 percent for homelessness.

## ATTRIBUTING RESPONSIBILITY TO INDIVIDUALS

An individual's responsibility for his or her economic station because of laziness or a lack of motivation or effort, was commonly invoked as an individual attribution to explain why some groups were in a bad financial situation. This code accounted for 21 percent of the first responses to explain unemployment, 13 percent for poverty, and 9.5 percent for homelessness. But the belief that the rich had earned their wealth through their own hard work, dogged determination, motivation, and effort accounted for a full 30 percent of the first responses to explain why some people are rich.

For example, one teen said that unemployed people were "lazy, and the US is for the working people, not the people that don't want to work," and another that they "did not have the will power to get a good job." A lack of will power was also invoked by a youth who felt that the unemployed "do not want to better themselves or get ahead. I feel everyone is in control of what happens to themselves so they can get a job if they want to." In contrast, the wealthy deserved their station because they had "worked hard for the money and they earned it."

Besides hard work, an individual's irresponsible choices and bad habits were used to explain why some people were homeless or poor. According to one middle schooler, some people were homeless because "People pay for cigarettes instead of saving up for apartment or house. They waste their money on junk." A white tenth grader explained that the homeless deserved their fate, although he grudgingly alluded to some potential structural causes for the problem: "some have dug their own graves so to speak with drugs alcohol and violence but *very few are homeless because their business failed or their homes were ruined* [italics added]." An African-American eleventh grader felt that the homeless "do not want to take responsibility like paying bills" and proposed the solution of having "a shelter just for the homeless and teach (them) how to be responsible." In contrast, she felt that the rich "make it their responsibility to get everything they want in life *without relying on others* [italics added]."

Economic success was traced to personal motivation, goal setting, and aspirations, although typically those future visions were rather nebulous. According to one teen, rich people "finished school and took care of what they had to do; they had a goal and reached it. They knew they had to start working towards their future at a young age," and another that "People who are rich worked hard, got what they wanted, had a good education, wanted to be *someone, not a nobody* [italics added]."

A lack of motivation and future planning distinguished those who did not succeed from those who did. People might be poor because they "didn't try hard in school and their future wasn't important to them"; or they made bad choices: "married young and went on welfare"; or lacked the moral fiber to succeed: "They were bestowed with no desire or strength to make themselves better." One teen stated his view of the unemployed even more harshly, "They probably didn't think of their future as youngsters but they now should *pay back by being unemployed* [italics added]."

Setting goals and aspiring to greatness were proposed as solutions, ways that the down-and-out could achieve the American dream. One

African-American female sounded like a motivational speaker: "Set a goal while you're young, try hard as you can to succeed at that goal. Don't give up and when you do these things you can't be *a homeless loser* [italics added]. You'll come out on top always."

## Formative Influences

### School

Education figured prominently in discussions of inequality. Sometimes the system was blamed for providing unequal access to educational opportunities: "employers now a days are looking for highly educated individuals and some cannot afford a better education." More often individuals were held accountable for their failure to apply themselves in school. But consistently the theme of formative influences in school that set the stage for success in adulthood came through. People were rich because "they went to college for a long time and made something out of their life" or "The reason why people have good jobs is because they work for 17–20 years in school." In contrast, the poor, according to a seventh grader who himself planned to be a teacher: "it is their own faults, they chose that lifestyle when they did not take school or whatever seriously." When asked what he thought was the main purpose of education, this boy replied, "to teach people so they can *survive* [italics added]. Without an education you will go nowhere."

His belief that it is imperative to get an education if one wants to survive echoes the dominant discourse on the purposes of education in the era of No Child Left Behind, the reauthorization of the Elementary and Secondary Education Act signed into law by President George W. Bush in 2001. Whether in discussions of the role of education in placing the United States at a competitive advantage or in economists' calculations of the lifetime earnings returned to individuals for each additional year or even semester of schooling, the instrumental goals of education have held center stage. This conversation has crowded out perspectives on the intrinsic value of learning that could have implications for students' motivation to continue life-long learning: as research on adolescents' theories of education has shown, when teens believe that the purpose of education is to increase status and wealth, they are more alienated academically and less committed to learning. In contrast, when students believe that the purposes of education include social responsibility and an understanding of the world, they are

more committed to the intrinsic value of learning and more likely to believe
that academic success results from personal interest, effort, and from collaborative learning.[8]

Several adolescents argued that habits of a lifetime were formed in school
and that this explained why some people were rich while others were poor:
"Some did not work hard in school and still are not trying hard now that
they are out of school." A seventh-grade Arab-American, who aspires to be
either "a basketball player or doctor," argued that people's dispositions are
formed through habits learned in the early years, "if they do not go to school
when they're young when they are older it is hard to learn." But even if
people do stay in school, an eighth-grade Latino, who hoped to land in a
"medicine job," worried about the lack of rigor in schools. According to him,
schoolwork may not convey how hard life can be: "When they were going
to school they were taught everything is easy so they did not had to study.
Now they grew up they see that life is different." Staying in school was also
invoked as a way to solve inequality. One student suggested, "put out a new
law that you cannot quit school at age 16," and another offered, "if you are
in school, stay in school. Attain all the knowledge you can and go to college.
Finish college and at least you will have a degree in order to find a job. Also,
if you dropped out of high school or college, go back."

*Families and Neighborhoods*

The formative role of families and neighborhoods also was noted, but in
contrast to most responses for schooling, individuals were less likely to be
blamed for being born into a poor family. However, their parents were often held accountable for the formation of character traits, habits, and ultimately, economic outcomes of their offspring. People might be poor because, as one Native-American seventh grader put it, "parents did not
encourage them to do anything." In contrast, another teen said that people
who are rich "obviously take education, motivation, & intelligence very seriously. Somewhere in the family someone had to work hard to get where
they are—a trait that should & is passed down in the family."[9]

Others felt that the die was cast at birth: "Most of these people were
born into poverty. There [sic] fate can be blamed on their ancestors," or
"Many (of the poor) were born that way, no hope, no motivation," whereas
wealthy people "had a good education, confidence, family wealth, worked
hard." One white male high school senior felt that the poor were "born into

it. Others do drugs and alcohol." An African-American tenth grader said, "One reason could be there [*sic*] background. Or maybe they just want to settle for less." That student was from a district that, in 2010, Arne Duncan, the U.S. Secretary of Education, referred to as "ground zero" in the nation's education system where, according to some estimates, less than 40 percent of ninth graders earn a high school diploma in four years. Other teenagers mentioned the poisoning influence of "bad neighborhoods" and the bad luck of growing up in one: "They grew up in a bad area and they screwed up and got bad breaks." Still another was doubtful about the upwardly mobile ladder: "not everyone receives the same skills or training and encouragement when they are young, some are born that way and it is hard to get out."

Family background was mentioned in 3 percent of the explanations for unemployment, 8 percent for poverty, and 4 percent for homelessness. But the advantages of being born into a wealthy family accounted for a full 18.5 percent of the explanations for why some people are rich. These included statements about inheriting parents' wealth and the benefits in social connections and social capital that birth into a wealthy family bestowed. Rich people "have good jobs and were probably left a lot of money when their parents died," or "have a good education or good connections in the world," or "some worked hard and went to school and others just were born into a rich family and when their dad dies they got sixty billion dollars." A Latino seventh grader said that "they were born into riches or they worked hard all of their lives," and a Latino fifteen-year-old high schooler from a well-educated family said, "They worked hard and set goals or were born into it." The fact that teens were more likely to mention the advantages of family background to explain wealth suggests that they recognize some inherent weaknesses of the meritocratic rules insofar as some people begin life with a leg up on others.

## Beliefs in a Just World and Theories about Inequality

Personal motivation, future orientation, goal setting, and commitments to hard work (especially in school) were recurring arguments explaining the pathway to economic success. But the character of those who make it or fail was a subtext. Unemployment was considered a just dessert, a punishment for sins committed in childhood when one failed to "plan ahead." Not only were self-discipline and the work ethic learned in "good" families; these traits were undoubtedly passed down in the DNA and replicated across generations. And getting a good education was linked to an individual's motivation to be "somebody," not a member of the crowd who's never noticed—a "nobody." Interestingly, although these teens' statements predate the libertarian political scientist Charles Murray's 2012 book, they resonate with his argument about the loss of basic American values of hard work and individual responsibility in white working-class families that, according to Murray, is now being passed down to younger generations.[10]

These teens' theories about inequality reflect ardent commitments to the American dream that success can be attained by anyone who is willing to apply themselves and to work for it. Most American adults hold such beliefs with large majorities in international surveys endorsing statements that anyone can escape poverty if he or she works hard enough.[11] This image of American society as a meritocracy is so strong that many will legitimate the status quo and the principles that support it even when their own family is barely making it.

## ATTRIBUTIONS TO SYSTEMIC AND STRUCTURAL FACTORS

However, individual responsibility was not the only attribution for inequality. Government policies and global forces also were listed as factors, especially to explain poverty and homelessness. People might be homeless because of a "bad housing plan, run down buildings and large cities and expensive rent" or because "Government abolished 2.5 million in low income housing which lessens the chance for the poor to be sheltered. Little money is provided towards shelters. ⅓ of homeless are mentally ill incapable of holding a job without medicine." Others noted mitigating circumstances that made it difficult for individuals to succeed. For example, people might be unemployed because they "might not have anyone to watch their kids" or "got divorced, lost job, or are disabled."

Insofar as this study was conducted in the industrial heartland, it is not surprising that many teens were aware of structural changes and the forces of globalization. Plant closures, layoffs, and the competitive advantages of "cheap labor" were mentioned; for example, "a lot of plants and jobs are being sent overseas or just being shut down"; "companies move to different states and countries"; and "business close down and they (the unemployed) aren't willing to help themselves, the government won't help them." One youth provided his own take on the phenomenon of the discouraged worker: "Some just don't have enough education for the job they want so they quit looking for a job and take the easy way out or the plant they work for closed down."

At times it seemed that an adolescent had a very personal awareness of the implications of structural economic change. In response to an item in the survey asking respondents, "What is your reaction if you hear on the news about a plant closing down?" one youth wondered, "is my mom or dad going to lose their job?" and another, "how am I going to succeed?" Ironically, in another part of the survey, this same young person described a good citizen as someone who "abides by the rules of a country." Other adolescents offered less personal but nonetheless empathic responses to news about a plant closing, saying they would feel "upset for those people out of work, too many live pay check to pay check" or "saddened about the newly unemployed and uneasy about the fallout of the new global economy." One teen commented that even dedication and hard work were no job insurance policy in the new economy where competition and profit drove decisions about the bottom line: "in a place where every one is trying to get ahead of everyone else people will let a hard worker go in order to hire a cheaper one."

In contrast to the ardent belief in the American dream of upward mobility, many felt that a natural rate of unemployment should be expected in any society, including the United States. As a male Asian-American put it, "no country has no unemployment, America is no exception." Similarly a European-American male felt that "our economy cannot support everyone working and still be healthy; it is true of any nation. Due to technology and global competition some unemployment is inevitable."

The belief that a reserve pool of unemployed labor was a natural state of affairs, a cost for the benefit of a global economic edge, was complemented by a belief that there were simply too many people vying for a limited supply of jobs. This "mismatch"—too many people, too few jobs—was mentioned in 18 percent of the responses for unemployment, 14 percent for poverty, and 5 percent for homelessness. "Sometimes there are no jobs available because there are too many people"; "job competition, everyone can't win;" and some are "unable to compete in the modern workforce."

In light of the dwindling supply of jobs, educational credentials and an ardent work ethic were considered even more important for determining who might land a job: "Times are tough, some folks have really bad work ethics"; "they do not have the proper schooling; they do not have the ambition, there isn't enough jobs." One seventh grader described in her own words what economists refer to as a redundant worker: "There is too much workers and they are not needed," but then she added, "Unemployed people are probably the people that cannot stand being bossed around so they had good jobs but they quit." But few were quite as callously deterministic as the following teen who explained, "In every society there are going to be poor people. Darwin's theory holds true—survival of the fittest. The smartest and most motivated earn the most money."

The picture of a shrinking pool of jobs was bolstered with references to increasing competition for jobs, to the imperative for individuals to hedge their bets for the leaner economy by getting more education and training suited to the tighter market, and to the reality that employers would be choosier: "There are so many people here and so little jobs. Everyone is competing and there are not enough jobs to go around. Those with less education and training get shut out and are unemployed." "Some did not graduate from high school therefore it is hard to get a job and jobs here are becoming scarce." "The US does not have jobs for everyone and usually the more educated and more fortunate are able to retain jobs." Some poor people "have not put all of their efforts into their education or aren't fit to take a position in the *ever competing job place* [italics added]." However, a few teens suggested that getting more education or training might not be the answer as some who are well qualified are shut out of jobs: There are "more people than jobs, hard to accept because some have higher qualifications." The bleak economic picture did not bode well for upward mobility in the younger generation. As one teen put it, "Most born poor will stay poor especially with the competition in modern business."

Reasons given for the shrinking pool of jobs included imports of foreign-made products and cheap labor outside American shores: "People buy products made in other countries so there is less work in the US, we need to buy American made." One suggestion for solving the unemployment crisis was "maybe by people supporting their country more and buying more American made." Mechanization of industry also was discussed as a factor explaining unemployment. One white male who planned to go into military service observed that "the economy is getting bad in America and many jobs are not hitting as many people anymore and machines are taking over the world." His solutions were to "stop using as many machines and America should stop giving things to other countries and not letting any more people come to America and live here and start focusing on our own people."

Such protectionist sentiments sometimes took the form of blaming "outsiders": "people from other countries are taking over," or "the immigrants come over here and take all of our jobs." Global capital's quest for cheap labor was mentioned as well: "They (the unemployed) are lazy or uneducated or they shut down the plants because Mexicans work for less."

A few teens mentioned various forms of discrimination as systemic causes for inequality. To explain unemployment, an Arab-American high school senior said, "People lose their jobs because closed mindedness and racism, or are not born with money." Others felt that "we have a lot of people here and we have discrimination," or that "There are not enough jobs for everyone and a lot of people decriminate [sic]." Racial discrimination was invoked to explain why some people are rich and others are poor. For example, one eighth grader of Arab descent held that "Most rich people are White and White people get a better chance in this world than Black's [sic] and arabics." Another teen alluded to ageism as an impediment for those seeking gainful employment: "The economy is sometimes tough and their age is a problem." And a white seventh grader noted the challenge for non-English speakers: "some people do not know how to talk the language well enough to get a job, other people just do not get employed, some are unemployed because their job just closed or are fired."

But teens were at least as likely to argue that discrimination was no excuse for slacking off. One student discussed his own experience of discrimination but also felt that racism, while it exists, should not be used as a crutch—"people should not give up and keep trying. If they wanted to succeed they can and they have to put in all their efforts, they can't just say yeah we have the opportunities but some people are racist and won't hire us. Then, I believe they should not give up and keep trying until they get what they are after." At another point in the survey, he noted, "I have been called a camel jocky [sic], and been told to go back to my country and I have also been faced with prejudice about my religion as though my culture and religion were the same." In short, his personal experience of discrimination seemed to have little bearing on his belief that opportunities to succeed in America were available to anyone willing to work hard.

The Panel Study on Income Dynamics (PSID) is a nationally representative study of families in the United States. It began in 1968 and has continued to follow individuals and their descendants. Among the many findings of the PSID is how dynamic family income actually is. Like the PSID, several teens in my study did appreciate that an individual's economic status was not static, that some people who had once been successful may have experienced catastrophic events that spun them into a downward spiral. Others traced the pathways of downward mobility—from job loss, to missing house payments, to homelessness: "Some people are homeless because they lost their jobs, can't pay bills, lost their home," or "they couldn't pay the mortgage, so got kicked out." One seventh grader gave a rather sophisticated structural argument for homelessness: "I would say that because of low paying jobs and high taxes and rents that people are kicked out of their existing homes." Still others noted the Catch-22 of being homeless and trying to find a job without a permanent address: "the homeless have no address to put on an application," and "It is hard to get off the street when you need a house to get a job and a job to get a house."

Among those who mentioned structural roots of inequality, several suggested structural solutions. For example, an African-American eleventh grader who planned to be a nurse proposed educational policy solutions: "Some people doesn't [sic] have an education. I think free adult education is the best idea to help poor people." Employment advantages of a green economy were suggested by a seventh grader, "They should have factories that help nature like plant trees and grow crops all around the world which would mean there are more jobs people could have." Solutions to unemployment included cutting back on overtime: "we pay too many people to work over time" and equalizing the pay differentials between supervisors and workers: "Cut out the high paying manager job and make 3 salaries for other workers." Solutions to poverty also included spreading the wealth around. For example, "Congressmen should give up some of their money to help. They make more money than they deserve or need."

Egalitarian measures also were recommended to address homelessness. An eighth-grade Latino proposed, "I would like to tell the people in America that the homeless people should be helped there are a lot of people who has a house with 5 rooms and they only use two rooms." A fellow student at the same school recommended "taking vacant houses and making shelters for the homeless," and a seventh grader proposed government loans for the homeless: "The mayor or the president can make up a program where you loan the homeless money for a job and home."

## Class Consciousness

These data were collected prior to the Occupy Wall Street protests in 2011 in the United States that brought national attention to growing inequality. Nonetheless, several of the structural or systemic attributions for inequality revealed an empathy for the struggles of poor people, an awareness of the ways that the system is stacked against them, and a scornful attitude toward those rich people who ignore the poor. For example, to explain poverty, one teen said that "poor don't have jobs and sometimes jobs can be hard to find and you cannot have a house with only making $4.25 per hour and having kids," and another that the unemployed "have gotten laid off or retired and they *are not given the money they were promised* [italics added] or are on welfare." A third teen observed that government policies further advantage the already advantaged: "A lot of rich people are successful in what they do, but they also benefit from the U.S. government. There is not enough focus on homeless people and also the government doesn't make it better for them." Still others criticized the country's priorities for ignoring inequality: "our country is focused on maximum production not equal opportunity and balancing the standard of living," as well as capitalism: "*in a capitalist country some people are on top and some are on the bottom. The money in our country is not distributed equally* [italics added]." Despite her critique of capitalism, she seems to believe that people's economic status is a matter of luck: For the rich, "the odds happened to be in their favor," whereas for the poor, "the cards dealt them a bad hand."

In many of the adolescents' statements, rich people were not only revered, they were also reviled. For example, one teen from a very poor community felt that people might be rich because "They either work hard to get what they deserve, *or they rob the poor* [italics added]." Another felt that some wealthy people worked for what they achieved but others lived off the labor of those under them: "*They succeeded in life. They wanted to be rich. They set a goal and succeeded. On the other hand others sit back and make money off other people* [italics added]." Arguments that the wealthy deserved their status because they had worked to attain it were balanced by challenges to meritocratic principles (i.e., people who were rich might have inherited their money, hit the lottery, or exploited other people).

Many responses reflected vexed sentiments toward the wealthy: "Some of the rich worked hard, others inherited, some manipulate and take from others"; "Three ways that people get rich—hard work, luck, and manipulation of people and laws." One white seventh grader, who planned to be a "trained police officer" when he grew up, felt that some people were rich because they "work hard for their money they do not go out every night and buy liquor" but also that "some people own a business and they will not give the homeless the time of day." One teen proposed that inequality could be curtailed if society were to "place limits on unbridled wealth or tycoons: antitrust laws, progressive income tax." But in general, adolescents were less outraged about inequality itself than they were about the fact that some (of the wealthy) do not play fair. Distrust of the wealthy and how they managed to make their wealth, which was mentioned by these teens, is also noted by Kevin Phillips in his history of wealth in America. According to Phillips, there is plenty of evidence that Americans have distrusted economic elites. However, only at certain periods in American history have democratic politics been used to curb the abuses of the very wealthy.[12]

## UNCONTROLLABLE FORCES

About 15 percent of the explanations for poverty and 12 percent of those for wealth referred to uncontrollable factors. The good fortunes or luck of the rich accounted for all of the 12 percent, with hitting the lottery the most common statement. Uncontrollable reasons for poverty included references to illness (2 percent), such as "People might be poor because they are disabled, ran away as kids, or their home was taken because they had an alcoholic mother"; bad luck (7.5 percent), such as "their house burned down"; and the volatility of income (6 percent), that is, that some poor people were formerly members of the middle class but some misfortune (war, divorce, job loss) had turned their fates. For example, "Many were in wars and now cannot do well so they are poor." Income volatility was also a common explanation for unemployment (6.5 percent), whereas references to mental health problems and drug and alcohol abuse accounted for nearly 9 percent of the explanations for homelessness.

Some youth noted the fragile and tenuous position of the working poor and lower middle class: "They are just a few pay checks from getting back on their feet"; "they lost everything they ever had and went into debt." There was a palpable sense in these responses of the slippery slope on which some people lived and of the life-long consequences of one risky choice. An African-American from a low-income community said of the homeless, "They took for granted that what they had was secure, some invested all their possessions into something that failed them"; a Native American stated, "Homes burn, lost job, can't pay bills"; and an Arab-American said of the poor, "Once they had everything but life turned on them." The psychological defeat associated with unemployment was expressed by another high school student who said, "They lost their jobs and can't find another and then they lose everything and maybe they feel they're a failure and just give up." The teens' impressions that one negative event can devastate a working family are supported by ethnographic work that shows how precarious the economic fortunes, especially of the working poor can be when life events like a medical emergency, a divorce, or the loss of a job quickly whittle away at one's savings.[13]

## Get Real: Lower Aspirations

The open-ended questions that I posed to adolescents did not ask them to propose solutions to inequality; however, some did. (I have already mentioned a few of these.) Among the "solutions" to poverty and unemployment were admonitions that these groups should cope by learning to settle for less. For example, a white eighth grader living in a privileged community whose career goal is to be an international banker, said, "Although some people are disabled and unable to work most either did not finish their education or they feel they are too good to work for minimum wage at a place like McDonalds." According to her, we could solve our unemployment problem *"If everyone stayed in school and realized that a job paying minimum wage is better then no job at all* [italics added]." Another teen felt that there were solutions to job loss and poverty, "but it is going to take time and people are gonna have to be willing to work for very minimal wages." Adolescents from privileged communities were not the only ones who recommended that those at the bottom of the ladder learn to settle for less, as the remarks of an African-American twelfth grader who attended school in the shadows of one of the largest auto plants in the United States suggest. This young woman who wanted to be a corporate lawyer by the time she turned thirty, observed, "many people do not have enough education to hold a permanent good paying full-time job and instead of working in a fast food restaurant where there is always work they remain unemployed hoping to find a job where they can do the least amount of work for the most money."

Jennifer Hochschild, a Professor of Government and African and African American Studies at Harvard University, has described four key beliefs that comprise the American dream: (1) everyone can participate equally and can always start over if they need to; (2) it is reasonable to anticipate success; (3) success results from individual actions and traits that are under the individual's control; and (4) success is associated with virtue and merit, whereas failure is linked to lack of talent or will.[14] Many adolescents questioned various tenets of this dream. Those giving structural as well as uncontrollable explanations raised doubts about whether economic success really resulted from actions that were under individual control.

In contrast, some of the youth who held individuals accountable for their economic station believed, at least in the abstract, that the playing field was level, that everyone could succeed if they applied themselves. But the "lowering of expectations/settling for less" group previously discussed suggested that everyone may not be entitled to the American dream (i.e., even with hard work and will, the shrinking pool of "good jobs" may mean that it is not reasonable for everyone to anticipate a share of the American dream). Those displaced by the new economic realities may have to buck up, take jobs that pay minimum wage, and settle for less.

Were adolescents' theories about poverty and wealth internally consistent? In roughly half (54 percent) of the cases, adolescents' theories based on their first responses were internally consistent, that is, they used similar attributions to explain poverty and wealth. Considering only first responses, 29 percent invoked individual, 23 percent systemic or structural, and 2 percent uncontrollable factors to explain why some people were poor while others were rich. For the other 46 percent of first responses, teens attributed poverty to one cause and wealth to another. In other words, for roughly half of the respondents, the first factor that came to mind when they thought about poverty was an attribution to a different underlying cause than the factor that first came to mind to explain wealth. For this group, theories about why people may have poor economic outcomes are not simply the inverse of why others are rich. Insofar as only 29 percent attributed inequality to individual factors (hard work, effort, intelligence), it seems that meritocracy is only one among several beliefs that figure in teens' theories about inequality.

## ADOLESCENTS' THEORIES ABOUT INEQUALITY: COMPLEXITIES

Initial responses are one indicator of how people think about an issue. As the first thing mentioned, psychologists tend to assume that this is the most cognitively available or salient. Consequently, it is thought to capture what is most meaningful or "true" for that individual. Another way to understand teens' theories about inequality is to code multiple responses. Doing so reveals that many teens consider the contributions of many factors to inequality.

Adolescents often mentioned more than one way that people become rich, poor, unemployed, or homeless. For example, in the following statement, the adolescent mentions multiple causes for homelessness, invoking structural issues including job loss and welfare reform as well as individual factors such as drug use: "I would say that a lot of them got laid off and could not afford their homes anymore some of them were on welfare but got cut off and the rest would be people who got into drugs and alcohol and some who ran away from home." Another example comes from an adolescent who mentioned multiple ways that people might become rich: "they are rich because they had a good education, and they have a good job. Or they have great connections, or they're drug dealers."

Overall, adolescents gave a greater number of responses for economic success than for various forms of economic loss or failure; they also had more to say about unemployment than about poverty or homelessness. Not only did they give more responses to explain how people might become wealthy, they also invoked different categories in their attributions. Scoring of their responses using integrative complexity techniques revealed that, in general, teens had a more complex understanding of ways that people could become rich than ways they might become poor. They had higher scores on integrative complexity, indicating that they had a fuller appreciation of the different ways that people might become rich. Scores based on integrative complexity coding ranged between 1 and 3 with only a handful of teens scoring 4. Higher scores indicate that more perspectives on an issue were considered. Means and standard deviations for the integrative complexity scores were: 1.97 (.96) for wealth, 1.87 (.95) for unemployment, 1.72 (.90) for poverty, and 1.69 (.90) for homelessness. Another indicator of complexity is the percent of responses that reached a level of 3: forty-four percent of the responses for wealth, 38.4 percent of those for unemployment, 29.3 percent for poverty, and 28.8 percent for homelessness.

As an aspect of societal cognition, an adolescent's theory about inequality is socially mediated (i.e., adolescents select their ideas from those that are widely shared, discussed in conversations and enacted in the everyday practices of mediating institutions). These beliefs are profoundly shaped by information available through the media. Studies show that the wealthy get far more media time than the poor and matters that concern the wealthy (society pages, stock market performance) take up a large share of the attention.[15] So we should not be surprised that, in general, teens knew more about wealth than about poverty. Entertainment shows also provide coverage of the rich and famous and ways to become more like them. A teenager flipping through channels, remote in hand, can learn "How to Become a Millionaire" or about "Lifestyles of the Rich and Famous." Routes to wealth include, as the teens in this study noted, hitting the lottery, having a rich father (think Paris Hilton), or swindling others out of their life savings (think Bernie Madoff).

Furthermore, according to media studies, stories about the poor and the wealthy typically use an episodic (case study) rather than a thematic format. Thus what the public learns about inequality focuses on individuals and downplays political and economic factors. But even this episodic format discounts poverty. The poor get little airtime, and stories about them tend to be seasonal (during holidays when stories about food banks and homeless shelters appeal to the charity of viewers) or to follow upon natural disasters.[16] However, according to some scholars, the public's insulation from the plight of the poor may have grown worse in recent years. In his 2008 book, *Unequal Democracy: The Political Economy of the New Gilded Age,* the political scientist Larry Bartels draws attention to the reviews of Barbara Ehrenreich's book *Nickel and Dimed,* in which she describes the daily lives and challenges of the working poor. Bartels notes that reviewers described her account as "illuminating, jarring, explosive, frightening" and suggests that the reviewers' words point to "the remarkable insulation of America's comfortable class from the realities of economic inequality."[17]

Teens in my study were less insulated. Living in the industrial heartland meant that they were like the canary in the coal mine, more cognizant than the rest of the country about economic restructuring and industrial downsizing. Although they knew less about poverty than about wealth, they had plenty to say about unemployment and, undoubtedly, were more aware than the average American about the implications of economic change and growing inequality for their own futures.

## CORRELATES OF TEENS' THEORIES ABOUT INEQUALITY

Older adolescents offered a greater quantity and a wider range of perspectives on inequality than did younger adolescents. In addition, youth who participated in family discussions of politics and current events offered a more complex array of attributions for inequality. Teens also were more likely to report that they engaged in such family discussions *if* their parents had higher levels of education. But it was discussions and not parental education that increased the likelihood that teens would mention *different* factors contributing to inequality.

## Family Discussions

The following short excerpt from one adolescent's survey suggests that such discussions may introduce different perspectives into teens' views about the world. Note that this excerpt does not concern inequality. Rather, the item asks adolescents whether they have discussed with their parents or grandparents what life was like in their day—when the older generations were young—compared to what life is like for teens growing up today. This teen responds, "My parents talk about it being safer when they were my age. There was no HIV, AIDS, not as many drugs or guns. But then my grandparents remind us how before that, when they were young there was a holocaust and oppression." The "but then" phrase is an indication of the teen's perspective-taking skills and is used in scoring for integrative complexity.

The phrase is a clue that the teen recognizes that some aspects of the olden days were better but other aspects were worse.

In another part of the survey, adolescents responded to items asking how often they discussed current events and politics in their families. Those young people who reported that family discussions of politics and current events are a common occurrence in their families were significantly more likely to give several reasons and different bases for inequality. Family discussions of politics and current events also were related to the likelihood that youth would invoke systemic causes for inequality. Why? One explanation comes from "system justification theory."[18] As John Jost and his colleagues argue, people typically accept the way things are rather than try to challenge the system. Accepting the way things are, or "justifying the system" requires relatively little cognitive effort whereas challenging the system implies a capacity to see alternative perspectives to the way things are and to critique the system in light of those other possibilities. Thus, family discussions of politics and current events may introduce adolescents to alternative points of view and enable them to take a more critical perspective.

Furthermore, these discussions may communicate something other than information insofar as the practice also reflects a political value, that is, that current events and political issues are important and that it matters for people to pay attention and to take a stand. Other scholars have identified this practice as a significant predictor of adolescents' civic commitments (that is, the personal importance that teenagers attached to taking a stand on civic issues). In their longitudinal study of low-income and ethnic-minority high school students, Joseph Kahne and Susan E. Sporte found that civic commitments increased over time *if* the adolescent discussed civic issues with their parents and if she or he lived in a civically responsive neighborhood where adults engaged and networked with one another and supported young people.[19] In short, it appears that young people become committed to doing something about our collective problems when adults engage them in solving those problems and communicate that there's something we can and should do together to solve our problems.

## Social Class and Beliefs about Equal Opportunity

There were significant differences in teens' theories about inequality based on their parents' level of education and on the social class composition of their school districts: students who listed individual or uncontrollable factors for poverty were more likely to be from low- and middle-income school districts, whereas those who listed structural or systemic causes tended to be from high-income school districts. In addition, their attributions were consistent with their beliefs about the social contract in the United States. Specifically, compared to those who mentioned structural reasons for poverty, adolescents who held individuals accountable for being poor, unemployed, or homeless were more likely to believe that the United States is an equitable society where the playing field is level, hard work distinguishes those who succeed from those who fail, and government safety nets promote dependency. These different political theories are similar to those held by adult conservatives and liberals, with the former more likely to hold individuals rather than society responsible for inequality. The more committed a young person in this study was to a particular ideological position (i.e., attributing many forms of inequality to the same cause), the stronger was his or her belief about America being (or not being) an equitable society. Although political views are unlikely to harden during adolescence, these results suggest that adolescents already are forming political theories that are in sync with their views about the opportunity structure in the United States.

## Personal and Family Values

The study also revealed consistencies between teens' personal values and their lay theories about inequality: those who provided structural explanations tended to endorse civic values indicating a concern for others—social responsibility for the common good, compassion for the less fortunate, concerns that economic disparities were growing in society, and altruistic values (i.e., a willingness to give up some personal luxuries in the interests of more equitable distribution for the common good). And these were not artifacts of the teen's social background because parents' education was controlled in the analyses. The teens who provided more structural explanations also were more open-minded toward "others," in particular, immigrants, endorsing views that immigrants enriched American society and should be encouraged to maintain and celebrate their language and customs.

But the adolescents' theories about inequality also reflected broader views about the world and how the terms of the social contract operated for people "like them." Those adolescents, disproportionately from working-class and poor families, who held individuals accountable for being poor tended to see a world where individuals were on their own and needed to jockey for position: both measures of social privilege (i.e., whether based on the level of parental education for the individual adolescent or the average household income of the district where the teen attended school) were inversely related to the adolescent's materialist aspirations and to his or her endorsement of a self-reliant ethic. Youth from the most disadvantaged families endorsed more materialist values, saying that, when they thought about their future, making a lot of money and having nice things were very important.

Adolescents from the most privileged backgrounds were the least likely to believe in the logic of opportunity. One interpretation of these results is that sociocentric understanding is associated with the advantages of education and income. Another is that the results reflect the distinct realities of youth growing up under different sets of circumstances in the United States. Materialism may be a less important value for those who have attained such goals but it appears to be highly valued by those who have not. Other studies have shown that children from disadvantaged families within the United States are more likely to endorse materialist values and that, across nations, populations are less likely to embrace post-materialist values until their more basic needs are met.[20]

The youth from disadvantaged families also were more likely than those from privileged families to report that their parents admonished them that they should work twice as hard as others if they wanted to get a job; that people have to create their own opportunities since nobody hands them to you; that they couldn't blame others for their problems; and that if they didn't succeed in life, they would have only themselves to blame. This view of a world of ardent self-reliance with no safety nets was more often endorsed by teens from disadvantaged backgrounds.

The notion that we live in a meritocracy is a lesson that most children in the United States learn as they grow up. But it may be even more incumbent on the disadvantaged to embrace such beliefs. For people "like them" with few connections, safety nets, or second chances, there is no other way (short of fundamental changes in social policies) to succeed except through intense self-reliance and hard work. In fact, perceptions about the basic fairness of the terms of the social contract may play a bigger role in the aspirations and behaviors of those who are disadvantaged by its terms. Among adults, disadvantage is associated with a greater likelihood of calibrating pursuits of long-term goals to one's beliefs about societal fairness. Thus, for disadvantaged groups, beliefs about societal fairness may offer self-regulatory benefits.[21]

Let me remind readers that adolescents who participated in this study were recruited from middle and high schools and that those schools in the poorest communities had drop-out rates exceeding 50 percent. For students in those districts who stayed in school justifying the system may have provided some consistency between their actions and beliefs. Their decision to stay in school, despite high levels of dropping out, is consistent with their belief that individuals are responsible for their fates. Conversely, if the system is the problem, ultimately they could be its victims.

According to proponents of system justification theory, there is more evidence (in the historical record and in psychological studies) that disadvantaged groups acquiesce to and defend the status quo rather than rebel against it. In part their support of the system is based on a need to maintain a favorable self-image, to feel validated in their actions, and to feel that their behaviors are consistent with their beliefs. Thus disadvantaged youth who apply themselves, studying hard in high school and aspiring to college, have to believe that their efforts will pay off—that the rewards of a meritocratic system will accrue to people "like them" who follow the rules. Legitimizing the system restores a sense of confidence and control, especially for those who are confronted by and do not have other ways to manage uncertainty.[22]

Adolescents in the study who grew up in more privileged circumstances were more likely to criticize the system, the very system that advantaged them. However, unlike their peers growing up in disadvantaged communities, they were unlikely to personally feel the brunt of the unequal system that they were criticizing. They enjoyed multiple safety nets—family connections, good schools, opportunities for nonformal learning through community organizations and groups, high school preparation to pursue college tracks. Consider the sophisticated and critical but detached perspective of one European-American female whose father teaches college. She explained that unemployment exists "because it is a capitalist economy and is healthiest (for everybody else) if at least a certain number of people are unemployed. In a rich country, our wealth is not evenly divided." When asked about her plans after high school, she responded, "go to college, see how I like it. Maybe transfer colleges, spend a year abroad as a student. Graduate school? Depends on what I want to do."

Her cavalier attitude toward college would be anathema to a young person from a less privileged background. However, there are more safety nets and second chances for the children of privilege. Their schools are not the inferior ones. If they decide to take time off from school, their families can afford to support them while they explore a gap year. But the theories of the poor reflect the realities of lives without safety nets (i.e., an intense belief that people's fortunes turn on their own efforts). The contrasting emphases in the values and world views reported by adolescents reflect different versions of core American value orientations—one framing a world in which self-reliance and material achievements are essential, the other reflecting a world of relatedness and social responsibility. The correlation of these value orientations with the social backgrounds of the participants should give us pause.

Furthermore, this study is not the only contemporary one to identify class differences in young people's theories about inequality. Other scholars have found that even in elementary school, children from disadvantaged backgrounds are more likely than those living in privilege to hold individuals accountable for being poor.[23] The class differences in youths' theories about inequality are in stark contrast to those summarized by Leahy more than three decades ago in which he emphasized age differences in endorsements of meritocracy and downplayed class differences in children's theories.[24] However, as previously noted, times have changed: both social policies and the extent of inequality between the haves and have-nots have changed over the past three decades. Today it is more incumbent on individuals and families to manage risk and uncertainty on their own.[25]

## The Erosion of Safety Nets and the American Dream

Risk (of job loss, illness, natural disasters) is part of life. To deal with this aspect of human life, a society can create political and market institutions that pool risks associated with the human condition. Alternatively, a society can decide that individuals and families should manage the uncertainties and bear the burdens of risk. Compared to other modern welfare states, the United States has always expected that individuals should shoulder the risks of uncertainties in life. Nonetheless, during most of the twentieth century, government and employer-provided programs that were legacies of the New Deal and Great Society provided safety nets for many Americans. Private workplace benefits such as health care, unemployment compensation, and retirement pensions had been part of the safety net to which many American workers and their families had been accustomed. However, as Jacob Hacker argues in *The Great Risk Shift*, over the past three decades, we have witnessed a massive erosion of the network of government and employer-provided programs and a transfer of the responsibilities for managing risk to individuals and families.

> The old contract—never enjoyed by all workers and almost always implicit, yet still a powerful private standard whose influence belied its less-than-complete reach—said that workers and employers shared the risk of uncertainty in the market as well as the gains of productivity from skills and innovation. . . . On the worker side, shared risks meant a certain degree of loyalty to the firm, a certain degree of commitment to the pay and welfare of fellow employees, a certain degree of restraint in demanding benefit and pay increase when times were good so that the fallout would be less painful when times were bad. On the employer side, shared risks meant an emphasis on the development of workers' skills, the provision of generous workplace benefits like health care and pensions, and the buffering of workers from the risks of fluctuating demand. The bargain held because it worked for both parties—workers received job security, guaranteed benefits, and good pay; employers got loyal, productive workers who invested in skills specific to their jobs and didn't jump ship when times got tough.[26]

It would be wrong to generalize the results of the study summarized in this chapter as if they reflected beliefs held by all teens of all times. In fact, reminding ourselves that these adolescents' theories about inequality are historically embedded and emanate from their lives in the industrial heartland make more visible the social processes and historical conditions that underlie their lay theories about inequality. But the teens' theories about inequality point to the new realities of economic insecurity that younger generations face, uncertainties that the sociologist Richard Sennett argues have become normalized as part of everyday life. In his 1998 book, *The Corrosion of Character,* he reflects:

> Through most of human history, people have accepted the fact that their lives will shift suddenly due to wars, famines, or other disasters, and that they will have to improvise in order to survive. Our parents and grandparents

were filled with anxiety in 1940, having endured the wreckage of the Great Depression and facing the looming prospect of a world war.

What's peculiar about uncertainty today is that it exists without any looming historical disaster; instead it is woven into the everyday practices of a vigorous capitalism. Instability is meant to be normal.[27]

Sennett's observations capture the dilemmas that younger generations face as they negotiate a world where they are on their own to manage lives made precarious by flexible capital and by what Jacob Hacker documents as the increasing privatization of risk management.[28] Furthermore, psychological costs in anxiety and self-doubt are likely for those individuals who imagine only private solutions to the insecure nature of jobs and the economy, personal costs that also have consequences for social trust and democracy, a point I take up in the next chapter. Sennett proposes a solution to the corrosion of character brought on by flexible capital: "A larger sense of community, and a fuller sense of character, is required by the increasing number of people who, in modern capitalism, are doomed to fail."[29]

chapter seven

# Trust

THE COVER OF *Time* magazine published on January 28, 2002, featured an infant, gazing innocently and outwardly at the reader. The prospects that the editors imagined about the world in which she would grow up were summarized in large print on the cover: "So many choices and no one to trust. In today's world . . . *You're on your own, baby.*" This particular issue of *Time* was published in the wake of the Enron scandal in which employees lost their pensions and many shareholders their savings through the shady accounting and investment schemes of company executives. *Time*'s cover plastered a set of questions across the infant's forehead: "Could an Enron happen to me? Is my phone service ripping me off? Who's looking after my 401(k)? Can I count on my broker?" Trust—in fellow human beings and in the institutions of our society—was at the heart of all of these questions. But *Time* also tapped into a collective anxiety brewing in the country about the unpredictable world in which younger generations were growing up and about the unraveling of the social contract on which earlier generations had relied.

Trust was again on the national agenda in the fall of 2008 when we experienced a massive crisis of confidence in our financial institutions. As the financial crisis took on global proportions, the Nobel Prize–winning Princeton economist and *New York Times* columnist Paul Krugman explained why international cooperation was called for: "Because we have a globalized financial system in which a crisis that began with a bubble in Florida condos and California McMansions has caused monetary catastrophe in Iceland. *We're all in this together, and need a shared solution* [italics added]."[1]

These two examples of collective crises of confidence provide a context for the topic at the heart of this chapter—adolescents' social trust (i.e., their beliefs that people generally are fair and trustworthy rather than out for their own gain). Psychologists' interest in trust often has been stirred by the collective anxieties associated with social changes such as threats of nuclear war or rising divorce rates.[2] Major social changes challenge widely held assumptions about the way the world works. The world is less reliable and the threats of uncontrollable forces cause us to be more vigilant, attentive to what might happen next, what steps others might take, and what we might do about it.

Long before the crises of confidence induced by market speculators, there were signs that social trust was on the decline. In 1960, when a national sample of American adults was first asked whether "most people can be trusted," 58 percent of the respondents felt that most people were trustworthy. By the mid-1990s, only a third agreed, and the figure has never returned to the levels of the 1960s. These trends are based on representative samples of American adults, but it is noteworthy that younger generations contribute disproportionately to the declines.[3] Declines in social trust were especially marked in the 1980s and 1990s, a period that also saw increasing endorsement of materialist values among high school seniors. In contrast to the sense that "we're all in this together," there was a greater sense of looking out for oneself, of having more money and things, and of doing better than others.[4]

Why should we care about declining levels of social trust? For more than fifty years scholars have noted that trusting other people is an important foundation for democratic governance. In the 1950s when the sociologist Morris Rosenberg first developed a scale to measure social trust, which he referred to as "faith in people," he argued that this belief was implied in the democratic doctrine's assumption that people are capable of governing themselves. In democracies, social order is not maintained by the state's coercive measures or even by legal constraints. Rather, because authority is vested in the people, because the people govern their own (collective) affairs, it follows that the people should feel identified with and committed to their common good. If most people are committed to the common good, then we can assume that they are trustworthy people of good will who will follow rules that benefit them and other members of their community.

Trust is never certain because it is premised on people's freedom. And that is the reason that trust is a foundation for democratic governance. In other words, our confidence in the democratic process reflects a fundamental belief that people who are free to make their own decisions will choose for the common good (in which they share) rather than for their more narrow self-interest.[5] Although we can never know all of our fellow citizens, believing in rule by the people reveals our faith that they share with us a set of norms, values, responsibilities that bind us to one another.[6] Obligations that arise from trust are not enforceable by law or sanction, but through pressures that arise from communal relationships.[7] In fact, this realization of sharing in a common fate is the foundation that Aristotle argues is essential to sustain a polity. According to Aristotle, laws and institutions cannot support governance in the absence of the comity and trust of citizens who appreciate that they share a common fate.

Democratic dispositions—to be open-minded, to trust others, to be committed to finding common ground that transcends differences—do not happen by default. People are not born with democratic dispositions. Rather, formative institutions and experiences are critical. Consistent with a civic republican or strong democracy vision, citizens obtain their freedom by being members of and participating in political communities and deliberating with fellow citizens to determine how, collectively, they want to live.[8] In fact, the very process of deliberation socializes self-discipline and restraint. In other words, we learn, by the deliberative process, to listen to others, to police ourselves, to refrain from judging others prematurely, to be open-minded in the interests of finding common ground.

Social trust has been called a democratic virtue, a psychological disposition that is essential for the operation of democratic societies because it is related to tolerance and civic engagement.[9] In other words, people who believe that other human beings are generally fair and trustworthy tend to vote, join organizations, lead groups, and actively support the rights of others to hold and express their own religious beliefs, cultural traditions, and lifestyles. Social trust also strengthens civil society because it is a basis for cooperation. When people have faith in fellow human beings, they need not spend time and energy maintaining their own competitive advantage. Instead, they can turn attention and devote time to working together for the benefit of the whole community.

Social trust also is correlated with other virtues that benefit democracy. For example, people who trust others whom they do not know tend to be trustworthy themselves: they say that it's hard for them to lie. They seem to value honesty and fair play and consequently hold themselves to such standards of behavior. Yet they are not more gullible or exploitable than non-trusting persons.[10] In fact, those with high levels of trust are good at discerning when to place their faith in another and when caution is warranted. Such "social intelligence" may be honed through social interaction insofar as people who stick to themselves (social isolates) have lower levels both of social trust and of social intelligence.[11] In addition, loners are less likely to trust others and to believe that others trust them, despite the fact that this perception does not correspond to reality.[12] At the same time, trusters do not judge people before getting to know them. Instead, they are open-minded, giving the benefit of the doubt to people they have never met.

Trust is a complicated phenomenon. Social trust is different from trust in familiars. We can predict the behavior of people we know and thus decide how much to trust person $A$ versus person $B$. The sociologist Eric Uslaner has labeled this form of trust in familiars "strategic trust." Based on our experiences and knowledge of those with whom we are familiar, we can make an informed judgment about whether we can rely on them, whether they will keep their promises. Later I will make the case that we learn about the phenomenon of trust through the many and varied experiences that we have with other people, familiar and unfamiliar to us. Nonetheless, the so-called strategic trust that we have in people we know is quite different from the trust we have in those we do not.

Unlike familiars, people we do not know are less predictable; we lack knowledge about them. Social trust, then, is a leap of faith, a decision to believe that human beings will be fair and trustworthy, although they may not be. We cannot be sure. So, in making that leap of faith, we leave ourselves vulnerable to the possibility that other people may disappoint us. In fact, they *could* take advantage of us. Social trust, then, is a gauge of our willingness to give people whom we do not know the benefit of the doubt. It is the decision to include them in our moral community and to treat them based on the Golden Rule, as we would wish them to treat us. For this reason, Uslaner has referred to social trust as "moralistic trust."[13]

A classic essay by the sociologist Mark Granovetter summarizes the distinction between the bonds of trust with those we know and the trust we have for others we do not, what he refers to as strong versus weak ties.[14] According to Granovetter, these ties differ in their level of intensity and familiarity but also in how homogeneous or heterogeneous the membership in these networks tends to be. Members of networks with strong ties tend to share the same social backgrounds. They tend to be of the same social class, ethnicity, or religious affiliation. Thus the trust we feel for people in networks of strong ties is based on knowing them well *and* on being able to predict their behavior based on how similar they are to us. These groups play an important psychological role—in affirming and supporting us, especially through tough times. But it is weak ties and trust in others we do not know well (social trust) that sustains a diverse, democratic society.

## DEVELOPMENTAL FOUNDATIONS OF TRUST

For the last fifteen years, research on social trust has been mainly the province of sociologists and political scientists and has focused on adults. That work tells us little about the mechanisms whereby the disposition to trust others develops. Although it seems reasonable to assume that there are early formative influences on our beliefs about whether people generally are fair and trustworthy, we know little about how our faith in humanity, in people we do not know, takes shape. Seeking answers seems all the more important when we consider that these beliefs tend to be rather stable in adulthood. What we believe at age twenty-six about people being basically fair and trustworthy is highly related to what we believe about people's trustworthiness seven years later, and that correlation gets stronger by midlife.[15] At the same time, levels of social trust are lower, on average, in late adolescence and emerging adulthood than in middle or late adulthood. The lower levels of trust may be due to the unpredictable nature of this period of the life course. Social trust may increase as people settle into adult roles and the predictable routines associated with those roles.

The period when youth come of age also shapes their initial levels of social trust as they enter adulthood. In other words, norms, values, and beliefs that are widely shared in society when a cohort comes of age act as a set point from which that cohort's level of social trust develops.[16]

Psychological research on trust has focused more on interpersonal than on social trust. Nonetheless, the work is relevant for understanding the phenomenon of trust in general and its psychological correlates specifically. Further, theories of psychosocial development are useful for helping us generate hypotheses about the developmental foundations of social trust.

Erikson considered trust fundamental to our ability to thrive as human beings. He contrasted feelings of insecurity and self-doubt with a sense of basic trust that he referred to as the "most fundamental prerequisite of mental vitality" and the "cornerstone of a vital personality."[17] Focusing on the processes whereby this basic trust developed in infancy, Erikson argued that trust springs from a confidence that caretakers *are there* for us. The child learns to trust his own instincts because the world is a *predictable place, because others who inhabit it are basically benevolent; they have the child's best interests in mind.*

According to Erikson, when an infant can rely on caretakers assuring a safe, reliable world, that infant feels free to reach out to the world, to turn attention to exploring its possibilities. Thus, trust is a foundation for learning, a point I will develop later when discussing trust and schools. When early experiences do not engender a basic sense of trust, self-doubt and feelings of insecurity become more integral to the self. Vigilance about the world can ensue.

Erikson emphasizes the importance of a feeling of continuity between the emerging sense of a distinct self with the broader community of which the infant is a part. The reciprocal relationship between trust and trustworthiness is learned even in this preverbal period. In short, in explaining how essential trust was to being human, Erikson emphasized the fundamental interdependence between human beings: "By trust I mean an essential trustfulness of others as well as a fundamental sense of one's own trustworthiness."[18]

Besides the foundational importance of trust in infancy, Erikson held that trust was integral to an adolescent's search for ideologies that she believed in, for traditions to which she could be faithful, and for a community of others who shared those commitments. When discussing fidelity as the cornerstone of identity, he alluded to the reciprocity between trust and trustworthiness, arguing that in seeking ideas and others who share our beliefs, values, and worldviews, an adolescent needs to feel that he is true to himself, a trustworthy person.

Erikson considered trust so fundamental to human existence that he nominated it as the foundation for the human being's need to have hope. He referred to the sense of trust that was nurtured in the infant's relationship with caretakers as "the ontological source of faith and hope."[19] But he realized that there would be times when our trust in others would not be reinforced, in fact, that it would be impeded, or even foiled. Sometimes people may not live up to the faith that we have placed in them. It is then, Erikson contends, that we must maintain a higher sense of hope: "Hope is both the earliest and the most indispensable virtue inherent in the state of being alive. Others have called this deepest quality confidence, and I have referred to trust as the earliest positive psychosocial attitude, but if life is to be sustained hope must remain, even where confidence is wounded, trust impaired."[20]

In summary, Erikson nominates trust as the foundational virtue for our ability to act as human beings, to explore, to learn, to find our place in a community with fellow human beings, to live lives of hope and purpose, and to make commitments. And he locates its foundation in our reliance on others who care for us.

## FRIENDSHIPS AND PEER RELATIONS

In contrast to the infant's one-sided dependence on caretakers, friendships are defined by mutuality and interdependence. As Jean Piaget argues, friendships are premised on horizontal relationships between peers. As such, they tend to be more egalitarian than are adult-child relationships and thus are critical for moral development.[21] I believe that peer relationships, especially intimate ones between friends, also are critical to understanding—intellectually and affectively—the phenomenon of trust.

Friends need one another, and because they are peers, neither should control the other. Consequently, in friendships we learn a great deal about the phenomenon of trust, and much of it is highly relevant to the personal vulnerability inherent in the leap of faith implied in social trust. The bonds of friendship are cemented by being loyal to one another, doing what we promised, even when we don't feel like it. Just like the benevolent caretaker for the infant, friends "are there" for us. By being reliable, they prove themselves worthy of our trust. And we reciprocate if we value the friendship. Reliability is one of the bases of interpersonal trust.

In friendships we learn about the reciprocal relationship between trust and trustworthiness: Friends hold one another accountable to their word.

Being true to our word means doing the things we said we would do, even if we don't feel like it—because our friends are counting on us and because we care about them and we want them to trust us. By living up to the expectations of our friends that we've *got their back, that we are "there" for them,* we become trustworthy persons. Keeping promises adds order and predictability to a relationship. Being true to our word means doing the things we said we would do—because we value our friendship and because we hold ourselves to a moral standard of dependability. When we break a promise, we lose face—with friends and in self-respect. We know the standards to which our friends hold us—and we do not want to disappoint them if we value our friendship. Not only would that disappoint our friends, it would violate the image we hold of ourselves. According to the social psychologist Morton Deutsch, the trustworthy person is aware of being trusted, cognizant of this standard of his character and therefore bound by the trust invested in him.[22]

The political scientist C. Douglas Lummis notes not only that we learn about trust but that *we become trustworthy persons* through the repeated commitments and honoring of promises we make to fellow human beings. He refers to trust as a democratic virtue and describes the everyday relationships that teach us about and reinforce this virtue. Relations of trust "are established in the web of human relations by thousands of promises and contracts, some explicit but most not, which people make in their daily dealings with one another over the years and over generations. Trust is not morality, but it produces virtuous behavior and virtuous persons."[23]

Alluding to the social contract that binds members of a civil society together, Lummis adds that "the act of making and keeping a promise is a conquest of the chaos that would come if each of us followed our individual passions from moment to moment wherever they lead. It is a conquest that establishes order without placing humankind under a punishing God, a punishing leviathan, a punishing conscience, or a punishing order of exploitative work."[24] In sum, keeping promises (i.e., keeping faith with one another) may be a means by which teens learn the meaning of the social contract, the ties that bind us together.

For the social contract of a democratic society to work, certain psychological underpinnings are necessary. Specifically, it is essential that democratic dispositions be nurtured in the younger generation. Those dispositions include an open-mindedness toward others with whom we disagree, a willingness to seek common ground, and a commitment to deliberate and work together to realize the kind of society we envision together. Through the repeated interactions with others who are reliable and loyal, *who are there for us*—we develop trusting dispositions. And because those relationships are reciprocal and we hold ourselves to standards of reliability and loyalty, we also become trustworthy persons.

In friendships we also gain practice in taking an *other's* perspective and thereby develop our capacities for empathy and compassion. Yet because our friends are typically people who are like us, these relationships may not be a basis for developing social trust. Furthermore, the bonds of trust between friends can be reinforced by stereotyping out-groups as less trustworthy. For example, elementary age children are more likely to trust peers of their own race and to believe that same-race peers would be more likely than peers of an opposite race to keep promises and tell the truth. Similarly, children's same-sex friendships are maintained by trust that results both from sharing secrets with one another and from maintaining beliefs that peers of the opposite sex would not keep secrets.[25] Nonetheless, in friendships we come to value certain virtues (loyalty, reliability, empathy, a cooperative spirit, honesty and authenticity) as standards to live by. If the virtues learned in friendships become integral to one's identity, then compared to loners or social isolates, youth who have had close relationships with friends should be better prepared to extend the boundaries of those they trust to a larger segment of their community.

At the same time, friends can disappoint one another. They are not always loyal or reliable. They are even free to choose whether to remain our friends. It is precisely because individuals are free and consequently unpredictable that we need trust. Trust implies taking a chance on others and accepting some level of personal vulnerability in that process. The essence of trust is the belief that "others" are fair, that they will not take advantage of us, *although they could*. When friends disappoint us we learn that vulnerability might be a cost of placing our faith in others. And that painful experience is critical to our capacity to understand the meaning of trust. Trust is premised on freedom: it is precisely because people are free to make their own choices that placing our trust in them is an act of faith. We can never be completely certain. Trust, as we know from disappointments in our closest relationships, implies the other's freedom, and consequently, our vulnerability.

Lummis discusses the dilemma of freedom and trust as the

essential paradox of trust. The only proper object of trust is people, *because* people are capable of untrustworthiness; only people are capable of untrustworthiness, *because* they are trusted. . . . Trust—and trustworthiness—was invented as a way of dealing with the uncertainties of human beings, who are free. It does not change the uncertainties into certainties. *Trust is not a proof but a judgment and a choice* [italics added].[26]

## STUDYING THE PHENOMENON OF TRUST AS IT DEVELOPS IN ADOLESCENCE

Our research team set out to learn more about the correlates and predictors of social trust by conducting a three-year longitudinal study of a socioeconomically diverse sample of more than eleven hundred early, middle, and late adolescents and their parents. Adolescents reported on processes in families and in schools that affected their social trust. Parents reported on processes in families and also discussed their perceptions about the trustworthiness of major social institutions including schools.

Concerning the family, we asked adolescents and their mothers two of the classic items used in national studies to tap "social trust": whether they believed that "most people can be trusted" and that "most people are fair and don't take advantage of you." In addition, we asked mothers and teens about the values emphasized in their families, in particular values about how one should treat other people. For example, teens indicated how strongly they agreed or disagreed with items tapping their family's emphasis on compassion, openness, and social responsibility for others such as "My parents have taught me to pay attention to other people's needs, not just my own" and "My parents have taught me to treat everyone equally." Parents, for their part, reported on similar values that they emphasized in raising their children (i.e., I tell my children not to judge people before you get to know them). Besides values of openness and social responsibility toward others, parents and teens also indicated the extent to which caution or vigilance toward other people was emphasized at home. For example, parents endorsed items such as "I warn my children that you can't always trust people."[27]

I cast a broad net in exploring the developmental bases of adolescents' social trust and began with the following assumptions: First, that our beliefs about others are not fixed but are formed in the course of development and, like many social categories, are more malleable when we are younger than when we are older.

Second, that interpersonal trust is a necessary foundation for social trust but that intelligence about the social world develops as we mature. Consequently, between childhood and the end of adolescence, we distinguish trust in those we know from trust in people in general.

Third, that parents play two important roles in the development of children's social trust: (a) they are moral guides, admonishing children about relationships with fellow human beings and how one should treat them (i.e., "don't judge people before you get to know them" versus "be on your guard lest other people take undue advantage of you"); (b) at the same time, parents play a role in the development of children's social intelligence (i.e., in their capacity to discern times when people are worthy of their trust and times when greater vigilance may be called for). Social intelligence, what we might consider a mature sense of social trust, also is informed by the diversity of our experiences with other people.

Fourth, that feelings of trust in other people should be learned by specific kinds of interactions with fellow human beings: (a) interactions through which youth gain a sense of group (collective) identity, a feeling of being part of a mutually caring community; and (b) interactions that broaden the circle of humanity with whom youth have contact and allow them to extend their beliefs about how trustworthy people in general are to groups of people with whom they rarely have contact.

Let me begin by describing what social trust looks like in early versus late adolescence. Our longitudinal data meant that we could assess change over time in the same teens' beliefs. We learned that, even by the fifth grade, an individual's belief about the general trustworthiness of people in one year is highly predictive of that belief in the next. However, these beliefs were more hardened in late than in early adolescence. For sixteen- to eighteen-year-olds, the correlation over one year's time was .63 whereas for eleven- to twelve-year-olds it was .49. The early adolescents' views about humanity (about people in general) also were more affected by interpersonal trust in their friendships, which was not the case for late adolescents. Interpersonal trust with friends was a measure of interdependence, tapped by the teen's reports that he had close friends who could be trusted to keep secrets and promises, friends who also could count on the fact that such loyalties would be reciprocated, that is, that friends could count on the teen himself to keep promises, or to be reliable. In short, a mark of friendship is that friends have one another's back. Between early and late adolescence, the trust and loyalty that a teen reported in his friendships was gradually distinguished from the teen's faith or trust in people in general: the correlation between interpersonal and social trust was .41, .26, and .13, respectively, for early, middle, and late adolescents. Note that these are all positive but that the association between trust in friendships and social trust (in humanity) weakens between early and late adolescence.

This weakening association suggests that between early and late adolescence, the abstract social category, "most people or people in general" (humanity, if you will), is gradually distinguished from the category of people one knows well, that is, from one's personal friendships. In early adolescence this distinction is weaker, whereas trust in these two groups is distinct for the late adolescent. The late adolescent is more capable of the kind of civic friendship that Aristotle describes as an interdependence of mature citizens whose goal is enhancing the common good. In contrast to the early adolescent who still conceives of "other people" in somewhat personal terms ("friends or people who are like me"), the late adolescent distinguishes the category, "people in general," from friends with whom she is most familiar. This distinction is important because civic friendship is not premised on similarity but rather on realizing the interdependence of one's desires and fate with the fates of a diverse array of fellow citizens.

The age-related distinction between interpersonal and social trust likely reflects underlying development in social cognition between early and late adolescence and the capacity to conceive of social categories or abstract groups such as the generalized other, "most people." Compared to an early adolescent, an older adolescent is more competent in thinking about abstract categories, distinguishing these groups from her personal relationships. In addition, as adolescents mature, they engage in a broader set of contexts and with more diverse groups of people. This may be why we found that faith in humanity declined as kids got older.[28] Even over the short duration of our study, growing older had a negative impact on the average adolescent's social trust. For early, middle, and late adolescents, reports of how trustworthy and fair they believed people generally were declined between year one and year two. In contrast, trust in friendships, was higher (above 4.0 on a 1–5 scale) than social trust for all age groups and did not decline with age.[29] Further, mothers' beliefs about whether other people are generally fair and trustworthy did not differ by the age of their adolescents. Thus, something about adolescents' lives as they get older is associated with declines in their beliefs that people generally are trustworthy and fair.

Trust is not gullibility, and experience helps us distinguish the two. Several decades ago Julian Rotter wrote that trust that is untempered by some skepticism is naïve and, in the absence of good judgment, is no more than gullibility.[30] Or, as Lummis puts it, "Democratic faith is not simply trusting everybody equally; it is not sentimental foolishness. It is grounded on a lucid understanding of the weaknesses, follies, and horrors people are capable of. It is precisely because of those weaknesses, follies, and horrors that something so weighty as faith is called for."[31]

The age trends in our studies point to an increase in social intelligence and to a deeper understanding of the phenomenon of trust. As the sociologist Toshio Yamagishi argues, trust reflects social intelligence.[32] As teens mature, they distinguish interpersonal from social trust and, while the former remains high, the latter declines with age. The age-related decline in social trust likely reflects the wider range of experiences with "others" that accrue between early and late adolescence. But the age-related declines in social trust also suggest that some cynicism about humanity may be a cost of growing up, although what it is about growing up is unclear. It is likely that families engage in more cocooning, monitoring, and protection of their early adolescent children but loosen the reins by late adolescence, allowing their older children more independence, or more latitude to be "on their own."

Reports about family communication from the adolescents in our study support the likelihood of more cocooning in early adolescence: compared to middle and late adolescents, the early adolescent group reported higher levels of parents' communicating with them about other people—admonitions from parents *both* to be compassionate and attentive to other people *and* to be vigilant lest other people take advantage of them. The early adolescents also were more likely than middle or late adolescents to say that their parents respected their opinions and considered those opinions when making decisions. Objectively, this scenario is probably not the case, that is, parents are more likely to give latitude in decision making to older adolescents. However, the nature of the decisions that parents and adolescents are negotiating varies as teens get older: whereas early adolescents may want to have friends over, late adolescents want the car keys to go out with friends. Taken together, the results suggest that more parent-teen communication takes place in early adolescence and that parents may have a greater influence (relative to other factors) on teens' social intelligence during this period than they might at a later stage of adolescence.

Adolescents' experiences in schools also differ, depending on the teen's age. Schools tend to be less competitive settings in early adolescence than in late adolescence. Further, late adolescents are more likely to face decisions about their futures—whether to seek work, to apply to college—questions about what they are going to do with their lives. Others have found that as they get older and have more experience with the adult world, adolescents' aspirations concerning the work they might do become more limited and that this is especially marked among African-American females.[33] In effect, the possibilities that they imagine for themselves become more realistic, for want of a better word, as they learn more about the terms of the social contract. These "reality tests" may dampen social trust.

Facing decisions about one's future also may raise doubts and cause anxiety, psychological states that are inversely related to trust. Many of the experiences of late adolescents also would remind them of the competitive nature of life: if one's view of the world reflects a limited and competitive pie, "others" are more likely to be seen as a threat to one's competitive advantage. The developmental imperatives of late adolescence may leave youth somewhat at loose ends. Greater vigilance about others may be a psychological protection when one feels like he is "on his own."

Whatever the mechanisms, as teens mature, their social worlds enlarge and their naïve understandings are replaced with some skepticism about other people. It is also possible that late adolescence is a particularly vulnerable time for social trust. In another study in which late adolescents were followed into the third decade of life, my colleagues and I found that respondents reported lower levels of social trust in late adolescence but that they gradually became more trusting by their late twenties. The increase in social trust between late adolescence and the end of the third decade of life was consistent across multiple historical cohorts, pointing to an underlying developmental trend. Perhaps the nature of everyday life is different in late adolescence when compared to the late twenties: in late adolescence, life tends to be more episodic and uncertain compared to the late twenties when individuals settle into social roles and life becomes more routine.[34]

Insofar as late adolescence was identified in both studies as the period when social trust was at its lowest point, we can infer that something about this time of life makes individuals less trusting of other people. Likely suspects, in my view, are the sense of being on one's own rather than, borrowing Krugman's phrase, "in this together," of worry about making one's way in the world, and of uncertainty about the direction of one's future that are common features of the late adolescent period. In the past few decades, late adolescence and the transition into adulthood has become a more protracted time: youth move in and out of education, combine work and schooling, frequently move their place of residence, and marry and start families at a later time than was the case in earlier generations.

The developmental psychologist Jeffrey Jensen Arnett sees the protracted period that he has called "emerging adulthood" as a developmental opportunity—a time when youth can explore who they are and what they seek in life.[35] From a civic standpoint, one could argue that the diversity of settings and people to which youth are exposed at this time may challenge their existing worldviews. Ultimately, reexamining beliefs that have been taken for granted should result in more open-mindedness—a disposition that is good for democracy. However, the process of questioning existing beliefs may feel destabilizing. Lower social trust may point to a more generalized sense of uncertainty, a loss of faith in old beliefs and of anchors to old ties. In short, late adolescence may bring with it a heightened sense of vulnerability and of being at loose ends. Increased vigilance about other people may serve a psychologically protective role.

One of the items on the survey in my study asked adolescents how much they agreed with the following statement: "In the long run, the only person you can count on is yourself." Teens who endorsed this view had lower scores on social trust. Although moderately correlated, this relationship does suggest a consistency between teens' views of a world where they are on their own rather than, as Krugman contends, "all in this together" and their views about whether they can trust other people. It is worth noting that fifty years ago, when Morris Rosenberg developed items to measure "faith in humanity," he included items tapping the belief that "you have to be vigilant or people will take advantage of you" as well as the belief that "no one really cares much what happens to you." These items suggest that Rosenberg saw a connection between trust in others and a sense that one mattered to other people and that like Erikson's trusting infant, you had significant others in your life who cared deeply about you and your welfare. Social connectedness and social support fulfill very basic human needs for belonging.[36] They also may be essential for maintaining social trust.

## SOCIAL TRUST AND GROUPS AT THE PERIPHERY OF SOCIETY

In research with adults and across different nations, there is consistent evidence that social trust is lower among ethnic minorities, the economically disadvantaged, and those who have recently experienced negative life events such as being the victim of a crime. Robert Putnam interprets the body of evidence in this way:

> In virtually all societies *have-nots* are less trusting than *haves,* probably because haves are treated by others with more honesty and respect. In America blacks express less social trust than whites, the financially distressed less than the financially comfortable, people in big cities less than small-town dwellers, and people who have been victims of a crime or been through a divorce less than those who haven't had those experiences.[37]

In his analyses of group differences in social trust, sociologist Tom Smith coined the term "groups at the periphery" to capture the position, or standpoint, of ethnic minorities and the socially disadvantaged vis-à-vis mainstream society. Smith's data also reveal that changing economic conditions are likely to have an impact on social trust: in his analyses of the General Social Survey, people who had recently lost a job and those who experienced a downward intergenerational occupational trajectory or a recent worsening in their financial situation had lower social trust.[38]

Whereas African-American adults contend that most other black people can be trusted, their trust in white people is much lower.[39] And, as already noted in Chapter 4, research on racial socialization indicates that as they reach adolescence, African-American youth hear more cautions from their parents about people outside their networks, especially if the parents themselves have experienced incidents of prejudice in their own lives. Thus the social trust of African-American youth is likely to be tempered by preparatory socialization, so-called cocooning, meant to protect them from and also prepare them for the realities of racism.

In my longitudinal study, levels of social trust were lower among African-Americans in early adolescence but not in late adolescence. These age differences contradict those found for the whole sample and may be an artifact of the sampling strategy in which we recruited adolescents through public schools: perhaps those ethnic minorities who remain in school into the high school years have more faith in the system and in fellow human beings.

Regardless of age, teens from ethnic-minority backgrounds did hear different messages from their parents about the terms of the social contract. Compared to white youth, ethnic minorities were more likely to say that their parents told them they would have to work twice as hard as other people if they hoped to find a job; ethnic-minority parents also warned their children that they could not depend on the system or other people to bail them out if they failed. Similar results also were obtained when we compared youth from economically disadvantaged families with those living in more privileged families. I believe that the greater emphasis on self-reliance that teens "at the periphery," to borrow Smith's term, heard reflects their parents' assessments of a social contract without safety nets, one where they were on their own to make it.[40]

We also found gender differences in adolescents' social trust with females reporting lower levels than their male peers. Females also were more likely to report that their families emphasized *both* responsibility for *and* vigilance toward other people. Mothers' reports confirmed their teens' observations: mothers of daughters were more likely than mothers of sons to say that they told their children to be responsive and compassionate toward other people but also that they should be guarded, lest others take advantage of them. These gender differences may simply reflect the fact that mothers and daughters have more conversations about people and relationships. According to studies of family communication and socialization, parents are more likely to discuss relationships and emotions and to emphasize prosocial behavior with daughters than with sons. They also are more likely to restrict or cocoon their daughters.[41] Even among young political activists, parents are more likely to restrict their daughters than their sons from engaging in more militant action.[42]

In summary, the socialization of daughters seems to involve more attentiveness to other people and to times when one should respond to them with compassion versus times when one should protect oneself by being more guarded, lest others take advantage. Taken together, the gender patterns in social trust, family values, and restrictiveness raise interesting questions about different routes whereby social intelligence develops: whereas females may learn to "read" other people because their parents emphasize such attentiveness to others, males may develop their social intelligence via a wider range of public venues and encounters with different groups.


## PARENTAL INFLUENCES ON TEENS' SOCIAL TRUST

Notably, among female and male adolescents, there was a positive, albeit small, correlation between reports that values of compassion or responsibility and vigilance or caution were communicated in their families. Note that the items measuring vigilance and caution are not a polar opposite of social trust: by communicating them, parents are not endorsing the belief that *all or even most* people are untrustworthy. Rather, parents would be telling the child that there may be *some* times when or with *some* people that a more cautious attitude would be called for.

Relatively few parents said that they communicated one view of people (treat them with compassion and social responsibility) but never mentioned the other (treat them with caution). The important difference was in *how* parents combined these admonitions. Roughly 35 percent of parents communicated *both* high vigilance and high social responsibility messages. In other words, they told their children to be cautious because there are some people in this world who will take undue advantage *and* they told their children to be compassionate and responsive to other people's needs. An equal number (roughly 34 percent) were in the low-low category, that is, families in which parents communicated very little about the importance of compassion or guardedness toward other people. It may be that this group of families engaged in relatively little communication about other people and how one should treat them. The other 30 percent of the sample was divided between two groups: one with high caution or vigilance and low compassion or social responsibility, and the other with low vigilance and high responsibility.

Two-thirds of the parents reported some combination of vigilance or guardedness and compassion or responsibility, which points to an interesting role that parents may play in developing teens' social intelligence, that is, their capacity to discern times when people may or may not be worthy of their trust. A mature sense of trust reflects social intelligence, that is, an individual's ability to "read" people. Sometimes people do take advantage of us and parents are likely to help their children distinguish between times when the teen should be open and helpful to others and times when he should be more guarded.

According to mothers' reports, social trust and values emphasized in child rearing were logically consistent: mothers with higher social trust were more likely to endorse compassionate values, whereas those with lower levels of social trust tended to endorse more vigilance, urging their teens to be guarded about other people and warning them against too much kindness.[43] In other words, mothers' views of their own parenting appear to be internally consistent—there is a concordance between their beliefs about the trustworthiness of people and how they admonish their child to interact with people (i.e., if I don't trust people, I also warn my child to be wary about people. If I do trust others, I urge my child to be responsive to other people's needs.) Independently, adolescents confirmed these findings, that is, adolescents were more likely to say that their parents emphasized compassion and responsibility for other people in families where mothers reported higher levels of social trust. Conversely, adolescents were more likely to say that their parents urged them to be cautious, lest people take advantage of them, in those families where mothers believed that people generally were not trustworthy.

Importantly, it was the values that adolescents reported hearing at home and not those that mothers said they emphasized that had the most significant impact on the teen's social trust. In analyses over a two-year period, adolescents' reports that their parents emphasized compassion and responsibility for other people increased the teen's social trust in year two—over and above the levels of social trust the teen had reported in the prior year. The impact of the values the teen heard were stronger in middle and late adolescence, but the positive trend was the same for all three age groups.[44] The greater impact of teens' versus mothers' reports of family values on adolescents' social trust does not mean that parents have little effect on these beliefs. It does mean that the message that the parents believe they are communicating is not the whole story. As a large body of research on parent-child communication indicates, other factors—such as the quality and warmth of the relationship, the teen's desires to emulate or distinguish himself from the parent, the teen's attentiveness and receptivity to adopt his parents' values—influence the relationship between what the parents believe they say and what the teen believes he hears, so that the reports of parents and teens tend to be only moderately correlated.[45]

Which patterns were related to adolescents' social trust? Telling your kids that they have a responsibility to help other people is positively related to teens' social trust, even combined with cautions about the costs of too much kindness or admonitions that sometimes people might take advantage. Conversely, telling your kids to be careful in dealing with people but *not* also telling them they have a responsibility for others seems to promote a misanthropic view about humanity. In other words, an emphasis on responsibility for the welfare of others ("You have an obligation to help others, especially those who are less fortunate than you") enhances faith in humanity even if your parents also remind you to be vigilant in your dealings with others ("There will be times in life when you have to look out for yourself because some people might take advantage of you").

The majority of parents provided a nuanced picture of humanity. According to mothers' and adolescents' reports, parents who admonished their children to respect people no matter who they were and to be responsive to others' needs also warned them to be careful because you can't always trust people. In the end, adolescents' beliefs that people generally are trustworthy do not appear to be damaged by also learning that they should be attentive to the way others treat them including warnings that other people might sometimes act unfairly. Learning that *sometimes* people may not be worthy of their trust need not depress the teen's belief that *most people* are generally trustworthy.

Besides the values that were emphasized in families, the respect that teens felt from their parents was also positively, although moderately, related to the teen's social trust. Teens reported on whether the parents listened to their opinions, respected their views, even when the parent disagreed with the teen's point of view. I have already discussed the reciprocal relationship between trust and trustworthiness, that people tend to live up to the standards of trust that others place in them. But this result points to a different interpretation, one that is relevant to the socialization of democratic dispositions in youth. When teens felt that their parents listened to and respected their autonomous opinions, that respect actually boosted the teen's beliefs that people were generally worthy of their trust. A similar finding was reported in a longitudinal study of a 1965 high school cohort that was followed into midlife. According to that work, high school students' reports that their parents and teachers (adult authorities who wield power over the adolescent) respected their autonomous opinions positively predicted their levels of social trust in midlife.[46]

The results that I am reporting are actually a more stringent test insofar as we used teens' reports of their social trust at Time 1 as a control on levels of social trust at Time 2, a year later. This is a stringent test because beliefs about the trustworthiness of other people are highly correlated over this one-year period. These analyses revealed that once social trust measured at Time 1 and other background factors (age, parental education, gender) were controlled, the teen's reports of how democratic her parents were, specifically, whether the parents listened to and respected the teen's opinions, significantly *increased* levels of social trust in the following year among early and middle adolescents. For late adolescents, democratic parenting did not boost social trust in Year 2. Thus, for the early and middle adolescents, we can conclude that parents' modeling of trust in others (in this case, the parent's demonstrating trust in the teen) translates into gains over time in the teen's own faith in humanity. The lack of a boost resulting from democratic parenting practices on late adolescents' social trust may be due to the crystallization of beliefs about most people that occurs by late adolescence or may mean that beliefs about other people are affected by experiences that vary according to the developmental imperatives and contexts at different stages of adolescence. It does *not* mean that parents no longer matter. In fact, the family values of compassion that late adolescents reported hearing in their families did boost their sense of trust in other people over the period of the study.

In summary, the results of the longitudinal analyses of family processes point to three ways in which parents affect their child's social trust: first, based on the values they emphasize in child rearing (especially those that, according to the teen's reports, sink in); second, through the respect that parents demonstrate to the child and his opinions; and third, by encouraging a balanced view of others and attitudes both of compassion and caution in one's dealings with other people.

Social trust or faith in humanity is communicated in families through everyday actions and admonitions about what one should believe about humanity and how one should treat other people. Basic values, such as "You shouldn't judge people before you get to know them. People deserve second chances. You should look out for others, not just yourself," shape the teen's views about the world and her relationships and obligations to other people in that world. Social trust also develops when parents listen to the views of their teens and treat them as worthy of trust, in other words, when they practice what they preach and model how one should treat fellow human beings. The results also point to an interesting role that parents may play in helping their children to develop from naïve to intelligent trusters. Specifically, most parents told their teens that there would be *some* times in life when people might take advantage of them and that it would be wise to be cautious, lest they get hurt. As long as they also emphasized the child's social responsibility for fellow human beings, these cautions about other people, warnings that likely prepare the child to navigate life, did not diminish the adolescent's beliefs about the trustworthiness of fellow human beings.

## PARENTS' VIEWS OF A CHANGING WORLD

The results of a June 9–12, 2008, Gallup Poll compared the American public's confidence in institutions in that year with the public's confidence in 1979, the year that President Jimmy Carter declared a "crisis of confidence." With the exception of the military (which enjoyed a 17 percent gain in public confidence), the public's confidence in other major institutions had declined: organized religion down 17 percent, public schools 20 percent, newspapers 11 percent, Congress and the Supreme Court down 22 percent and 12 percent, respectively.[47]

What might be the implications in families of declining faith in major social institutions? We addressed this question first by asking 967 parents in our longitudinal study to rate five major social institutions (work, schools, media, religion, and government) on a five-point scale based on whether they felt each institution was *more* (5) or *less* (1) trustworthy, safe, or secure or about the same (3) as it was when the parent was a child. Sixty-six percent and 56 percent, respectively, of the parents felt that religion and the government were about the same or even more trustworthy as those institutions had been when the parents were young. Forty-seven percent and 41 percent, respectively, felt that work and the media were as or more trustworthy, and only 37 percent felt that schools were as or more trustworthy, safe, and secure as schools were in the parents' youth. Note that this summary is not an absolute judgment about how trustworthy each institution is today. Rather, parents are making a comparison, judging each institution today vis-à-vis that institution during their youth. Thus parents who feel that government is about as trustworthy as it was in their youth may feel that the government has never been trustworthy.

I have provided the percentages for all five institutions but my focus will be on schools with parents' assessments of the other institutions a useful barometer. Of all five institutions, schools suffered the biggest drop in parental confidence: sixty-three percent of parents felt that schools were less safe, secure, and trustworthy than schools were when the parents were young. This negative perception of schools is troubling for several reasons, not the least of which is that young people spend large portions of their time at school. What takes place in schools has a significant formative influence not only on children's knowledge but also on their dispositions and beliefs. In addition, according to analyses of trends in school safety, this stereotype about schools as less safe, secure, and trustworthy belies the facts.[48] Despite the media's attention to several high-profile incidents of violence in schools, on an everyday basis, schools are actually safer and more secure than ever.

In the following discussion, I compare the 37 percent of parents who felt that schools were equally or more safe and secure (dubbed "school trusters") with the 63 percent of parents who felt that schools had become less safe, secure, and trustworthy (dubbed "school nontrusters"). Only two demographics distinguished the two groups of parents: the nontrusters were more likely to be married and to have continued their education beyond high school. In other words, middle-class parents with relatively more stable marriages and greater educational advantages felt that schools had become less trustworthy institutions compared to what schools were like when they were children. Again, in light of the comparative nature of the question (compared to when you were young), it is possible that working-class parents felt that schools in their day were not safe and that nothing has changed since that time.

Importantly, parents who perceived contemporary schools as less safe and trustworthy were not just more anxious people. For example, they were no more likely to feel concerned that their child would fall in with the wrong crowd. Nor were they more pessimistic about their child's future educational and occupational prospects: they were no more worried than "trusting" parents that their child might have trouble getting into college or finding work. Nor had their teenagers or the teen's friends been victims of bullying or exclusion at school. One concern raised by the less trusting parents was the perception that drugs and violence had increased—in society generally and in the community where they were raising children.

More troubling, in my view, however, were the significant differences in parents' and teens' perceptions of dynamics at the child's own school. In those families where parents had stereotypes about schools as less safe and trustworthy institutions, *both* the parents and the adolescents perceived relationships at the teen's own school in a more negative light. They reported that most students at their (their child's) school felt little sense of pride in the institution and cared little about fellow students. Both the parents and the teens also felt that teachers at their school made little effort to create a civil climate where students were encouraged to express their own opinions and listen to the views of fellow students. Parents' stereotypes about schools even had a significant impact a year later on the parents' and the adolescents' reports of the climate that characterized the school that the adolescent attended. They felt that students at the teen's school generally had little sense of pride in and belonging to the school and that teachers made little effort to create a civil climate for learning, this despite the fact that most of the teenagers had actually changed schools between the first and second years of the study. Thus, the majority of parents were reporting on different schools than they had reported on in the first year but their negative stereotypes about schools persisted and affected perceptions in both years.[49]

When asked why they felt that schools had become less trustworthy, 35 percent of the parents mentioned problems with the younger generation in the schools (i.e., more gangs, substance use, violence and bullying, and general character deficiencies). There was a perception that youth today are different than youth were when the parents were young. For example, parents coded in this category said that kids today were "a different type of adolescent"; "more troubled", "so much meaner now than I remember from when I was in school"; "more daring in a dangerous way." One mother said, "Kids today do not care as much as we did years ago. Therefore there is more fighting, meanness and hurt kids in our schools today. I volunteer a lot and I see it."

Perceived changes in the institution were invoked by 28 percent of the parents who felt that schools were more dangerous, bigger, violent, more impersonal, and that teachers and administrators less caring and responsive to students. Interestingly, 17 percent of the trusting (those who felt that schools were at least as or more safe and trustworthy) mentioned the same features with the opposite attribution (i.e., felt that schools today were safer because there were more security measures, policy changes to ensure safety, a better climate, and more involvement and caring on the part of teachers and administrators).

The media frenzy about students bringing guns to school had clearly affected perceptions of some of these parents, as remarks from this European-American mother of a fourteen-year-old daughter conveyed: "You can't even feel safe as a parent these days to send your children to school because of shootings and drugs. It's scary," or from this Native-American mother of an eleven-year-old son, "Because there are guns, drugs, alcohol, gangs in our school and it's hurting our children. They live in fear in school. Very Sad! It's scary." According to others, declining trust in schools also was due to a loss of community, of people not knowing one another. As one parent put it, "Much larger population—not everyone knows each other—students, teachers, and administration included." According to some parents, this lack of familiarity bred mistrust between families and schools over disciplinary measures. As another parent put it, "schools in general don't step in and take control, afraid of trouble from parents or law."

Another 6 percent of the parents referred to changes in parenting, some holding individual parents accountable and others the increasingly stressful lives that many parents were living: "With parents working longer hours and or several jobs, they tend to spend less time with their children. Some children take their problems out on their school mates." The negative views of a few parents were associated with changing demographics in their communities and the fact that unfamiliar people, "outsiders," were moving in. One parent noted that there were "Many people moving into our area and bringing bad elements with them."

Seven percent of the responses referred to general problems in society (moral decay, less religion, increasing poverty, more complex, more violent society, increasing numbers of "outsiders" and "foreigners" in local communities) that spilled over to make schools less trustworthy institutions. The following statement by a European-American mother of a ten-year-old son is illustrative: "I really don't know the 'catch all' reason. I suppose there are many influences here. Drugs, moral decay, TV and video game violence, divorce rate, depression and behavioral problems in children, etc., etc., etc."

That parent's broad misanthropic brushstroke—"etc., etc., etc."—paints a picture of a world replete with reasons to be more vigilant and less trusting.[50] Despite the negative views of schools held by many parents, we will see in the next section that certain practices in schools increase teens' social trust over time.

## BOOSTING SOCIAL TRUST: POTENTIAL OF SCHOOLS AND COMMUNITIES

Is an adolescent's faith in humanity fixed, or can it be boosted by experience? Studies of adults show that social trust and membership in community organizations are intimately linked, so much so that Putnam has referred to this relationship as a "virtuous circle," reciprocal and reinforcing.[51] The direction of effects in this relationship has been a bone of contention, and the best evidence is that it is adults with trusting dispositions who join organizations. Typically, joining an organization results in little change in trust in a generalized other because, for the most part, adults join organizations where the members tend to be people *like them*. However, an adult's social trust is boosted by joining particular kinds of organizations—those with diverse membership and those that engage in charitable work. Compared to adults who participate in other types of community groups, those that participate in voluntary community service report higher levels of hope, optimism, and trust.[52]

Adolescence is a time when political views and beliefs about other people are still forming. Consequently, experiences in institutions and organizations should impact teens' social trust. Dewey argues that it is through communication, through getting to know and bond with one another, that we create a sense of the public and transform local community experiences into what he called the "Great Community." He writes, "Without such communication the Public will remain in eclipse. Communication can alone create a great community."[53] In other words, our sense of ourselves as a people will remain in the dark unless we get to know one another and work out ways to address our collective community needs. How might communication and relationships in schools and other community institutions enable teens to envision themselves as members of the public, co-creators of a *great community?*

In the United States, public schools are *the* public institution with a mandate for incorporating younger generations of Americans into the polity. In fact, universal public education is America's great experiment. Many state constitutions justify public school financing based on the role of schools in fulfilling the mandate of educating an informed citizenry, capable of self-government. Often the justifications refer to the content of instruction, including the basic skills that enable individuals to interact and function in society. While instruction is important for advancing the civic mission of schools, knowledge and skills alone cannot promote civic interest, action, and commitment. Students also need opportunities to work together, to voice their views and to hear those of fellow students, to construct their identity as a group, a public.

There is a large body of literature on the psychological benefits of schools for the well-being of individual students and for the social incorporation of younger generations. That work can be summed up with the following statement: to the degree that students feel that the school welcomes and includes them, that they are an integral part and that they matter to other members of the institution, their academic motivation and achievement will be higher, and they will be less likely to engage in risky behaviors that compromise health. According to national longitudinal studies, students' sense of institutional connectedness, their sense that they belong and are an important part of their high school, is a significant predictor of various forms of political and community engagement (voting, volunteering, joining community based groups) in young adulthood.[54] Building on this work, I have argued that the school functions as a mini-polity, a space where, collectively, teachers and students and, by extension, families work out what it means to be a "public" in a democracy.

We know from research with adults that social trust is positively related to a sense of shared norms and a feeling of being part of the same "moral community."[55] In addition, a sizable body of psychological research shows that when the need to belong is satisfied, it has a positive effect on our perceptions of others and that trust in others improves when groups foster a spirit of cooperation and interdependence.[56] To assess whether adolescents' experiences in schools might boost social trust, I used the longitudinal data and focused on the following dimensions of students' school life: students' sense of solidarity with fellow students and their perceptions that teachers create a civil climate for learning at their school.

School solidarity captures students' feelings of belonging to and identification with their school and with fellow members therein. It is measured with items tapping adolescents' perceptions that students at their school feel proud to be part of the institution, feel like they count, and generally care about the welfare of fellow students, not just their own social clique. So it is not just the individual adolescent's personal sense of belonging but his projection of that feeling onto the student body.

Analyses of our longitudinal data revealed that adolescents' reports of school solidarity predicted significant *increases* in social trust in the second year of the study *over and above* the levels the teens had reported in the first year. In other words, even with the very strong stable relationships between social trust at Time 1 and Time 2, feelings of school solidarity *boosted* social trust in Year 2. These patterns were the same for early, middle, and late adolescents. My interpretation is that solidarity with fellow students and feelings of pride in being an integral part of the institution help teens to appreciate what it means to be a member of the public. By a "sense of the public," I mean her sense that she, like other students at school, is an integral part of a community where people care about and look out for one another, and where the human need to belong and to be cared for is satisfied.[57]

The civil climate measure taps students' perceptions that their teachers listen to and respect students' opinions, insist that students respect one another's opinions, and put a stop to any acts of intolerance or bullying. As I have already noted, longitudinal studies have shown that social trust is higher in adulthood for those persons who in adolescence had parents and teachers that respected them and their rights to hold autonomous opinions, even if they conflict with the adults' opinions.[58] Furthermore, by establishing shared norms of respect, teachers are conveying to students how members of a civil society should treat one another.

The teacher's insistence on a civil climate for learning communicates several lessons of relevance to trust. First, as the adult authority in the classroom, the way that a teacher handles that power is key to building social trust in students. By treating students' opinions seriously, teachers convey their faith in students, that is, their belief that students are capable of handling their right to dissent and their responsibilities to be tolerant of others' opinions. Second, teachers who engage students as collaborators in the learning process show that they are willing to accept the vulnerabilities and uncertainties that such open climates for learning entail. As Deborah Meier argues in her book *In Schools We Trust,* teachers who adopt such practices reveal that the best way to learn is to be public and open, trusting fellow learners enough to leave oneself vulnerable to their judgments: "The trustful relationship with the world that this acceptance of uncertainty allows—with respect to people, ideas, and things—is at the heart of learning."[59]

Adolescents' reports that their teachers created a civil climate at school affected the teens' social trust indirectly, through their feelings of solidarity at school. In other words, when youth felt that teachers at their school respected students' autonomous opinions and encouraged a respectful exchange of views, it increased their sense of solidarity and identification with their school that, in turn, led to higher social trust. Teaching practices that encouraged students to attend to one another's perspectives increased students' sense of collective identity that, in turn, enhanced their faith in humanity. This interpretation fits with the results of laboratory studies using the prisoner's dilemma to investigate how cooperation among strangers can be enhanced. According to this work, cooperation is increased and competition and rivalry decreased when a period of discussion precedes the task of allocating limited resources.[60] Apparently, Dewey was correct in asserting that "communication alone can create a great community."[61] A tantalizing question from these results is whether there is a sequence of mechanisms underlying them—that is, might a sense of the public created by civil climates of mutual respect in turn boost identification with others in the institution and ultimately boost a sense of one's identity as part of the public in youth?

In summary, the foundations of social trust or the inclination to give others the benefit of the doubt is nurtured in schools where students feel included, where they conceive of themselves as part of a collective, "We the student body," and where they learn that fellow students are basically trustworthy and fair. The feeling of being part of the collective, the student body, is enhanced when teachers respect students' views and ensure a climate of tolerance in their classrooms. Other analyses showed that the sense of community that students felt in schools characterized by civil climates was associated with their beliefs that America is a fair society and with the teens' commitment to patriotism and service. In short, teens' diffuse support for the American polity and their commitments to serve that polity are nurtured in mini-polities—in this case, schools—where youth gain a sense that they are part of something that is larger than themselves.

My graduate students and I also examined whether teenagers' reports of solidarity and civil climates at school would be associated with their willingness to stick out their necks and do something to prevent harm from happening to others at school. We presented a dilemma to the middle and high school students in the longitudinal study—a dilemma similar to one that had a tragic ending at Columbine High School in Littleton, Colorado. Students in our study were asked to imagine that a fellow student had plans to do "something dangerous" at their school and then to report what actions they would take. The students' sense of belonging at school and of the trustworthiness of their teachers was critical in their decision to act: those who reported a sense of inclusion and solidarity with others at school were more likely to say they would either deal directly to stop the student's plans or confide their concerns about the student to a teacher or principal. If students believed that confiding in a teacher or principal would just cause more trouble because the adults would not trust them, they were more likely to say that they would ignore, or be a bystander to, a peer's dangerous plan.[62]

Schools serve as mini-polities where feelings of membership in the institution, of camaraderie with and caring for fellow citizens, and of mutual respect for differences of experience and opinion shape the democratic dispositions and inclination to act on behalf of the common good in younger generations. Public schools provide public spaces where members of the public, especially younger members, gather. It is in the relationships, the invitation into learning and inclusion in the spaces where learning is enacted, that a "sense of the public" develops in younger generations.


## COMMUNITIES

The boost to social trust from teens' sense of solidarity felt at school also was found for their sense of belonging and positive regard for their local community. As part of the survey, adolescents were asked to think about the neighborhood or community in which they lived and then report how much they agreed or disagreed with the following observations about that community: "Adults are nice to young people," "People feel safe," "Most people try to make this a good place to live," "Most people trust each other," and "When someone moves here, people are nice to them." Agreement with these perceptions of community reflects a positive view of fellow members of one's community, a view consistent with a civic republican philosophy that liberty is defended when people work together to solve collective problems.

Like the impact on social trust that feelings of solidarity at school had, teens' social trust also was boosted by these positive views of their communities. With stringent tests controlling for social trust in the first year as well as family influences (mother's reports of social trust and teens' reports of trusting relationships with parents) and for demographics, positive views about fellow members of one's community increased teens' social trust in the second year.

Analyses of Add Health, the premier national study of factors related to the health of American adolescents, point to teens' reports of community connectedness—personal feelings of belonging to key institutions in their communities and of mattering to others in those settings—as a protective factor against a host of health-compromising behaviors and negative health outcomes (from smoking and drinking to teen pregnancy).[63] Longitudinal analyses of these same data show that teens' feeling of connectedness to key community institutions is a significant precursor to their later participation in multiple forms of civic action (including engagement in volunteer community service, voting, involvement in social action or solidarity groups, environmental and conservation groups, and education groups).[64]

Other work has shown that teens' reports that they lived in a civically engaged and responsive neighborhood can boost their own civic commitments. In a two-year longitudinal study following students, primarily of low income and ethnic-minority backgrounds, educators Joseph Kahne and Susan Sporte found that, controlling for demographics and prior commitments, high school students' civic commitments increased if they discussed civic issues with parents, engaged in extracurricular activities other than sports, and *lived in a civically responsive neighborhood where adults engaged and networked with one another and supported young people.*[65] Teens' perceptions that people in their community care enough to work together and get things done and that those same people support youth signals that civic issues are concerns shared by fellow citizens, that it matters to take a stand, and that adolescents are welcome to be part of the solution.

## PUBLIC HOPE AND THE SOCIAL CONTRACT

I opened this chapter with the worldview presented in *Time* magazine, one in which younger generations are on their own with little support from society or its institutions and have every reason to believe that there's no one to trust. I close with the responses of parents to a question that we posed to them in the wake of September 11, 2001.

September 11, 2001, was a defining moment in United States history. It reminded us collectively of our vulnerability as a people and made salient our mortality as individual persons. Not only was the first year of data collection for the three-year longitudinal study just six months after 9/11, two out of the six communities participating in the study had close connections to the sites of the attack: one was near Shanksville, Pennsylvania, where the third plane crashed, and another was near New York City with many of the parents in our study working in the city. Parents participating in the longitudinal study were asked to share their reflections on whether the events of 9/11 had had any effect on the way they were parenting their children. We posed the following open-ended prompt: "Many people have said that September 11th changed everything in the United States. But nobody has asked parents if it had any effect on the way they are raising their children. As a parent, what are your thoughts? Have you talked to your child about it?" There were 1,198 parents who completed surveys for the study, and 972 of them answered the open-ended questions about whether and how the events of September 11, 2001, had affected their parenting.

Similar to other national studies indicating that three out of every four parents in the United States talked to their children about 9/11, we found that the majority of parents indicated that they had discussed 9/11 with their children. Furthermore, although we had not mentioned trust or anything related to it in the question we posed, many of the parents' reflections are relevant to understanding trust. For example, one group of parents interpreted these events as a call for greater vigilance. Some admonished their children to be more aware in everyday life—"be constantly on alert" and "be extra careful." Others indicated that they had become more vigilant about their teen's safety: "I am more worried about what, where, and who my child is with and where she goes. I guess it made me more cautious." Generally, this group of parents interpreted 9/11 as a sign that their children would grow up in a more dangerous and unpredictable world.[66]

The psychological research on 9/11, including that on parenting, has focused disproportionately on how people coped with the attack. Our team took a broader view to understanding what a major defining moment such as 9/11 might reveal. Our sense was that, whereas we typically function on automatic pilot and have little occasion to sit down and examine the beliefs and values we hold most dear, major events such as 9/11 shake us up. They cause us to reflect on our core values and beliefs, on the things in life that we cherish, on the kind of world we live in and want our children to inherit.

Although studies are few and far between, there is reason to believe that such major events may function as defining moments in families, giving parents reason to pause, to discuss, and to interpret the event for their children. Temporary shocks that are caused by major political or historical events such as war, economic downfall, natural disasters, or terrorist attacks have been shown to play significant roles in shaping people's political orientations, values, and behaviors.[67] Events such as 9/11 produce anxiety, partly because of the threat they pose to our sense that we have control over our life. Indeed, such events make our very mortality more salient and that induces a sense of fear and dread in us. According to terror management theory, facing the threat of our mortality causes us to reflect on our core beliefs, values, and worldviews.[68]

Anxiety and dread about uncontrollable events that threaten one's life were themes in the parents' reflections. One European-American father of a sixteen-year-old daughter said, "Yes we have talked about it—there is a fear in our children—not knowing if and when something like that could happen again," as did this Latino-American father with a thirteen-year-old daughter, "Worries about security and more terrorist attacks." And another European-American father, also with a sixteen-year-old daughter, "Yes. Children were told about this dangerous world, which will get worse before it gets better." His pessimistic outlook about the future was echoed by another father of a twelve-year-old son, "I feel that it (9/11) has changed the outlook of our future. It seems that it is always in the back of our minds now, the uncertainty of what lies ahead." These fathers' global statements were more tempered in the worldview of this European-American mother of a fifteen-year-old daughter, "Yes. Try to teach them that the world we live in isn't always a safe place." Basically, her "isn't always safe" pointed to the replacement of a naïve view of a safe world that one could take for granted with one more tempered by reality.

Two other groups of parents interpreted 9/11 as a call to admonish their children about "other people" and how children should treat them. The first of these were admonitions to be more vigilant. As this European-American father told his twelve-year-old, "I told my son there are terrible people in this world." Another European-American father was more precise in admonishing his eighteen-year-old son about exactly which people one should not trust, "Don't trust foreigners. If they're not speaking English, they are not trustworthy." And the threat of "foreigners" also was raised by another European-American mother with her eighteen-year-old son, "Be more conscientious of foreigners." And a white mother of a twelve-year-old daughter said that 9/11 had made her "more concerned about strangers." Another white mother of a thirteen-year-old daughter drew the circle of trusting relationships into the confines of the family, "My children need to know about how people hurt people and you cannot really trust anyone. They need to know that the only people they can trust is their family." Finally, a white mother of an eleven-year-old daughter reflected that 9/11 had reinforced lessons about trust she already followed, "Not everybody can be trusted. I've always grown up not to trust everyone and I still don't."

Diametrically opposed to these reactions were admonitions to give unfamiliar others the benefit of the doubt. One white mother of a thirteen-year-old son felt that 9/11 had made her even more earnest in emphasizing the value of tolerance, "It hasn't changed the way I am raising my children, except for the fact that I'm placing more emphasis on them tolerating others' ethnic, religious, and political beliefs." Tolerance also was a theme that another white mother with a fifteen-year-old son raised, "Sept. 11 has necessitated a lot of discussions with my children on tolerance. We've talked a lot about what causes people to hate others and respecting the rights of other individuals."

Similar views were voiced by an African-American mother of a fifteen-year-old son, "Since the event of 9/11—I have expressed to my children how important it is to stand together as one nation under God, and to support your fellow man, no matter what race or religion." A white mother of a fourteen-year-old son, also referred to diversity as a strength, "We emphasize the value of family, faith, life. We need to love and respect one another and be open to the diversity that surrounds and strengthens us." Another European-American mother with an eleven-year-old son was cognizant about the negative views of humanity that could result from such a terrible event and purposefully tried to provide a more balanced view for her children, "We have talked about 9/11 but we have tried to show them the positive things that have come out of this terrible experience. Although we need to be cautious it is important not to let fear cloud our ability to relate to people of all races and creeds." Finally, one white father raising a fourteen-year-old son considered 9/11 a clarion call for human beings to improve their world, "It has reiterated our responsibility as human beings, members of the family of man and residents of this planet, to make this world a better place."

One of the most basic things that parents do is interpret the world for their children. At an early age, they tell them what things are, how, and why they work. As children age, parents continue to interpret events in the world—major events such as 9/11 or mundane events such as why the child wasn't invited to a peer's party or what the child should do if he witnesses bullying at school. Parents are moral guides for their children. I suspect that most parents would consider this one of the more significant roles they fulfill. Yet, although we know a good deal about the processes whereby parents' socialization of values is more or less effective, we know less about the content of the values that parents emphasize in their child rearing.

Research on family communication, conducted in the wake of Hurricane Katrina in the southern United States, suggests that family conversations about these life-shattering events help children to process and crystallize the hodgepodge of information that is "out there" in the media and in everyday conversations. African-American youth who had conversations with their parents about Hurricane Katrina had more consistent views about the causes of the disaster and the government's response to it when compared to their peers who did not discuss the event with their parents.[69] In other words, those conversations helped children to develop a lay theory about the event.

Besides major events in life, there also are points in the life course when people tend to reflect on their core beliefs and values. And adolescence is such a time to take stock. So Erikson's belief that trust emerges as an important psychosocial issue at this developmental juncture is not surprising. In his work, he contends that as young people explore identity, the "who I am" question inevitably raises the "what do I stand for" question. An adolescent, he argues, cares about being authentic or true to himself, faithful to his ideals.[70] If adolescence is such a time, it seems all the more important that we enable teenagers to reflect on and discuss with others the "what do we stand for" questions.

In *Radical Democracy*, Lummis makes a distinction between private and public hope. By private hope, he means an individual's belief that her own life will go well, that she will earn a good living and achieve personal success, even if others do not. Public hope, by contrast, reflects a belief that if people pull together, they can effect change that will benefit them all. Consistent with a civic republican tradition, public hope means investing one's time and energy in building, as Sennett put it, "a larger sense of community."[71]

Lummis closes his book with reflections on the social contract and the leap of faith implied in the willingness of individuals to give up personal freedoms in order to live in a democratic community with others—like and unlike them.

> Faith in human beings is the hardest faith, yet we all have it in some degree. We have to, to live. It is the very stuff out of which our personal lives are shaped; it is so common we barely notice it. . . .
>
> Democratic faith is the decision to believe that a world of democratic trust is possible because we can see it in each person sometimes. It is the decision to believe in what people can be on the basis of what they sometimes are. It is the decision to believe that each polity and each person contains the possibility of a democratic version of itself. It is the belief that as people are free, they are free to become that, too. None of this has been proved, but neither can it be disproved. One is free to believe either way.[72]

chapter eight

# Community Service

SERVICE LEARNING IS a form of experiential learning in which students engage in community service and learn through reflection on those actions.[1] Although far from institutionalized in public education, service-learning programs can be found in at least 30 percent of high schools in the United States. There is now an impressive body of research documenting both the academic and civic benefits of young people's engagement in community service and service learning.[2] Of course, programs vary in content and quality, and although requiring students to engage in community service as part of their high school experience continues to be a thorny issue, whether service is mandated or voluntary appears to have no impact on students' civic and academic outcomes. What matters is whether the adolescent engages in service with an organization that provides direct service for groups who need the service rather than just filling required hours by performing functionary or busywork.[3]

Whereas others have documented the *fact* that young people learn from community service, the goal of this chapter is to uncover *what* they learn about themselves, about fellow members of their community, and about the ties that bind them together. I draw from adolescents' verbatim responses to *what they learned from their community service experience* for two reasons: First, although there is mounting evidence that engaging in community service in one's youth is positively related to community and civic involvement in adulthood, we know less about the developmental processes underlying these links. Second, to draw from teens' responses about what they learned is to address criticisms that youth engagement in community volunteer work may substitute in the minds of many young people for engaging in the political fray.

Concerning the first, we know that engaging in community service in high school is a good predictor of volunteering and voting in adulthood.[4] Why? Several developmental mechanisms may be involved. First, the adolescent years are typically considered a time for exploring and consolidating identity. Relationships and interactions with other people are at the core of this identity exploration process and community service offers a unique niche for such exploration. As in-depth work by the developmental psychologists Miranda Yates and James Youniss showed, service projects can be an opportunity for teens to explore issues of social justice, to enlarge the boundaries of their civic community and their responsibilities for fellow members of that community. These scholars followed high school students over the course of a year's project for a class on social justice in which the students volunteered in a soup kitchen for the homeless. During the course of the year, Yates and Youniss documented a process of identity transformation for some (not all) of the students. The process occurred in stages as students became aware of the humanity of homeless individuals, compared their own more privileged circumstances with the conditions that the homeless faced, and ultimately achieved what the authors referred to as a more transcendent identity, an enlarged sense of their responsibilities for fellow citizens.[5]

Second, organizations are the main route through which youth get engaged in community service projects. According to research with American adults, membership in one organization enhances the likelihood of getting recruited into additional forms of public life. If people are asked to volunteer or to join an organization by someone whom they know, they typically say "yes."[6] The likelihood of being asked to join or volunteer is higher if one is already involved in an organization that does community service. So, simply by virtue of "being there" in such an organization, a teen is more likely to get recruited into additional civic projects. In summary, both the civic pathways to adulthood and the civic identities of the young people are formed through community service work.

Community service or service learning also has its share of critics who worry that, if youth engage in direct service to people in need but never learn about the deeper structural or political roots underlying the need for service (e.g., lack of health care, hunger, homelessness, environmental degradation), they may not appreciate the importance of engaging in the political fray.[7]

In earlier eras of our history, community service was often a bridge to politics. A classic example is provided in the work of Jane Addams, who co-founded Hull House in 1889 to serve the needs of the mostly immigrant poor in Chicago. Like other community-based organizations, Hull House provided direct services to meet basic needs of families including food, shelter, child care, and activity clubs for children—services that neither the state nor the private market were providing for the very large waves of new immigrants coming to the United States at that time. But, like other organizations that constitute civil society, Hull House was also what Sarah Evans and Harry Boyte have referred to as a *free space*—a place where people could gather in public, work out ways to meet their common needs, and create plans to challenge the state and the oppressive norms of the dominant society.[8] So Hull House became a public space for meetings of groups such as the Nineteenth Ward Improvement Association as well as a site where the Public Library Board located a branch reading room. Bridging to the political arena was often a logical next step from the meetings of associations and from the informal connections between municipal authorities such as the police and the work of Hull House staff. For example, one of the services that Hull House staff provided to the community was to serve as unofficial "guardians" of delinquent youth. When the Cook County Juvenile Court was established in 1899, its first probation officer was the very woman who had been informally providing that service for many years from Hull House. Jane Addams considered it the true mission of groups such as Hull House to galvanize public consciousness around community needs and then to challenge government to provide for those needs, a sentiment she articulated in her book *Twenty Years at Hull House*:

> So far as a settlement can discern and bring to local consciousness neighborhood needs which are common needs, and can give vigorous help to the

municipal measures through which such needs shall be met, it fulfills its most valuable function.[9]

The concern today is that these links—between community service and political mobilization—have been severed and that younger generations may come to see community volunteer work as an alternative rather than a complement to or motivator of political mobilization. In an incisive essay, the political scientist William Galston, points out that, whereas in direct service, youth feel that they can make a difference in the lives of others, many consider the political arena corrupt and ineffectual and one in which they could personally have precious little impact.[10]

In this chapter, I propose a developmental argument about the potential of community service for the formation of what I call "a sense of the public" in adolescents. Specifically, I draw from teens' open-ended responses concerning what they learned from doing volunteer work to argue for the potential of service to enlarge teens' concepts of their community, of fellow citizens in their community, and of responsibility for their common good; to alter the group stereotypes teens hold through contact with members of stereotyped groups; to enable teens to see how their fates are tied to the fates of fellow citizens; and to engender in teens a feeling of efficacy in taking civic action.

In two studies in my program of work—the project on intergroup relations and beliefs about social justice (discussed in Chapter 3) and the longitudinal study (discussed in Chapter 7)—I included items asking teens about their involvement in community service projects. Here I use the longitudinal data to compare the trajectories over time in social trust and social responsibility for teens who engaged in community service with their peers who had not. However, the lion's share of the data reported in this chapter were drawn from teens' reports in the project on intergroup relations and beliefs about social justice.

In that study, adolescents answered three items about their involvement in extracurricular and volunteer activities: First, they simply checked whether they had been involved in any clubs, extracurricular activities, or volunteer work during the past year. Second, if they said that they had done some community volunteer work, they were asked to state what they had done. Third, if they had indicated that they had done some volunteer work, they were asked, "Did you learn anything about yourself, about others, or about your community by doing this volunteer work?" Those who indicated that they had learned something from volunteering were asked to report what they had learned. In this chapter, I am concerned primarily with what the teenagers said that they learned from engaging in community volunteer work. Later in the chapter I use the teens' reports of involvement in extracurricular activities and clubs as a basis for comparison with the groups who report engaging in volunteer work.

Of the 1,031 teens who responded to the three items listed above, 783 reported that they had engaged in some volunteer work during the past year. Of those, roughly 70 percent said that they had learned something from that experience. This group, whose reflections are the basis for this chapter, volunteered on a more frequent basis than the 30 percent who felt that they had learned nothing from volunteering. In other words, more frequent volunteering is positively associated with the adolescents' perceptions that they had learned something from the experience, a finding supported in other work on service learning.[11]

## WHAT TEENS LEARNED FROM THEIR COMMUNITY SERVICE EXPERIENCES

I turn now to a more in-depth look at the teens' statements about what they had learned. The teens' responses are organized sequentially—based on whether the teens primarily focused on what they had learned about themselves; about relationships with others; about fellow members of their communities whom they served through their volunteer work; about the community itself and adult role models therein; and finally about collective work and the common good. Concerning the three broad categories (learning about self, about others, and about your community) that formed the open-ended question that the teens answered, the responses were evenly distributed across these three broad categories.

## Learning about Oneself

Service learning in public schools has, at times, been promoted as a means for students to gain vocational knowledge—the argument is that this experiential form of learning provides students information about careers or vocations they might consider and a first-hand assessment of what they're good at, what they like, and what they might like to do in the future. Some of the teens' statements coded as "learning about oneself" suggested that they did make certain vocational assessments—reflecting on what they learned about the job, how those experiences might serve them in future endeavors, and whether they learned what they were good or not so good at. For the most part, teens did not discuss their experiences as if they were "career" preparation for particular jobs. Rather, as the teens' following statements reveal, the volunteer experience helped them realize what they are capable of doing, how they interact with different groups of people, and what their limitations may be.

For example, a white male ninth grader whose mother had not finished high school had volunteered with the theatre at school and felt that "I learned how theaters work and this will better prepare me if I get cast for a performance." Others reflected on their capacities for working with different groups or managing various challenges. One white female twelfth grader whose parents terminated their education after high school reported that she "helps out an older friend with hospice work" and learned that she had a strong constitution: "I get along very well with children and disturbing things (medical) do not bother me." Some teens learned that the work was not simple. For example, a fourteen-year-old male of Asian descent learned the challenges of managing young children: "I learned how difficult it can be to control a group of people." In contrast, caring for young children was the means whereby his white female peer learned "that when something goes wrong or something bad happens, I can take charge and do the right things." Finally, a fifteen-year-old Puerto Rican female reported, "I join clubs and try to do as much community service as I can, whenever I have time. I learn what I'm capable of doing, how far I can go, the different kinds of people I can work with, stuff like that."

Most of the teens' reflections on what they learned about themselves did not speak directly to vocations. Instead, they learned about things they valued, about their dispositions, competencies, limitations, and about how working with different people and in diverse settings revealed things they had not known before, for example, "that I respect nature"; "that I can handle a crisis"; "how to work with different people"; and "what I'm capable of doing, how far I can go, the different kinds of people I can work with, stuff like that." One teen who volunteered in activities "w/ youth group fundraisers & Internet service club at school" learned that "although I am shy, I can work well with people if I try. I can be a leader in some things, but others are unsure about following me."

Often we think of the civic actions that young people do as *preparatory* for the time in the future when they will *really be citizens*. In this sense, adolescents are like citizens on hold or citizens in the making but not real or full citizens. Adolescents also are regularly reminded that they lack power, simply by virtue of the fact that they are minors (i.e., dependents of adults). But one of the possibilities offered by community service is the opportunity for agency, the chance for young people to see first-hand that there's something they can do as citizens *here and now*. Insofar as teens are neither independent nor age eligible for certain forms of civic action such as voting, participating and leading community-based volunteer efforts are venues available to them.

The following two quotes reveal ways that through community service, the teens saw themselves in mature roles as civic actors. A white female ninth grader learned that, even at her relatively young age, she could be a civic role model for others: "I help with community clean-ups. I volunteer at a day care, help at senior citizen homes. When I volunteered at the day care I had little kids looking up to me. I didn't have a lot of self-esteem but know I was a role model for some kids and I want to work at the day care next year." A sixteen-year-old African-American male said, "I volunteered in the past week to be a role model for the fifth graders and I learned that by teaching someone your mistakes may help them not make that mistake." Another fifteen-year-old distinguished *individual* responsibility—which is the kind of responsibility we most commonly teach in the United States from *social* responsibility, a more civic form. From her tutoring of children, she learned "I can be helpful to others, *not just myself* [italics added]."[12]

Social responsibility refers to an individual's sense of obligation to others and to the common good shared with other people—whether citizens or fellow human beings. In my program of work, we have measured this construct by tapping into teens' endorsement of personal goals and family values that reflect such things as commitments to helping people in need, to taking actions to preserve the environment for future generations, and to serving one's community and society. In several studies, we have looked at the correlates and predictors of teens' sense of social responsibility. In

Figure 8.1, I draw from data in the three-year longitudinal study to illustrate developmental patterns in social responsibility for those teens who, in
the first year of the study, had engaged in some form of community service
with their peers who had not. Note that the "volunteer" group includes all
teens who reported some form of community volunteer work in the past
year, whether those teens felt that they had learned something or not from
engaging in the community service.

Figure 8.1 illustrates teens' endorsements of social responsibility—the
personal importance they attached to aiding others and contributing to
the common good—over the three-year period. On the x-axis, W refers
to wave or time of each survey administration. Thus, W1, W2, and W3 refer
to the three years of data collection. As the figure shows, teens' endorsements of social responsibility as an ethic that they live by tends to decline as
they get older. However, this age-related decline is less marked among those

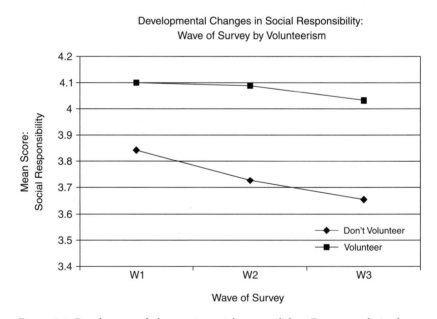

Figure 8.1. Developmental changes in social responsibility. Data were derived
from the longitudinal study on Social Responsibility and Adolescents. Scales were
based on the mean of items in each scale. The precise wording for all items is
provided in the Appendix.

teens who report that they engaged in volunteer work in their community. Not only do those teens start out at Wave 1 at a much higher level of endorsing social responsibility but they maintain that level over time.

Note that the groups (volunteer versus do not volunteer) were formed based on the teens' reports of volunteering at Wave 1. The figure does not capture any fluctuations in volunteering over these three years; so there is some error because some of the teens who report volunteering at Wave 1 may not be volunteering in subsequent years, Waves 2 and 3, and some who had not volunteered at Wave 1 may have done so in subsequent years. Yet research suggests that volunteering tends to be a habit—once people start, they tend to continue. For adolescents, there is probably a selection effect (that is, once teens have been part of a social network that engages in some volunteer work, they are likely to select in subsequent years into similar networks); whether or not those networks engage in volunteer work at a particular time, they are likely to have a prosocial orientation. Thus, the endorsement of higher levels of social responsibility represented in Figure 8.1 may be an indirect effect of volunteering and the prosocial networks of peers into which volunteering selects teens.[13]

## Learning about Relationships of Self, Others, and the Community

A growing body of research points to the psychosocial benefits of engaging in community service: benefits to mental health, well-being, and thriving have been documented in research, largely with adults but some with adolescents. Distress, anxiety, and antisocial behavior are lower and feelings of efficacy, confidence, empowerment, hope, and optimism higher among those engaged in helping and volunteering.[14] Many studies are correlational but even longitudinal studies point to reciprocal and reinforcing relationships: according to analyses of national panel data, people with greater well-being invest more hours in volunteer work *and* engaging in volunteer work further enhances life satisfaction, self-esteem, sense of control over one's life, physical health, and happiness.[15]

Importantly, adolescents' initial motivation for joining community organizations or projects may be for social reasons—because friends are doing it. Over time, they develop an affinity and identification with the mission and cause of the group, a change that sustains their involvement.[16] Of course, affinity for the organization is found for those youth who remain with the organization, not for those who left. The fact that some remain and others drop out of community organizations is consistent with research by motivational psychologists who find that the match between an individual's motivation for volunteering and the organizational work is critical for sustaining the volunteer's commitment.[17] In short, to stick with an organization or project that benefits their communities, young people have to feel that they belong, that they have a meaningful place and a voice, and that what they are accomplishing with others in their organization matters.

What might be the underlying mechanisms for these relationships? First, helping others may be psychologically rewarding in and of itself since knowing that one is contributing time, money, and effort to the provision of the public good is internally self-rewarding.[18] Those rewards may derive from the sense of benevolence one feels from helping, from the social benefits and the networks that form, or from the feeling of attachment and identification one derives from connecting with others in the community. Second, as research on happiness indicates, relationships and responsibilities are more psychologically beneficial for people than are independence and freedom.[19] Sidney Verba, Kay Lehman Schlozman, and Henry Brady's study of adult voluntarism provides important insights into the intrinsic rewards derived from doing one's part for the collective good. They point out that there are both social rewards as well as personal satisfactions derived from doing one's share:

> Joint activity can bring social rewards—the chance to interact with other people or to gain respect from others involved—or can be fun or exciting. Moreover, performing the act may be intrinsically gratifying: participants may derive a sense of satisfaction from promoting a cause in which they believe, doing their share, or fulfilling a civic duty. These benefits are sometimes termed "expressive" rather than "instrumental"—the benefit deriving from the performance of the act, not the consequences of the act. In these cases, costs and benefits are hard to disentangle, for paying the cost becomes itself a benefit.
>
> When the benefit derived from political activity includes—and we show that it does—the satisfaction of performing a civic duty or doing one's share to make the community, nation, or world a better place, the greatest reward is not necessarily achieved by the least cost. . . . In short, bearing the cost becomes part of the benefit.[20]

Consistent with Verba and colleagues' contention that there are personal rewards associated with contributing to one's community, many of the teens mentioned that they learned that it "felt good" to help others. One seventeen-year-old who helps out in soup kitchens for homeless people and also had volunteered in emergency relief efforts, said he learned "that I am fortunate for what I have. You get a great feeling of satisfaction in helping others. It feels good to give someone a little of what you have." The question is whether this benevolent feeling is satisfying in itself, whether giving a little of what you have taps a teen's sense of noblesse oblige (that is, because they enjoy relative power, wealth, or privilege, they have *some responsibility* to those who do not) or, alternatively, whether the awareness of privilege and disadvantage motivates deeper considerations of justice. In the following section, we see that although learning about inequality and their own relative privilege was a common theme, how teens interpret these *lessons* from their volunteer work varies.

*Reflections on Social Inequalities*

Exposure to the plight of others may induce a realization of relative privilege. In other words, teens may not grasp how easy their own lives are until they are prompted to compare their lot with that of others who face greater challenges. According to experimental work, young people's feelings of well-being can be enhanced by simply reminding them about things in their lives for which they should be grateful.[21]

Gratitude was a common theme in the teens' statements concerning what they had learned from service. Many became aware that they lived lives of privilege relative to the conditions and challenges faced by many others in their community. For example, a seventeen-year-old Puerto Rican male learned that "some kids have more & bigger problems than others." Two teens of Arab descent who attended the same high school used different words to express a common sentiment: "people aren't blessed w/ the things I've been given" and "I learned more about the less fortunate and become grateful for what I have." Two of their classmates who shared their ethnic background felt that they learned a moral lesson about how they should act: "There are lots of people out there who need help and are a lot less fortunate than I am so why not help instead of being selfish"; and "you learn that there are some people out there who are less fortunate than others. You begin to become less selfish." A seventeen-year-old white male from a working-class family, who had a long list of volunteer projects (soup kitchen, clean parks, help with children, visit elderly people), put the psychological concept of relative deprivation in his own words, "whenever I feel self pity, I think of those who have so much less than I do." And an eighteen-year-old who volunteered with patients at the Veterans Medical Center felt that he had "become a nicer person because I know that some patients at the hospital have very little family left and I try to entertain and amuse them so they will have more joy in their lives."

Here we might pause to remember Vygotsky's thesis that the ideas and beliefs these youth are internalizing—the "intrapsychological category," to use Vygotsky's term—are internalizations based on their experiences on the social plane, between people.[22] In their own words, these teenagers tell us that their service experiences—their interactions with people in need—caused them to reflect on their blessings, their good fortune vis-à-vis less fortunate members of their community. These experiences on the social plane also caused some—intrapsychically—to put their own problems and their own self-centeredness in perspective. Ultimately, these teens are commenting on the effect of service on their personal values, on the choices they are making, and on the kind of persons they want to be.

Other adolescents commented on the opportunities that service provided them to learn what life is like for others—people with disabilities, children, the elderly, those living in poverty—groups with whom adolescents rarely interact. Teens recognized the challenges that certain groups faced, the gaps in income between groups, all of whom aspired to the American dream. Some teens also observed that they had come to appreciate why such inequities in the social contract might lead people to become cynical and angry.

For example, one eleventh-grade white female from a highly educated family said, "I'm vice-president of key club & we do a variety of community services often centered around children. It has helped me to see just how hard it can be for some kids & some adults with disabilities." Another eleventh grader, a white male from an equally privileged family, said, "I work in a soup kitchen, at a food bank, and sometimes in a cleanup crew. It taught me how wide the gap is between just the middle class and the poor." And finally, a white eighth-grade male, who volunteers through his church, stated simply, "I see what people get angry about."

Besides social inequalities, other adolescents observed that they had learned about differences between generations or age groups in the challenges each faced. One tenth-grade male from a working-class family reflected, "I learned how our younger generations are growing up," and an Asian-American in the same grade said that he "learned about the treatment of the elderly."

*Questioning Group Stereotypes*

Dewey posed two standards for evaluating the democratic worth of various modes of social life: "How numerous and varied are the interests, which are consciously shared. How full and free is the interplay with other forms of association."[23] With these two simple criteria, Dewey reminded us that spending time in homogeneous groups, associating with people who are like us, does little to nurture democratic dispositions and has little effect on democracy. Instead, to nurture open-mindedness, trust, and commitments to a broad common good, we need heterogeneous associations. We need to see the world from others' points of view and to appreciate how their interests and ours intersect.

But adolescents' everyday lives tend to be rather homogeneous and trends in the past few decades may have exacerbated this reality. Since the early 1970s, both neighborhoods and municipal boundaries have become increasingly segregated along class lines. Between 1972 and 2004, Americans moved into increasingly homogeneous neighborhoods—in lifestyle, beliefs, and, ultimately, politics.[24] Most public school districts are drawn from neighborhoods of similar household incomes. School choice policies (vouchers and charter schools) have encouraged further tailoring and homogenization of the schools that students attend. Over this same period, the links between membership in organized religions and partisan political behavior have tightened. The result is an intensification of like-mindedness within religious congregations such that they act like a political echo chamber.[25] Not only does clustering of like-minded people have a self-reinforcing effect on our beliefs, it also has a polarizing effect on politics, intensifying and making more extreme the positions that people hold. Heterogeneous groups tend to be more moderate, restraining group excess.[26] New technologies also make it easier to tailor the news and views that we take in, streamlining them to our liking.[27]

But teens also make choices about how to use their free or out-of-school time, and it is in this context that community volunteer work may offer unique opportunities. Compared to clubs, extracurricular activities or other interest-based groups that young people choose, community service introduces them to a more heterogeneous group of other people. I submit that these encounters are relevant for the younger generation's evolving interpretation of the social contract because of their potential for extending the boundaries of the community with whom youth feel connected and for whom they feel responsible. As this seventeen-year-old observed about his volunteer work, "I met many different people and experienced what I would not have experienced elsewhere." Teens in this study noted that they learned "how to deal with different kinds of people"; "about what others think, how well I can handle a crisis, and who lives around me"; and "how different people really are and yet how similar everyone is to one another. We are all human." Adolescents also learned about community settings that would not be typical venues they would frequent. Some of the many institutions and organizations they mentioned included the local hospital, the assisted living center, the food bank, the day-care and after-school care facilities for children, and the different religious congregations.

As I discussed in the last chapter, people tend to trust others who are like them—in physical appearance or social background. When people seem "like us," we feel that we can predict their actions, assuming that they would probably behave as we would in similar situations. Even elementary age children are more likely to trust peers of their own sex and race, expecting that peers who are like them would be more likely than those who are different to keep secrets, promises, and to tell the truth.[28]

Can a case be made for the potential of community service to extend the boundary of other people whom one trusts and to build a generalized sense of trust in humanity? There are three reasons to argue for such a case. First, adolescents' beliefs about people are still forming and thus will be informed by their experiences. Second, in many service projects, adolescents are likely to interact with individuals who could be considered members of stereotyped groups, such as the elderly or the homeless, people with whom they would otherwise have little contact. According to contact theory, such encounters may reduce stereotypes if the adolescents gain first-hand knowledge about individuals in the group that disconfirms those stereotypes. Furthermore, the reduction in prejudice that results generalizes to other members of the out-group.[29] Third, community service projects fit the definition of the kinds of organizations (engaging in charity, heterogeneous membership) that research with adults indicates can boost social trust.[30]

*Stereotypes and Intergroup Contact*

I was surprised to learn the degree to which the elderly had been a stereo-typed group for many of the adolescents. Several commented that by engaging in volunteer work with the elderly, their preconceptions about this group had broken down. For example, a fifteen-year-old white female from a working-class family observed after volunteering at a nursing home, "I used to be afraid of the elderly. I understand them more and found out they are really nice and have a lot to share." And a seventeen-year-old female of Arab descent whose parents had not gone to high school volunteered to do "whatever needs to be done" at the local hospital and reflected, "I got to meet new people and now I respect the elderly more than I used to."

Besides the elderly, teens also noted that because of their service, they were questioning stereotypes they had held about other groups. For example, one fifteen-year-old African-American female from a poor inner city community said that she learned, "If you live in a rich area, it doesn't really mean that you're snobby." And a peer from her school said, "I learned all White people aren't stereo-types." Similar observations were provided by a sixteen-year-old white female from a well-educated family: "I volunteer at a nursing home and at a therapeutic center for disabled children and adults" and learned that "Just because someone is old or disabled it's no reason to be frightened of them." Getting to know the person behind the group stereotype was a theme voiced by two white females from different social class backgrounds: One said, "Basically you get to know people for who they are, not what they are." And the other noted, "Sometimes you can learn to get along with people in other age groups; can learn how to respect people for their individuality." Finally, a sixteen-year-old white female from a working-class family said, "I volunteer at the local soup kitchen and also for a youth theatre program. I learned that not all people who attend a soup kitchen are homeless. Some are just lovely old people who can't survive on social security."

My interpretation of these anecdotes concerning the potential of community service to change teens' views about the social contract is backed up by evidence in other work. In their longitudinal study documenting changes in adolescents' attitudes over a year of community service, Ed Metz and James Youniss found that, after a year of working in projects that served the needs of the poor, high school students were less likely to blame individuals for being poor and more likely to see the systemic bases of poverty.[31] This work raises the interesting possibility that youth's direct contact through their service—with poor people—enables them to question the deeper political roots of poverty.

In the 1950s, when Morris Rosenberg initiated his studies of social trust, he argued that trust should be correlated with one's stand on social policies such as whether the poor deserve public relief.[32] In other words, social trust, or faith in humanity, reflects beliefs in people's capacities for change. Consequently, it should be positively correlated with supporting social policies that would enable people to make changes in their lives. Furthermore, if they become sensitized to the plight of marginalized groups as a result of their community service, it is likely that teens will stay committed to the plight of those groups. Developmental studies show that children are more likely to help others in need if they feel high levels of sympathy for those others.[33]

### Engendering a Sense of the Public in Youth

As research on intergroup contact reveals, people perceive and process their experiences through the frames, or categories, they have stored from their prior experiences. Framing new experiences based on a customary set of categories is efficient; it allows us to move on with our lives. The previous quotes suggest that as contact theory predicts, getting to know individuals whom the teens had formerly framed as members of stereotyped groups (the elderly, people with disabilities, etc.) helped them to reframe how they thought about those groups. In short, the lens through which we filter experience matters for the way in which we process and learn from that experience.

Framing issues has caught on as a technique in community youth development—as a way to enable young people to interpret community issues. This technique was used by one of my graduate students who taught a group of teens from a working-class community how to use a 35 mm camera and conduct "person on the street" interviews about public issues. The teens were doing a project on substance use and decided to conduct interviews with several people in their community who were involved in a recovering addict program. Through the face-to-face interviews, young people understood that the stereotype "addict" actually applied to individuals who had real lives and roles (e.g., parent) in their community. In other words, those individuals might be struggling with addiction but they were not just addicts—

they were parents, workers, members of local congregations; they were fellow citizens. Consequently, the young people began to "frame" the issue of drug use as one that was a public or shared community issue rather than one that belonged to and was the fault of a distant and stereotyped "other." After filming, the teens started talking about substance use as "our" rather than "their" problem.[34]

Social problems are not resolved overnight and realizing that "we" have a public issue to tackle may seem like a very small step. I am not suggesting that youth engagement in community service is *the* way to solve public problems. Rather, it is a means through which teens can develop a sense of themselves as members of the public committed to tackling the public issues that we share and assuming the social responsibilities that we bear for one another: as a seventeen-year-old Arab-American male put it, "I was a summer school teacher for a Muslim school. I have learned to appreciate the youth in our society & also realized than everyone needs to put in some of they're [*sic*] own time into our community."

Exactly what one should do is not always clear but that one has a responsibility to figure it out is clear. For example, a sixteen-year-old white female who volunteered "at Sojourner House, a halfway house for addicted mothers & their children," said, "I have a lot of empathy for the people I work with at soup kitchens, & Sojourner House, and the mission trips. It's hard to figure out what my responsibility is in all this." Others expressed anger about the complacency of their fellow citizens in the face of the hardships that they witnessed. One sixteen-year-old who volunteered at the diagnostic lab of a local hospital felt that "when people are hurt they're afraid & they need your moral backup." He considered it unjust "when there is hardship that affects a good size of my town & nobody cares nor helps." A similar sentiment was voiced by a sixteen-year-old who volunteers at the YMCA, "a lot of people don't care and it's really sad. So I'm trying to change people's minds."

*Social Intelligence*

I have argued that community service provides an opportunity for interacting with people from different backgrounds and experiences than those whom teens typically encounter. If youth are open to these experiences and learn from them, it may boost their abilities to "read" and to "understand" other people. As discussed in the previous chapter, social trust—beliefs that other people are basically fair and trustworthy—is positively associated with social intelligence, that is, the capacity to read and to understand others and to discern when and whom one can trust. We also saw in the previous chapter that as adolescents age, they seem to become more cynical about people: compared to early adolescents, older teens report lower levels of social trust. Might involvement in community service moderate that age-related decline in social trust? If community volunteer work exposes teens to a wider array of "others" than they would meet in their more typical homogeneous encounters in everyday life, it might offer particular value for developing teens' social intelligence, social trust, and sense of the public. The following quotes suggest that in serving their communities, some teens learned that there are many kinds of people "out there" and that even the very same people can sometimes act in ways worthy and other times not worthy of our praise.

Several teens observed that by getting to know individuals in need, they had a better understanding of the person's situation and a better explanation for her behavior. One white sixteen-year-old female from a well-educated family observed that "a lot of people in the nursing home *aren't mean, just lonely* [italics added]. It's really interesting to talk to them." A twelfth-grade Puerto Rican female who herself had experienced prejudice reflected, "when we first moved here from New York City, we received a lot of letters telling us to go back to where we came from, no one wants any minorities here." In her new community, she did some volunteer work in nursing homes and learned, "People are different but they don't have to be an outcast." Another white female from a working-class community who helped transport patients to the hospital learned that people come from "different backgrounds and home lives" and that their backgrounds "can alter a person's first impression and attitude."

The political scientist Rogers M. Smith contends that we should insist that diverse intergroup contact be integral to national service policy. He writes about the components and potential of national service:

> But if national service is to enable Americans to grasp and shape their shared existence better, it obviously should not simply rehearse its participants in the civic knowledge they already possess, or indicate that existing arrangements are natural and unquestionable. Instead, it should be a vehicle through which Americans learn to take seriously the perspectives of Ameri-

cans different from themselves. That goal requires a measure of egalitarian-
ism in the internal organization of national service programs, for people
pay more attention to those who work with them rather than for them. It also
suggests that national service should seek to provide people with meaningful work they can usefully do in environments they do not usually
encounter. . . .

And in contrast to past programs that further accustomed Americans to
accept their places in ascribed hierarchies, national service thus reconceived
might help citizens to recognize the injustices that have so pervasively shaped
American life, the ways injustices are perpetuated today, and the practical
means by which they can be combatted. At a minimum, national service
would give more Americans more insight into the realities of the civic identity they share, so they can better decide what American citizenship should
mean now and in the future.[35]

In Figure 8.2, I summarize teens' beliefs about the trustworthiness of
other people, that is, their social trust, as discussed in Chapter 7. Like Figure 8.1 on developmental trends in social responsibility, these data are
drawn from the three-year longitudinal study. Here my point is to illustrate
that the developmental patterns of social trust over the three years of the
study differed for those adolescents who were involved in community service compared to their peers who were not involved in service. Figure 8.2
shows a somewhat simplified comparison insofar as it is based on the teens'
reports that they had participated in community volunteer work at Wave 1
of data collection. In this sense, it is not dynamic: some adolescents in the
study who had not reported volunteering at the first wave could have started
volunteering at the second or third waves. Nonetheless, the figure indicates
that the age-related declines in social trust that I discussed in the previous
chapter are less precipitous among those teens who had engaged in some form
of community volunteer work during the first year of the study. As already
noted, as teens get older, they are less likely to believe that people generally are
trustworthy or fair. However, those age-related declines in social trust are not
as steep for teens who engage in some form of community service.

The boost to social trust from interactions with diverse groups, noted in
research with adults, was obvious in the following teens' statements. A
white male tenth grader who did many community projects as a member of
the Boy Scouts learned that "People are a lot friendlyer [sic] & kinder than
they are made out to be." A seventeen-year-old member of the Young

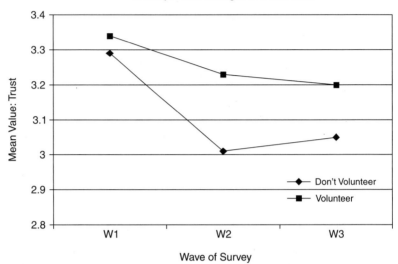

Figure 8.2. Developmental changes in social trust. Data were derived from the longitudinal study on Social Responsibility and Adolescents. Scales were based on the mean of items in each scale. The precise wording for all items is provided in the Appendix.

Muslim Association who, through his organization, worked "with young kids and volunteered with patients at the Veterans Hospital," learned that "all people are important and that everyone deserves the same chances." Three other teens specifically noted that some people are trustworthy and others are not: A seventeen-year-old who volunteered at the "VA and other hospitals" learned that "no matter what race, or religion some people are nice and some are not"; a fourteen-year-old learned that "there are a lot of nice people, some bad but most are just like yourself"; and an eleventh-grade male who "pushes wheel chairs and talks with people at the local assisted living center, learned "how willing some are to give and how some are extremely greedy." Finally, a sixteen-year-old female of Arab descent, who "tutored, cleaned up the streets of my community, and worked in a blood drive," related, "I learned that by helping someone you'll receive many rewards. The biggest reward is RESPECT."

But not all young people felt that their service work gained them respect. In fact, one eighteen-year-old Arab-American felt that despite his volunteering at the Veteran's hospital where he helped "to escort, feed, and take vital signs for patients," he learned "that there can be very ignorant people because even though I was helping out and taking time out from doing fun things, I still get comments about my culture and religion." This comment and that of a Latina volunteer remind us that not all of the learning that occurs in encounters with the real world is positive, which may explain the declines in social trust between early and late adolescence. This Latina volunteered as a candy striper in a hospital where she learned "what others think, how well I can handle a crisis, and who lives around me," but she also felt that opportunities to succeed in society were not equal because of prejudice, "Many people are ignored because of their backgrounds & experiences." She then went on to relate a very personal experience of discrimination, "my grandfather & I were walking down a street and some kids knocked him into the street, spat on him, & then proceeded to call us 'spics.'"

### Second Chances: Restorative Justice and Community Service

Youth themselves belong to a group that is stereotyped by many adults and that stereotype is especially difficult to dislodge.[36] A few adolescents commented on the potential of face-to-face contact for changing the perceptions that adults in their community held about young people. The following observations suggest that community volunteer work gave some young people a chance to prove themselves and to undo negative stereotypes about "youth," even about those youth who may have engaged in antisocial behaviors. In fact, community service is sometimes mandated as a way to reintegrate youth offenders back into the community. The hope of so-called restorative justice practices is that the young person will understand that their actions violated real people, fellow members of their community and that they have a responsibility to restore that community. Community volunteer work also is likely to expose young offenders to prosocial reference groups because those adolescents who typically engage in community service are less likely than other teens to be involved in antisocial behavior.[37] By putting young offenders into contact with adults in community organizations, the hope is that stereotypes about youth offenders may be undone. A few of the respondents in this study alluded to such restorative justice practices. One seventh-grade white male related, "I have to do community service for fighting and I work up at the bingo hall." A Mexican-American twelfth grader who volunteered at an ex-convicts rehabilitation center learned

"That there are nice considerate people out there that could still believe someone after they have done wrong."

Community service is a form of collective public action: typically, it is done through a community-based nonprofit organization and with others (fellow students or fellow members of a community-based nonprofit organization). Thus, community service should enhance teens' community connectedness. When people work together in collective action with a common purpose, it tends to increase feelings of connectedness. That feeling should satisfy what psychologists have identified as a basic need that human beings have to feel that they *belong,* that they have attachments and meaningful relationships with fellow human beings.[38] We know from national studies that adolescents' sense of connection to community institutions and of affective ties to fellow members of those organizations protects against a host of risk factors: regardless of other social background factors, teens who report such connections are significantly less likely to have physical and mental health problems or to report that they engage in a range of risky behaviors that might lead to psychosocial or health problems.[39] Further, according to longitudinal work, such ties to fellow members of community organizations increase the likelihood that teens from different racial or ethnic backgrounds will be committed to serving their communities and will be active in the political process in the early adult years.[40]

Not all of the young people who had engaged in community service in our study actually felt that they had learned something: thirty percent of those who had volunteered said that they had not learned anything from the experience. The data don't allow me to ferret out whether the 70 percent who felt that they learned something from their volunteer work were more open-minded to their experiences or actually had a better "learning" experience. However, as Figure 8.3 illustrates, compared to peers who learned nothing from volunteering, those who felt that they learned something from the experience had significantly more positive views of fellow residents of their communities.

The legend in Figure 8.3 lists three scales that capture the youths' perceptions about fellow residents of their community (that people in their community generally are caring, open, and effective). Each scale was composed of multiple items that teens endorsed using a 1–5 (strongly disagree to strongly agree) format. Items in the *caring* scale tap their agreement with items such as "if someone in my community has a problem, they can usu-ally count on others to help them out" and "most people try to make this community a good place to live." Youths' reports that theirs was an *open* com-munity included items such as "when someone moves here, people make them feel welcome." Finally, youths' perception that theirs was an *effective* community was based on items such as "if there is a problem getting some service from the government, people in my community could get the prob-lem solved" and "every town has some problems. In general, people in my town work together to solve our problems."

The columns in Figure 8.3 are based on group means for the 70 percent of youth who felt that they had learned something from their community volunteer work and the means of the 30 percent who felt that they had not learned anything from that experience. As Figure 8.3 illustrates, compared to youth who learned nothing from their community service, those who felt that they had learned something perceived their communities in a more posi-tive light: the "learners" were more likely to feel that people in their community

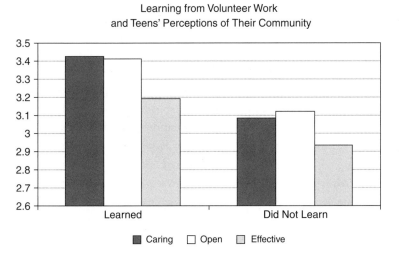

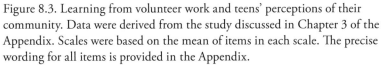

Figure 8.3. Learning from volunteer work and teens' perceptions of their community. Data were derived from the study discussed in Chapter 3 of the Appendix. Scales were based on the mean of items in each scale. The precise wording for all items is provided in the Appendix.

were generally caring, open to newcomers, and effective in getting things accomplished that would benefit the whole community.

These results remind us both that the civic learning opportunities in service experiences vary and also that what individuals bring to the community service experience is likely to play a role in what they get out of it. It is possible that the group who learned something from volunteering had more positive perceptions of their community to begin with, perceptions that might even have played a part in their decision to volunteer. Their motivations for volunteering may have differed from their peers who did not learn from the experience. We know that adults who participate in volunteer organizations have different motivations for participating and that their length of service depends in part on whether the experience fulfills their needs. Not surprisingly, they are more likely to stick with the organization if the service experience is a good match for their motivation for serving.[41] It is certainly possible that youth who say they learned from service work experienced a better match for what they expected to get from the experience. Alternatively, as others have noted, the specific content, that is, what the young person actually does in his service, has everything to do with the outcome. Compared to functionary work, direct service with people in need and work that addresses social issues is more likely to motivate adolescents' concerns about social issues and continued commitments to civic action.[42]

In the field of youth civic engagement, there has been consistent attention to youth involvement in extracurricular activities at school and in community-based organizations because such participation in one's youth is a good predictor of voting and of joining and leading community groups in adulthood. However, analyses of two national longitudinal data sets suggest that certain kinds of extracurricular involvement are more likely than others to lead to later civic engagement. Daniel McFarland and R. Jack Thomas report that although participation in extracurricular activities in one's youth is important for political engagement in young adulthood, involvement as a youth in voluntary associations that entail community service, public speaking, debate, and performance, and religious affiliations are the strongest predictors of political involvement in young adulthood. After controlling for multiple social background and selection factors, these scholars conclude that "youth organizations that demand time commitments and that concern service, political activity, and public performance have the most significant positive relation to long-term political participation."[43] In a similar vein, research with adults suggests that democratic dispositions such as social trust are more likely to be boosted by participation in certain kinds of community-based organizations, specifically, those that engage in community service and those with a diverse membership.[44]

Like Figure 8.3, Figure 8.4 summarizes teens' perceptions about how caring, open, and effective the people in their communities are. This time I compare four groups based on the teens' reports of whether in the past year they (a) were involved in any community-based clubs or extracurricular activities and (b) were involved in any community service projects. Four groups of teens emerged. Reading from the right side of the figure, these groups are (1) social isolates who responded "no" to both items (the neither group in the figure); (2) club members who were involved in some extracurricular activity but had not done any community service (clubs only group); (3) volunteers who had done a community service project but were not members of any club or activity (volunteer only group); and (4) those who both belonged to a club and also had done a community service project (clubs/volunteer group).[45]

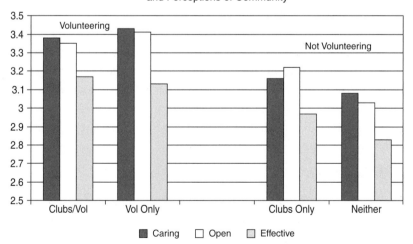

Figure 8.4. Types of youth engagement and teen's perceptions of their community.

Two conclusions can be inferred from these data. The first is that as a general pattern, some kind of engagement is better than none. The adolescents who are not involved in any extracurricular activity, community-based club or organization, or in volunteer work (the neither group) have less positive views of the people in their communities when compared to their peers who are in at least one club or do some form of volunteer work. This group may spend time in other pursuits such as paid work, family responsibilities, or hanging out with friends, but they are not involved in nonprofit community-based organizations. The second conclusion is that engagement in clubs and extracurricular activities—that I am arguing typically would select for youth with similar interests with no additional engagement in volunteer work—is associated with less positive perceptions of one's community than is engagement in volunteer work. In short, there seems to be something about engaging in volunteer work that is associated with more positive perceptions about fellow members of one's community as being caring, open, and effective in getting things done.

According to other work, engagement in community issues also is positively associated with adolescents' psychosocial adjustment. Mark Pancer's research on a large sample of Canadian high school seniors identified four clusters of community involvement: uninvolved in any helping behavior, responders to direct requests for help from others such as neighbors, community volunteers who were proactive in seeking out projects but were apolitical, and a small group of activists who were highly involved in a wide range of community and political activities. Compared to the first two clusters, the latter two were higher on measures of psychosocial adjustment (e.g., optimism, self-esteem), of identity exploration and commitment, and of discussions of a range of social and moral issues (religion, moral values, politics, friendships), suggesting that, as Erikson theorizes, they were using the adolescent years to explore different perspectives on ideological issues and to define their positions.[46]

*Adult Role Models*

Most service-learning projects take place in community institutions, settings that K–12 students might otherwise not enter. Insofar as those institutions welcome students and these public spaces become familiar, even comfortable terrain, the concept of "our community" becomes a deeper and more palpable one for the youth. From the perspective of the adults in the organizations, there should be a reciprocal boost to their trust and respect for teenagers as a result of the young people's participation in community-based organizations and service. As Shep Zeldin and his colleagues found in their work on youth-adult partnerships, the infusion of youth into community-based organizations can improve intergenerational relationships as adults come to appreciate the contributions young people make, accommodate their often-negative stereotypes about teens, and become more trusting of young people.[47] Of course, such changes are possible, not inevitable. Adults have to be open to the notion of partnering with rather than leading the younger generation and, even when they have the will, they need practice in changing their ways. But as one in-depth ethnography of three youth activist programs showed, there are different strategies that adults can use to guide the participation of youth, manage tensions between young people, and also meet the goals of the activist campaigns. According to an educator, Ben Kirshner, adults who are motivated to partner with youth use strategies of facilitation, apprenticeship, and joint work to support young people as they make decisions and assume leadership.[48]

In the research on community service and service learning, relatively little attention has been paid specifically to the interactions that youth have with adults who are public servants or human service providers. But public servants are exactly what their title implies (i.e., servants to the public). And the staff of human service agencies typically are not, as the misanthropic items in the social trust scales imply, out for their own gain at the expense of others. In fact, I would venture a guess that most human service providers in community-based organizations genuinely care about other people. Since nonprofits run on volunteer labor, it is likely that many of the adults in community-based organizations with whom teens would interact are volunteers themselves. Insofar as young people are still formulating ideas about the kind of adults they aspire to become and the kinds of careers they plan to pursue, interactions with those in public or human service organizations could be formative. Whether or not they choose to do similar work when they are older, youths' concepts of fellow human beings and how malevolent or benevolent they believe them to be should be informed by these interactions. As one young person reflected when asked what he had learned from the service-learning experience, "I learned that there are a lot of people who are kind, who care, and are willing to help others."

*Collective Work and the Common Good*

Adolescents also indicated that through their community volunteer work they had learned the importance of collective work for accomplishing goals. Regardless of their cultural or class backgrounds or whether they volunteered in "clean-ups with the Environmental Club," "church to help the community," "the 4-H park," "Big Brothers/Big Sisters, nursing home visits, fire company fund raisers," high school students related the following: "If you work together you can get things done"; "In order to achieve things everyone must work together"; "if we all pitch in even a little, this earth could be so much cleaner"; "I was able to grow closer to people at school and realize that team efforts make a difference"; and "we are bonded closer together than I would have ever imagined! we truly are a community!" Finally, one Native American student who volunteered to "do programs for schools to help them learn about my people" felt that volunteering "helps me bond with others and they help me see myself." Her statement points to another potential of community service—to enable adolescents to connect their own lives, needs, and interests with those of fellow citizens. In their own way, they are referring to what Frances Moore Lappé has dubbed "relational self-interest"—linking our own interests to those of fellow citizens. That link, according to Lappé, rather than altruism and charity, is the only way we can sustain an effective public life. Rousseau would concur. As he explained in his treatise on the social contract, "the undertakings which bind us to the social body are obligatory only because they are mutual; and their nature is such that in fulfilling them we cannot work for others without working for ourselves."[49]

Teens' engagement in community service holds some promise for informing their ideas about the social compact that binds them to others members of their society. For example, several teens learned about pooling resources, giving when they are able in the hopes that when they are in need, others like them will respond. For example, a fifteen-year-old from a working-class family who volunteered to "help old people in a home" reflected, "I learned that everybody's gonna get old and need some kind of help before they die. So it's good to help out others so maybe someone will return the help when I get older." Similar remarks were voiced by other high school students about the ethic of mutual responsibility that holds a society together: "You should always give help, because it will probably be there when you want it back, that it will come back to you at the end" and "by helping others you are helping yourself because when you need some help there will be people there for you."

In closing this chapter, I want to return to criticisms that community service distracts young people from traditional politics and from holding government accountable. To do so, I reiterate a point made in Chapter 7— that when teens are made aware of social issues and believe that it matters to take a stand, they will reflect on their position on that issue. The Swedish political scientist Erik Amnå has coined the term "stand-by citizen" to refer to adolescents who have an interest in and a motivation for politics but who are inactive.[50] The fact that they are aware means that when they feel the imperative, they will be prepared to take action.

In earlier chapters, I argued that this is why family discussions of current events may be associated with teens' interest in and knowledge of social issues. Here I make a similar point about community service, that is, when attention is drawn to a public problem, young people will want to do something about it—and they will want their government to take some action as well. The positive relationship between personal action and government accountability was brought home to me in analyses that my colleagues and I conducted of trends over time in adolescents' environmental activism.

Using data from the Monitoring the Future study that tracks trends among high school seniors in the United States, my colleagues and I found that, across the twenty-seven years of these trend data, cohorts of high school seniors were more likely to take civic action to preserve the environment during years when they believed that natural resources were scarce and that technology did not offer an easy fix for the problem. In other words, the teens were more prepared to take action, to do something about the problem, during periods when they believed that there was a real problem and that taking action mattered. Further, the personal resolve of young people to deal with environmental problems followed a similar trend with their resolve to hold the government accountable for the problem. In other words, in years when youth wanted government to act, they also were more committed to engage in civic action themselves and in years when youth did not want government to take action to preserve the environment, neither did the young people act in an environmentally responsible way in their personal lives.[51]

Political action need not be a trade-off. In fact, my point is actually stronger than that: for things that we care about and value (in this case, environmental quality), we will be motivated to act—to take personal actions to preserve what we care about and to urge elected leaders to enact policies that preserve what we care about. Politics does concern the "authoritative allocation of values," as Easton so famously put it.[52] The imperative, as the philosopher Peter Levine, director of the Center for Information and Research on Civic Learning and Engagement (CIRCLE), has urged, is for people to determine together those values that unite us and those normative goals that we want civic education to achieve.[53]

It is unlikely that the adolescents who shared their thoughts on what they had learned from engaging in community service ever heard of Hannah Arendt. Nonetheless, in their reflections, they are alluding to her notion of a public realm as outlined in her book *The Human Condition:*

> Only the existence of a public realm and the world's subsequent transformation into a community of things which gathers men together and relates them to each other depends entirely on permanence. If the world is to contain a public space, it cannot be erected for one generation and planned for the living only; it must transcend the life span of mortal men.
>
> The common world is what we enter when we are born and what we leave behind when we die. It transcends our life span into past and future alike; it was there before we came and will outlast our brief sojourn into it. It is what we have in common not only with those who live with us, but also with those who were here before and with those who will come after us. But such a common world can survive the coming and going of the generations only to the extent that it appears in public.
>
> Through many ages before us—but now not any more—men entered the public realm because they wanted something of their own or something they had in common with others to be more permanent than their earthly lives.
>
> For the *polis* was for the Greeks, as the *res publica* was for the Romans, first of all their guarantee against the futility of individual life, the space protected against this futility and reserved for the relative permanence if not immortality of mortals.[54]

# Coda

I OPENED THIS book with Timothy E. Cook's critique of the early political socialization research in which he attributed its demise to "a loss of confidence about what it is we are measuring and then what it all means."[1] In that same essay, Cook urged scholars interested in the developmental roots of political thinking to attend to psychological theories of human development and focus less on system stability and more on how younger generations *develop* within a political system. I have tried to take seriously Cook's critique. Although I do not purport to have solved the mystery, I hope that we have come some way in understanding how political and personal development intersect during adolescence. I have argued that exploring civic and political identities and beliefs is an integral part of the process of identity exploration in adolescence. As they consider who they are and who they want to become, adolescents will inevitably make assessments about their society and world—about the options that seem possible for people *like them* but also about the kind of world they want to inherit, to inhabit, and to pass on.

Adolescence is a period when political theories are developing, but the content of those theories depends on who the adolescents are and on the social context in which they are constructing those theories. Consistent with domain approaches to social cognition, I have argued that politics is a domain of knowledge and understanding, but one that is much broader than the electoral or partisan arena and one in which emotions and identities are intertwined with cognition. To emphasize the social foundations of adolescent political theories, I have relied on Vygotsky's thesis that our ideas and beliefs are internalizations of social, collaborative practice. Politics is not done in private but in relationships and collaborations with others—within particular economic and political systems and at particular historical junctures. In summary, to understand political development, it is important to attend both to the characteristics of individuals (their age, gender, social class, ethnic identity, etc.) but also to the political and economic system in which teens experience the terms of the social contract that bind them to other members of their communities.

Throughout the book, we saw that adolescence is a period of growth in understanding the political domain. Whether discussing democracy, laws, or inequality, compared to their younger peers, late adolescents had more accurate information, a wider range of views on issues, and as indicated by their higher integrative complexity scores, an ability to integrate diverse perspectives. In explaining inequality, older teens understood that there could be different factors that would explain why some people are poor while others are rich; they mentioned a greater number as well as a more diverse set of factors. When considering laws, late adolescents were more likely to endorse both individual rights and the need for government protections for people. Older adolescents also are better at distinguishing abstract political concepts from personal experiences; but at the same time they appreciate ways that the personal and political intersect. For example, compared to early adolescents, late adolescents differentiate their trust in familiar others from the social trust they express for people in general. Older adolescents also see more sides to issues and understand the connections between personal experiences of prejudice and structural issues of discrimination.

Older adolescents also were more cynical: not only does social trust decline between early and late adolescence, perceptions of fellow students, teachers, and of fellow residents of one's local community also become more negative. I do not wish to imply any causal relationships. In fact, the negative views about other people probably have more to do with the developmental demands that late adolescents are negotiating. At the end of adolescence, youth face pressures to make decisions about the pathways their lives will take; they also learn first-hand about the competitive nature of life—getting into college or post–high school training programs, competing for jobs. Late adolescents also may be aware of the negative stereotypes about "youth" that are held by the public. In short, an increase in cynicism may be a cost of maturing and of shedding the cocoons with families and friends that protect younger adolescents.

## DEVELOPMENTAL MECHANISMS UNDERLYING POLITICAL STABILITY AND POLITICAL CHANGE

I have used the term "mini-polities" to refer to the role that mediating institutions play as spaces where younger generations work out what it means to be a citizen of the larger polity. In mini-polities (schools, religious, community-based organizations), adolescents develop a concept of themselves as members of the public, practice being part of a sovereign authority in a democracy, listen to the perspectives of fellow members of the public, and negotiate what together people decide is their common good. It is in the practices and processes of mediating institutions that the social contract of a society is stabilized as well as challenged and changed.

Cook criticized political socialization studies for focusing on system stability and urged the field to attend to ways that younger generations develop within a political system. Taking a political *development* rather than a political socialization perspective actually helps elucidate those mechanisms that underlie political stability as well as those that underlie social change. Regarding the former (political stability), I have argued that societies are thinking systems, that younger generations generally come to adopt as fair and just the principles of the social contract to which they are accustomed and that cultural practices reinforce in younger generations beliefs about the system that are both widely endorsed and hegemonic. As Cook himself states, younger generations develop *within a political system.* Remembering that fact forces us to attend to ways that the principles of a political system infuse the practices of adolescents' everyday lives.

Transmission from older to younger generations is part of the process: throughout the chapters, we saw that family values and parent-adolescent discussions of current events were repeatedly associated with adolescents' political knowledge, perspective taking, and commitments. But parents don't transmit political orientations or partisan preferences or even a set of political beliefs intact. In fact, as the items in the measure of family discussions of politics and current events show, parents themselves are listening to the views of their teenage children. Political development can be a bidirectional process. As the research on Kids Voting USA has shown, children who are too young to vote can influence the likelihood that their parents will vote.[2]

However, if justifying the system were the only thing that people do, if transmission were the only mechanism, how would social change ever happen? How could we explain the Arab Spring or the Occupy Wall Street movements of 2011? Such major movements for social change are represented in the media as episodic events that happen suddenly and with no warning. Even in high school textbooks, major historical changes from the fall of the Berlin Wall to the end of South African apartheid to the Civil Rights Movement in the United States are reduced to simple stories of heroic individuals acting alone. Lost in this rendition is the fact that social change is hard work; it is accomplished by the collective actions of many people working in organizations (behind the scenes) over an extended period of time. As adolescents working in activist projects learn, social change means changing mindsets; social change can only be accomplished by working with others, and the process is as important as the goal, which can often be elusive.

The mini-polities of mediating institutions (schools, faith-based, community-based organizations) play a role both in political stability and in political change. With respect to political change, I have borrowed the concept of "free spaces" from Sarah Evans and Harry Boyte who coined the term to illustrate how black slaves in the United States transformed Christian services and symbols into visions of freedom and gained leadership and organizing skills by acting on those visions.[3]

Gay-straight alliances (GSAs) are examples of adolescents claiming a free space in high schools in the United States and of transforming the meaning of extracurricular activities. By forming an alliance of students who insist on tolerance and inclusion in public schools, GSAs accomplish several goals—challenging stigma, making high schools safer and more tolerant settings for all students, educating fellow students, increasing the sense of safety and well-being of sexual minority youth, empowering participants and enabling them to develop a sense of collective identity and commitment to a common good.[4] In short, such collective action is psychologically beneficial for the participants and creates a more open, tolerant, and democratic learning environment even for students who don't participate.

Claims of rights to full citizenship are the basis for both of these civil rights movements. According to Michael Schudson, the author of *The Good Citizen,* a rights-conscious or rights-regarding citizenship is the right model for our times, one that needs to be nurtured because it is an invaluable foundation for (although not the end of) political consciousness. For Schudson, "a rights-regarding citizenship implies respect for the rights of others and a willingness to engage in public dispute according to public norms and a public language."[5] Throughout the book, I have distinguished the liberal philosophy of individual freedom and rights unencumbered by civic responsibilities from a civic republican tradition in which liberty is defined by citizens deliberating together about their common good. What the civil rights struggles of African-Americans, women, or gays and lesbians remind us is that a rights-conscious citizenship is imagined, defined, and achieved by people working together. A rights-regarding citizenship implies not only a commitment to the rights of others but also a commitment to engage in public deliberations to define the ties that bind people together.

## GROUPWAYS: LINKING PERSONAL AND POLITICAL

To understand teens' political theories, we have to pay attention to who they are. Toward that end I have coined the term "groupways" to draw attention to the role of social identities and the standpoint of groups from which an adolescent experiences and interprets the social contract of his/her society. In Chapter 2 we saw that in the midst of the political and economic changes gripping the nations of Central and Eastern Europe, adolescents' ideal social contract as well as their perceptions of growing inequality reflected the political interests of their social class. These youth may not have conceived of themselves as a political interest group. However, like political interest groups, these adolescents understood how social policies affected people "like them" and how their fate was linked to the fate of others. "Groupways" refers to the accumulation of everyday experiences and relationships that are shared by individuals by virtue of their membership in particular groups.

Groupways captures the connection between the personal and the political in the experiences of ethnic-minority youth in the United States. The early formation of a political group consciousness can be seen in the fact that for ethnic-minority youth, an awareness of their ethnic identity was stronger among those youth who had experienced some personal instances of prejudice. This association suggests that they were making connections between the personal and political, between their experience of being prejudged by other people and their membership in an ethnic group that experiences discrimination in society. This greater awareness was a mark of their political consciousness—and it seemed to motivate the teens to action insofar as awareness of their ethnic-minority identity was positively related to the teens' civic commitments to help other members of their ethnic group and to promote intergroup understanding. Another example of groupways can be seen in the gender differences noted across chapters with females typically more likely than their male peers to be concerned about inequalities in their society and the conditions faced by marginalized groups. Finally, groupways was illustrated in the social class differences in adolescents' theories about inequality with those youth from disadvantaged backgrounds more likely to hold individuals accountable for their economic situation.

## MOTIVATORS OF CIVIC PARTICIPATION

Scholarly interest in the preadult foundations of political identities and commitments tends to increase when younger generations either rebel against or are apathetic and indifferent toward participation in conventional politics. Attention turns to those factors that might motivate civic interest and participation in the young. So what have we learned about the developmental precursors of civic engagement?

Based both on my own work and that of scholars in the field of youth civic development, I propose two mechanisms whereby an ethic of civic participation is inculcated in younger generations: first is an awareness that political issues are contested, that there are different sides or perspectives on any issue, and that it matters to take a stand; second is an internalization of certain norms or values concerning how responsible citizens should act. These are not mutually exclusive and, in fact, may be complementary.

## Controversy as a Motivator of Political Interest and Action

Concerning youth's awareness of controversy in political issues—we can interpret several findings discussed in the book under this general category. The previously noted connection between experiences of prejudice and the personal importance that youth attach to political participation is one example. Others detailed in various chapters that were related to teens' political theories, dispositions, and commitments include family discussions of current events and politics, classroom climates that encourage students to exchange different points of view, and community service experiences in which adolescents come face to face with the lives of individuals and groups with whom they typically have no interactions.

The experience common to all of these practices—and borrowing from Vygotsky, the political ideas that are internalized—is that there are different sides to every issue, that reasonable people may disagree, and that it matters to take a stand. In the very act of engaging in deliberations with others, adolescents are forced to reflect on their own position and to ask, "Where do I stand?" This process—of grappling with different points of view on issues—should shape the adolescent's disposition toward open-mindedness and tolerance. Politics is not always nice and, in fact, can be passionate and heated. The very fact of standing for something means that we oppose others' viewpoints. But, as the American legal scholar Robert Post emphasizes, a democracy without public opinion is a contradiction: democracies demand political discussions of different opinions.

And as psychological studies have shown, discussions with others who disagree with us tend to have a moderating influence, making us less certain and less adamant about our opinions. Homogeneous groups tend to reinforce within group opinion and exacerbate political conflict between groups. By spending time with people who think like us, we are convinced that our views are the right and only views and we are more likely to defend them against all others.[6] In contrast, heterogeneous groups where discussions raise perspectives that differ from our own have a moderating influence—making individuals more cognizant that theirs is only one among many views and that resolving the differences demands that citizens find some common ground.

Dewey was aware of these social dynamics when he posited two elements of groups that would nurture democratic dispositions in their

members: first, numerous and varied points of shared interest and the recognition of common interest as a factor in social control; second, continually
readjusting social habits in response to the new situations and free interactions between groups who were once isolated from one another.[7]

Intergroup contact and dialogue is the sine qua non for forming democratic dispositions and habits. It is mainly for this reason that I have argued
that community service projects can be a means whereby teens have contact
with individuals who are members of groups they would otherwise never
encounter. There is no question that there is a wide range in the quality of
community service programs and experiences. However, the case that I have
made for the value of community service is for its *potential* to enlarge adolescents' minds about the challenges faced by people who are not like them
and, ultimately, to engage their commitments to public policies that are
responsive to this wider world. National surveys of public opinion have
shown that even simple exposure to a highly stigmatized group such as
homeless people has a positive impact on public attitudes toward homeless
people.[8]

Schools can also be settings where adolescents learn to see the perspectives
of fellow students and to reconsider their own positions. In several chapters,
we saw the civic benefits for teens of civil climates for learning in which
teachers encourage respectful dialogue and diverse points of view. Adolescents' civic knowledge was broader when they had opportunities for exchang-
ing perspectives with fellow students. But even more importantly, adolescents were more committed to serve their communities and nation when
their teachers (the authority in the mini-polity of the school) insisted that all
students had the right to voice their opinions and that all students had to
respect one another's opinions. Such teaching practices boosted students'
sense of group solidarity at school, their trust in others, their beliefs in the
American promise, and their commitments to serve their country.

However, according to national studies, students are less likely to experience such civil climates for learning if they attend racially mixed schools.[9]
In other words, teachers may feel less comfortable with handling different
points of view in racially mixed settings. This finding is hardly surprising
insofar as teachers typically get no training in facilitating civil dialogues.
Those who do deal with controversy, as the educator Diana Hess shows, take
very proactive steps to enable their students to analyze and to use successful
discussion techniques and, through the process, to develop dispositions of

open-mindedness and tolerance.[10] Public schools are one of the few settings where younger generations might develop these skills. By failing to prepare teachers and to protect them as facilitators of civil dialogues, we forfeit the potential of public education for nurturing the democratic dispositions of younger generations.

## Civic Norms and Values

The second mechanism whereby an ethic of civic participation is inculcated is via civic norms and values. Throughout the book, we saw that the personal and family values that adolescents endorsed were consistently associated with their political theories. Across the six countries discussed in Chapter 2, adolescents' civic commitments, the personal importance that they attached to serving their country and community, were higher among teens who reported that an ethic of social responsibility was emphasized in their families.

In the other chapters that focused on adolescents in the United States, we saw significant associations between values and teens' political theories. For example, adolescents were far more likely to imagine a democratic society as one that was based on equality and the common good if they and their families embraced values of social responsibility and compassion for others. In contrast, individual freedom was a more meaningful aspect of democracy for those youth who valued material achievements and whose families were concerned about other people getting an unfair advantage. Adolescents' theories about inequality also were associated with their values: those who endorsed material values were more likely to hold individuals accountable for being poor or to say that the unemployed weren't trying hard enough to find job. In contrast, when teens endorsed social responsibility and compassion as values that were important to them, they were more likely to mention systemic or structural factors that contribute to inequality.

How can we explain the relationship between personal values and political views? I believe that it has to do with the process of identity formation. Identity has long been considered the psychosocial task of adolescence. However, when we consider the process of identity formation as one that includes adolescents' reflections on the values that define them and the purpose of their lives, then it is not a big leap to say that, as Youniss and Yates observed in their work on adolescents' civic identity formation, in the process of consolidating identities, youth are also constituting their society.[11] At the risk of sounding redundant, as adolescents reflect on who they are they also wrestle with the kind of world they want to live in. Those options are informed by the ideological alternatives that are swirling about as young people come of age.

Those ideas are profoundly affected, as hordes of developmental psychologists will attest, by peer norms. Peer norms and pressures are among the most studied topics in research on adolescence. All too often the field has conceived of peer pressure as a negative influence, encouraging risky behavior and discouraging social values that most adults might prefer. But it is equally clear that peers also exert positive pressures on one another—to do homework, to join extracurricular activities, even to value a sense of civic duty. According to the political scientist David Campbell, if a high percentage of fellow students in an adolescent's high school consider voting a civic duty, that young person is far more likely to vote when s/he is eligible to vote. In fact, the impact of the group norm in high school on voting in adulthood wipes out the effect of the individual adolescent's own belief about voting as a civic duty, leading to Campbell's conclusion that civic norms are inculcated within collectivities.

Our research team has found similar effects of shared values in a classroom on adolescent's prosocial behaviors. We asked students in middle and high school classrooms to report on the degree to which their families emphasize social responsibility as an important value. As I discussed in several chapters, this family value is a significant correlate of an individual adolescent's civic commitments, their dispositions to trust other people, and their theories about inequality. But the question is, if civic norms are inculcated in collectivities, might there be a facilitative effect of shared family values among the students in one's class? This effect is exactly what we found: when social responsibility was a family value shared by fellow classmates, it made it more likely that individual adolescents would act in socially responsible ways and endorse civic values. In other words, being in a class with other students whose families emphasize social responsibility increases the personal importance that an individual adolescent attaches to public interest goals (of serving the country, helping others, preserving the environment for future generations) over and above the effect of her own family values on those civic commitments. This contagion-from-fellow-classmates effect also extended to a teen's readiness to intervene and dissuade peers from engaging in risky substance use behaviors.

Perhaps this finding is not surprising in light of a recent meta-analysis of laboratory experiments using public goods games that found that cooperative behavior is contagious and has ripple effects on other interactions, increasing the likelihood that individuals in the cooperative interaction will cooperate in subsequent interactions with individuals who were not part of the original group.[12] In the authors' own words, "The results suggest that each additional contribution a subject makes to the public good in the first period is tripled over the course of the experiment by other subjects who are directly or indirectly influenced to contribute more as a consequence."[13]

I hope that this book has restored some confidence about what it is we are measuring in the civic domain and what it all means. I do not purport to have solved the mystery and am aware that there are limitations in the methods that I used and the questions that I posed to teens. However, I am confident that the interdisciplinary field of youth civic development will continue to add breadth and depth to our understanding of ways that political theories and identities take shape during the adolescent years. My confidence is based on the fact that the field starts with the premise that young people are assets to their communities and nations and proceeds with a commitment to scholarship in which researchers and practitioners collaborate in defining the questions and methods of inquiry.

As we move forward, our field would be enriched by taking seriously the challenge that Peter Levine and Ann Higgins-D'Alessandro put to us: that we have a public conversation about the normative reasons for the civic programs that we propose.[14] As adults involved in the civic arena, we wield considerable influence over the young people with whom we work and learn. We have an obligation to them and to society to be more explicit and to be more public about the civic values and dispositions that embody our vision of a "good citizen."

# Appendix

METHODS

THE DATA PRESENTED in this book are drawn from four studies. Chapters have been organized topically. In some chapters, data from more than one of these studies are presented. In this Appendix, I provide details about the methods for all of the studies. In the interests of saving space and trees, I first present an overall summary of methods used in the four studies, for example, the strategy of purposive sampling, chosen to address specific issues by examining them in the diverse ecologies in which adolescents were growing up (i.e., whether in the choice of nations for cross-national comparisons or the choice of communities within the United States that reflected contrasts in social class or racial-ethnic composition) or the procedures used to code the content and level of integrative complexity of the open-ended responses. Likewise, because some of the same scales were used in different studies, I have saved space by providing information about the scales only once. Measures of internal consistency were adequate for all scales. Following the general summary, I discuss measures and other methodological issues unique to the data discussed in each of the chapters. When the same data set is used in different chapters I report on the sample that responded to the items in each chapter. Additional details about sampling, methods, and measures can be found in the published papers from the projects that I have cited in relevant chapters.

Purposive sampling techniques were used in each study—with the goal of gaining insights into the perceptions of the social contract held by young people located in different positions of power or status in their society. For the chapters on democracy (Chapter 4) and on "we the people" (Chapter 3), I recruited schools in communities with a diverse array of cultural, racial or ethnic, and new immigrant groups. To understand adolescents' theories about inequality, I intentionally chose communities based on their social class composition. Consequently, in that chapter (Chapter 6) we hear the views of teens whose parents are doctors and auto executives as well as those of their peers whose parents are beauticians or online factory workers.

## RECRUITMENT STRATEGIES AND DESCRIPTIONS OF THE STUDIES

A similar procedure was used in each study to recruit participants. First, the purpose of the study was presented to school superintendents and principals and then discussed with teachers, typically teachers of social studies. The project was described to students and in letters sent home to their parents as a study of adolescents' opinions about their schools, their communities, and societies. Written consent was sought from parents as well as students prior to their participation.

It is important to remember that all of the data were collected from school-based samples. Thus, the voices of teens who had dropped out of school are missing. This fact is especially relevant in the chapter on teens' theories about inequality (Chapter 6), where some teens from the most disadvantaged backgrounds have remained in school, despite drop-out rates in excess of 50 percent in their schools.

With very rare exceptions—one being parents' reports included in Chapter 7, the chapter on trust—adolescents' responses are the sole source of information. I readily admit that this is only one perspective, a point that is most relevant in instances of reports of family processes where parents might provide very different perspectives. However, when it comes to adolescents' pro-social behaviors, it is their perceptions of the values that their families emphasize, in other words, the values that they hear and attend to, and not their parents' reports of family values that matter.[1]

## SURVEY ADMINISTRATION

Surveys were administered within groups in classes during regularly scheduled social studies classes. With rare exceptions, all of the students in the United States were literate in English. They completed the surveys on their own and were able to ask research assistants questions for clarification during the survey administration. The studies were described to students as opinion surveys (for example, the cross-national survey discussed in Chapter 2 had a title on the front cover, *Students' Opinions about Issues in Society*). Students were informed that opinion surveys meant there were no right or wrong answers but that their ideas and views were important and that's why they were being asked to share them. As the instructions on the cross-national survey explained, "Teenagers are not old enough to vote but they usually have opinions about issues in society. We're interested in your ideas."

To give them a context in which to understand the study and the importance of their views, adolescents at each site were informed about the larger study and who else would be included. For example, in the cross-national study, they were told that adolescents from other nations would also be filling out similar surveys in their country. In the study on what it means to be an American, participating teens were told, "We are interested in learning what teenagers think about some issues in America. Students from many communities and from many different ethnic and racial backgrounds are filling out these surveys and giving their views. Your generation will be the leaders of America someday. So your ideas are very important."

## CODING OF OPEN-ENDED RESPONSES

Adolescents' responses to open-ended items in various surveys are a large share of several chapters. I have made every effort to maintain adolescents' verbatim responses to the open-ended items, keeping the original spelling and grammar intact. In addition, when adolescents capitalized words or put them in parentheses, that formatting was maintained. In some instances, I italicized certain words or phrases to draw particular attention to them. In those cases, I have noted "italics added," meaning they were not in the original.

The same coding procedures were used for each open-ended question and those procedures are summarized here. Adolescents' (and in Chapter 7, parents') open-ended responses were coded by trained scorers who were blind to the hypotheses of the study and who had no knowledge of the respondents' characteristics. Open-ended responses were coded using a multistage content analysis process. In the first stage of the analysis, investigators from the team made a complete reading of the responses to note emerging themes. They then re-read responses to derive categories and developed a general coding scheme based upon the emerging themes identified in the data. Two researchers from the team then coded selections of the responses using the data-derived coding scheme, with each response permitted to receive several content codes in order to capture potential complexity and breadth. Discrepancies were discussed and codes were refined as necessary. Unclear responses were resolved through collective agreement. A subsample of responses was utilized to assess final inter-rater reliabilities that, in all cases, were satisfactory (ranging from .75 to .91). In most of the chapters, I provide examples for some of the discrete categories but organize the discussion based on collapsing the discrete categories into a set of a few theoretically derived macro or superordinate categories.

## METHODS UNIQUE TO EACH CHAPTER

Next I discuss the designs and sampling strategies for the studies summarized in the various chapters. Following that I provide information about the measures.

## Chapter 2

The data discussed in Chapter 2 are drawn from a cross-national comparative study that I conducted in the mid-1990s with colleagues in five other nations. Three countries (Bulgaria, the Czech Republic, and Hungary) were negotiating market and political transitions, that is, fundamental changes in their social contracts. The other three countries (Australia, Sweden, and the

United States) had in place stable institutional practices that matched their economic and political systems.

My colleagues and I recruited adolescents (twelve- to nineteen-year-olds with a mean age of 15.7 years) from schools in a large metropolitan area of each country and purposely sampled youth from high- and low-status family backgrounds in each country. The latter decision was based on our interest in understanding whether youth who are more or less *advantaged* by the social contracts in their nation would provide different insights into the terms of their nation's social contract. Further, in the Central and East European nations, some different groups stood to win or lose in light of the changing conditions of their nations' social contracts—especially due to the move from a social welfare to a private market economy.

To obtain comparable samples, we recruited in schools based on different school types (gymnasium or college preparatory, technical, and vocational) in Bulgaria, the Czech Republic, and Hungary. In Australia, Sweden, and the United States, we sampled schools that were located in working-class and low-income communities and middle- and upper-income communities. In addition, within each nation the level of maternal education (number of years of school completed) was used as an indicator of the individual adolescent's social class background. We obtained a total sample of 5,600 adolescents, roughly evenly divided across the countries and by gender within each country.

Surveys were developed after long discussions among the principal investigators (every PI was either a research scientist or a university faculty member) in each country about the social contracts in each nation and the policies, including the organizational and instructional practices of schools that flowed from the contract. Some items were developed specifically for the study, and others were adapted from the International Social Justice Project.[2] Items were developed in English and checked by each PI for validity, then translated into the principal language of each country after which each survey was translated back into English and checked for consistency across sites. Purposive sampling resulted in two measures of social status. The first was either the type of school an adolescent attended (in Bulgaria, the Czech Republic, and Hungary) or the average income of the community where the school was located (in Australia, Sweden, and the United States). The second (which was used in the within-country analyses) was a measure of parental education based on the average education an adolescent reported for his or her mother and father or parenting adults. Adolescents were asked to think about the adults (parents or other caretakers) with whom they spent the most time and to choose a number (from 1 to 20) to "show the highest grade that those adults finished in school."

## Measures

Adolescents indicated their agreement with items on the survey by choosing a number from a 5-point Likert scale ranging from Strongly Disagree (1) to Strongly Agree (5) or Not at All Important (1) to Very Important (5). These items were then formed into scales.

### MACRO-LEVEL JUSTICE BELIEFS

People have different views about the best way for a society to be organized. Here are some things others have said. What are your views? Remember there are *no right or wrong answers,* just opinions (1 = strongly disagree to 5 = strongly agree).

## Adolescents' beliefs that the government should provide for the welfare of citizens

- The government should provide basic services such as health care and legal services to everyone, free of charge.
- If people lose their jobs, the government should support them until they find new jobs.
- The government should make sure everyone has a place to live, whether a person can pay or not.
- Society should give financial help to families who are raising children.
- If people have children, they should find a way to support them. They shouldn't rely on society for help (reverse coded).

## Adolescents' concerns about the moral hazards of social welfare

- When the government provides services for free, people tend to get lazy.
- When the government provides services for free, people tend to cheat.

## Adolescents' views of the ideal social contract (emphasis on equality)

- It's not right for there to be very rich and very poor people in America (or Bulgaria, etc.). There should be more equality.
- It's only natural to have rich and poor people in a society (reverse coded).

## Perceptions of increasing social disparities

In my country . . .

- Economic changes are making the life of the average person worse, not better.
- A few individuals are getting wealthier but many people are becoming poorer.

## Perception that one's society is equitable

- Any person who is willing to work hard can make a good living in our country.
- In general, everyone has an equal chance of getting ahead in our society.

### MICRO-LEVEL JUSTICE BELIEFS

People have different ideas about how schools *should* be organized and about the *best ways for students to learn.* What are your opinions about the following statements?

## Adolescents' beliefs about the proper role for schools (single items, not a scale)

- Students should have a say in how their school is run.
- Competition in school helps students learn what competition in life will be like.
- Students become better thinkers if they are sometimes allowed to disagree with their teacher's ideas.
- Schools should help students find jobs.

Adolescents' perceptions of self-orientation among students
at their own school

At our school . . .

- Most students look out for themselves rather than help others.
- Students only care about their friends.

### MEASURING ADOLESCENTS' VIEWS ABOUT ROUTINE PRACTICES (CHILDREN AND CHORES)

In the future, you may be a parent. We are interested in your ideas about raising children. Some people think children should do chores. Other people
think children shouldn't have chores to do. First, let's talk about the kinds of
chores when children have to clean up their own things—like putting their
toys or clothes away or making their bed or cleaning up their part of the room.

The following four items were asked concerning children's responsibilities for *their own things* and then *for general household work*:

Now how about *general household work*—like doing dishes, sweeping
floors or other jobs around the house?

At what age do you think children should be expected to do
*general household work?*

(Circle *only one* choice)

- A. Never
- B. Under the age of 6
- C. Around 6 or 7, but not before
- D. Between 8–10 but not before
- E. When they're 11 or older

What would you say is the major value of having children do
household work?

(Circle *only one* choice)

- A. None. No value.
- B. It helps the parents. It takes away some of the parents' work load.

C. It's good training for the child in responsibility and self-discipline.

D. It helps children learn that they're part of a family and everyone should help the group.

## Do you think children should earn an allowance for doing such household work?

(Circle *only one* choice)

A. Yes. They should be paid for each job they do.

B. Yes. They should be paid an allowance as a general payment for the work they do.

C. Sometimes. They should be paid only for extra or big jobs.

D. No. They should not be paid for the jobs they do.

### ADOLESCENTS' CIVIC COMMITMENTS

When you think about your life and your future, how important is it to you personally to (response format 1 = not at all important to 5 = very important)

- contribute to your country
- do something to improve your society

### ADOLESCENT AND FAMILY VALUES

Choose a number to show whether you disagree or agree with the following (with 1 = strongly disagree to 5 = strongly agree).

## Adolescents' self-transcendent values

In the future when I'm an adult,

- I would be willing to work fewer hours and earn less income if that would create jobs for unemployed people.
- I would be willing to have fewer luxuries (like nice cars, clothes, or fancy houses) if that would help starving people in other countries.

- I would be willing to have fewer luxuries if that would preserve the earth for future generations.
- I would be willing to pay taxes to help the poor or homeless.
- Before I make a decision I try to think about how it will affect others.

## Family value of compassion/social responsibility

- My parents have taught me to be helpful to others, especially those who are less fortunate.
- My parents get upset when they hear about harm or injustice being done to others.
- My parents have taught me to be aware of other people's feelings and needs.
- My parents have taught me to pay attention to other people's needs, not just my own.

## Chapter 3

Chapters 3 and 4 are drawn from data collected as part of a cross-sectional study conducted in different communities within the United States. The main purpose of this study was to understand ways in which teens in the United States interpret their experiences as Americans and as members of different ethnic or cultural groups.

The data were collected in social studies classes from approximately 1,000 sixth to twelfth graders (53 percent female) who represented the following racial or ethnic groups: 17 percent were African-American; 13 percent Arab-American; 7 percent Asian-American; 3 percent Latino-American; and 60 percent were from European-American backgrounds. The sample also was socioeconomically diverse: 34 percent of the adolescents' parents had completed twelve or fewer years of schooling and 26 percent had professional or post-four-year college degrees. Not surprisingly, there were more recent immigrants in some ethnic groups than others. Whereas 95 percent of the European American and 88 percent of the African-American youth reported that their families had been in the United States for three or more generations, only 44 percent of the Latino-American and 31 percent of the Arab-American youths' families had resided in the United States that long.

## Measures

Here are the three open-ended questions that are the basis for Chapter 3:

- Besides being a citizen of the United States, how would you describe what it means to be an American?
- Sometimes a person identifies strongly with their ancestral or cultural group. Other times a person may identify more with being an American. Can you think of times when you felt very much like a member of your ancestral group?
- How about times when you felt very much like an American?

Adolescents could give multiple responses to each of these three questions that were coded into discrete categories to preserve as much detail as possible. Since the majority of young people gave only one or two responses, the first two responses are summarized in Chapter 3. There are good reasons to consider first responses because they capture what psychologists refer to as the "availability heuristic," a reference to the relevant information that comes to mind or is retrieved from memory quickly and easily.[3]

However, insofar as the first responses may not capture the adolescents' fuller meaning, we also coded second responses. First the teens' responses were coded into discrete categories that were later collapsed into three superordinate categories for further analyses. The three broad thematic (superordinate) categories included references to liberalism/individual rights, republicanism/common good, and patriotism/loyalty. Only a small percentage of the discrete responses could not be assigned to these three categories.

## Ethnic Self-Identification

Adolescents were asked the following: "People in the United States come from different ancestries. Some of these are listed below. Check what best describes your family's ancestry." Choices included the following: African/Black, Arab, Asian, European/White, Mexican/Latin American, Native American/Indian, Puerto Rican, other Caribbean ancestry.

## Ethnic Awareness

To assess participants' ethnic awareness, they were asked to respond to the following statement: "Some people are very aware of their racial, ethnic, or cultural identity. Others are not. How about you?" Adolescents responded by indicating they were either very aware or not very aware. This was followed by the open-ended item, "Describe some times when you felt like a member of your ethnic/cultural group."

## Experiences of Prejudice

To measure experiences of prejudice, adolescents were asked the following: "Have you or someone close to you ever faced prejudice?" This dichotomous (No/Yes) item was followed by an open-ended one, "If you answered yes, can you describe some of these times?" The open-ended responses were coded into categories based on content and context where the incident occurred.

In addition to the open-ended items, adolescents indicated their agreement with other items on the survey by choosing a number from a 5-point Likert scale ranging from Strongly Disagree (1) to Strongly Agree (5) or Not at All Important (1) to Very Important (5). These items were then formed into scales.

### ATTITUDES TOWARD IMMIGRANTS SCALES

The movement of people between countries has become more and more common in the world today. Some countries have a lot of people moving *into their* country. These people are called *immigrants*. Considering your own society, how strongly do you agree with the following statements?

## Immigrants pose a threat to our society

- Immigrants tend to bring crime into our country.
- Immigrants tend to take jobs away from our own people.

## Immigrants enrich our society

- Immigrants to our country should be encouraged to preserve their language and customs.

- Immigrants should have the same right to health care that citizens of our country get.
- The children of immigrants should have the right to a good education in our country.
- Immigrants enrich our culture.

## Immigrants should assimilate

- If they want to be accepted, immigrants should learn our customs and language.
- If we allow too many immigrants into our country, the American culture might be destroyed.

### PARENTAL ADMONITIONS ABOUT PREJUDICE

Adolescents were asked two sets of questions about the extent to which parents discussed prejudice or discrimination with them.

## Emphasis on tolerance

- My family tells me it is wrong to judge people before you get to know them.
- My family has taught me to respect people no matter who they are.
- My family has told me that everyone deserves a fair chance.
- My parents have told me to treat everyone equally.

## Prejudice may pose a barrier

- Some people in my family have been treated unfairly because of prejudice.
- Some people close to me have been denied opportunities because of prejudice.
- My family has told me about people who have struggled to get where they are.

## BELIEFS IN THE TENETS OF THE AMERICAN PROMISE

Items were developed for this study to gauge adolescents' beliefs that America is an equal opportunity society, that the government responds to the average citizen, and that the police mete out justice fairly.

### Equal opportunity

- In America you have an equal chance no matter where you came from or what race you are.
- Basically people get fair treatment in America, no matter who they are.
- America is basically a fair society where everyone has an equal chance to get ahead.

### Responsiveness of American government (note that items are reverse-coded)

- The government doesn't really care what people like me and my family think.
- The U.S. government is pretty much run for the rich, not for the average person.
- The government will do whatever it wants to, no matter what people like us feel.
- The government doesn't care about us ordinary people.

(Items in the following scale were included in a section of the survey in which adolescents were asked to reflect on their local community. The other *perceptions of my community scales* are described in the Appendix for Chapter 8. The school climate scale is described in the Appendix for Chapter 7.

### Police mete out justice fairly

- The police are fair to everyone.
- Everyone can rely on the police to help them.

## CIVIC COMMITMENTS

Adolescents were asked about the personal importance that they attached to a set of public-interest (as well as self-interest) goals. Here I present the items in three of the public interest scales: patriotism, improving race relations, and advocating for one's ethnic group.

When you think about your life and your future, how important is each of the following for you personally to achieve? Use the importance scale with 1 = not at all important to 5 = very important.

Patriotism

- Helping the country
- Serving the country
- Helping my society

Improving race relations

- Improving race relations
- Working to stop prejudice

Group advocacy

- Supporting my ethnic group
- Helping my people
- Standing up for my ethnic group

## Chapter 4

The sample for this chapter is the same as that discussed in Chapter 3.

## Measures

Adolescents' definitions of democracy were obtained via an open-ended question, "People have different ideas about what it means for a society to be a democracy. In your own words, what does democracy mean to you?" A total of three responses (including incorrect definitions) were coded so that the breadth of students' responses could be captured.

In addition to the open-ended items, adolescents indicated their agreement with other items on the survey by choosing a number from a 5-point Likert scale ranging from Strongly Disagree (1) to Strongly Agree (5) or Not at All Important (1) to Very Important (5). These items were then formed into scales.


## PERSONAL AND FAMILY VALUES

The next statements refer to families. When you think about *your own family,* choose a number to show how strongly you agree or disagree with each statement.

## Social responsibility

- My parents have taught me to be helpful to others, especially those who are less fortunate.
- My parents get upset when they hear about harm or injustice being done to others.
- My parents have taught me to be aware of other people's feelings and needs.
- My parents have taught me to pay attention to other people's needs, not just my own.

## Environmentalism

- In our family we try to recycle whatever we can.
- My parents have taught me not to be wasteful.

## Social vigilance

- My parents encourage me to stick up for my rights if anybody tries to push me around.
- My parents have warned me that people sometimes take advantage of you.

- My parents have taught me to know who my friends and enemies are.
- My parents have warned me you can't always trust people.

## Discussion of current events

- In my house we have many discussions about current events and politics.
- My parents discuss what's happening in the world with me.
- I tell my parents my opinions about events in the news.
- I am interested in the news.
- Sometimes I have different opinions from my parents about current events.
- Sometimes I argue with my parents about current events.

Adolescents' personal values were tapped using a 1–5 (Not at All Important to Very Important or Strongly Disagree to Strongly Agree scale).

When you think about your life and your future, how important is each of the following for you personally to achieve?

## Self-enhancing value: Materialism

- Earning a lot of money
- Having nice clothes
- Having a nice home

## Self-transcending value: Altruism

- I would be willing to have fewer luxuries (like nice cars, clothes, or fancy houses) if that would help starving people in other countries.
- I would be willing to have fewer luxuries if that would preserve the earth for future generations.
- Before I make a decision I try to think about how it will affect others.
- In the future when I'm an adult, I would be willing to pay taxes to help the poor or homeless.
- I get mad if I see someone being treated badly.
- In the future when I'm an adult, I would be willing to work fewer hours and earn less income if that would create jobs for unemployed people.

## Chapter 5

This chapter is based on data drawn from two data sets that focus on adolescents' perceptions of laws related to public health and their reflections on the rights of individuals to engage in risky behaviors. The focus is on laws and taxes, both actions on the part of the government that are meant to protect public welfare but that restrict individual freedom. The first data set, which is the main focus of this chapter, is based on the open-ended responses of youth to a set of hypothetical laws. The samples for both studies are socioeconomically and ethnically diverse, include approximately equal numbers of males and females, and include early through late adolescents. For the in-depth qualitative study, there were 64 seventh to ninth graders and 124 tenth to twelfth graders.

The second data set is a large longitudinal (three-year) survey study. The goal of the longitudinal study, conducted between 2002 and 2005, was to understand factors and processes related to the development of civic virtues including social responsibility and social trust. I have conceived of adolescents' beliefs about rights and responsibilities concerning their own and the public's health as an aspect of their civic understanding. In this chapter, I draw from the longitudinal data to show age differences in adolescents' endorsements of individual rights to engage in health risks and the government's right to enact laws that constrain individual choices.

Adolescents were surveyed annually in fifth through twelfth grade classrooms across eight school districts (reflecting diversity in ethnicity, social class, and urbanicity) in a northeastern and a midwestern state. At the first wave, 563 early, 506 middle, and 467 late adolescents ranging in age from ten to eighteen participated. The parents and teachers of the adolescents also completed surveys at each time point.

## Measures: Adolescents' Beliefs about Health

Six items tapped adolescents' beliefs about rights concerning health. Items were based on Likert-type (1 = strongly disagree to 5 = strongly agree) scales. Both exploratory and confirmatory factor analyses were performed on these items that resulted in two factors. Both scales had adequate measures of internal consistency: Cronbach's alpha of .78 for "individual right" and .71 for "public health."

## Belief in health as an individual right

- It's my body, I can do what I want with it.
- If I want to smoke or drink, it's my choice.
- People have a right to smoke; they are only hurting themselves.

## Public health belief

- If something is bad for your health, the government should tell you to avoid it.
- The government should make laws to protect society against drunk driving.
- Smokers need to be responsible, not smoke when little kids are around.

## The Vignettes

In the qualitative study, adolescents responded to three hypothetical vignettes that involved smoking, driving under the influence (DUI), and wearing motorcycle helmets. They were described as follows:

- Suppose there's a country where the government pays for health care for all of the people. A law is discussed which says that people who smoke must pay a special "smoking" tax to the government. The lawmakers say that smoking is bad for people's health and the government shouldn't have to pay for people's bad habits.
- Drunken driving accidents have become a big problem. A law is being discussed that says a person's license could be taken away for a year if their test showed that they were legally drunk.
- Studies show that if people wear helmets when they ride motorcycles, they are less likely to get killed or have serious brain injury if they're in an accident. So a law is discussed that would make it illegal to ride a motorcycle without a helmet.

For each of these questions, the respondent was asked "What do you think *would* happen?" as well as "What do you think *should* happen?" Note that the public implications of individual health risks and the government's argument for why the particular law was justified were made salient in each of the vignettes.

## Chapter 6

This chapter is based on data collected from the adolescents in the United States who participated in the cross-national study. Details about the sample of adolescents from the United States are provided here. Data were collected via survey administration in social studies classes of seventh–twelfth graders in a midwestern state. Six urban and suburban school districts were included in an effort to sample youth from a broad range of social backgrounds. There were two school districts in each of the low-, medium-, and high-income communities and, based on Census data, the average annual household incomes for those areas were $24,700, $54,100, and $110,000 respectively. The sample was evenly divided across the three types of school district. The sample ranged in age from twelve to eighteen (mean age = 16 years). Fifty-two percent were Caucasian, 21 percent African-American, 13 percent were Arab-American, and the rest were from other minority groups. Sixty-seven percent of the youth were from two-parent married families, 18 percent from single-parent, and the rest were from remarried families. Levels of parent education ranged from less than high school through professional or post-tertiary with an average level of some training beyond high school. Both parent education and the income level of the school district were used as measures of social class in this study.

## Measures: Explanations for Inequality

For the open-ended item, students were asked: "Suppose some people from a foreign country were visiting our country and they asked you to explain some things to them. If you had to explain why some people are unemployed, what would you say?" This same format was repeated for why some people are poor, rich, or homeless. A fixed order was used for the set of open-ended questions with explanations for unemployment followed by poverty, wealth, and homelessness.

Explanations for unemployment, poverty, homelessness, and wealth were coded as distinct questions. Responses were coded for specific detail and Cohen's kappa ranged between .80 and .88 for the four items. Subsequently, these detailed codes were aggregated into three summary categories based on whether they referred to (1) individual or dispositional factors (e.g., the unemployed don't try to find jobs; people are poor because they have problems managing money); (2) situational, societal, or structural factors (e.g., people are unemployed because companies are moving a lot of jobs to Mexico; the reason we have homelessness is the government doesn't provide enough low-income housing); or (3) uncontrollable factors (e.g., good or bad luck—hit the lottery, had a house fire and lost everything).

Because each explanation was coded for two references, it was possible that an adolescent's explanation would include references to both individual and situational factors. Some explanations that were coded at the detailed level could not be assigned to any of the summary categories. For example, the statement, "the unemployed don't have jobs," was coded as a definition. However, because inferences about cause could not be made, it was not assigned to any of the summary categories. Likewise, general references to education were distinguished from references to educational factors under individual control (e.g., "they didn't study hard") as well as from situational/societal references to education (e.g., "their schools weren't very good"). However, no inferences were made about cause implied in the general references to education, and thus general references to education were not included in the summary categories.

## Measures

Adolescents indicated their agreement with items on the survey by choosing a number from a 5-point Likert scale ranging from Strongly Disagree (1) to Strongly Agree (5) or Not at All Important (1) to Very Important (5). These items were then formed into scales. Cronbach's alphas were .70 or higher for the scales.

### BELIEFS ABOUT OPPORTUNITY IN AMERICA

These were the same items in several of the scales discussed in Chapter 2.

## The United States is an equitable society

- Any person who is willing to work hard can make a good living in our country.

- In general, everyone has an equal chance of getting ahead in our society.

## Moral hazard: Government support programs promote dependency

- When the government provides services for free, people tend to get lazy.
- When the government provides services for free, people tend to cheat.

## Family and personal values

### Compassion/social responsibility

- My parents have taught me to be helpful to others, especially those who are less fortunate.
- My parents get upset when they hear about harm or injustice being done to others.
- My parents have taught me to be aware of other people's feelings and needs.
- My parents have taught me to pay attention to other people's needs, not just my own.

### Self-reliance

- My parents tell me if I don't succeed in life, I'll have only myself to blame.
- My parents have told me I should be ready to work twice as hard as other people if I want to get a job.
- My parents have told me you can't blame others for your problems.
- My parents have told me I'd better be able to support myself when I get older.
- My parents want me to have a better life than they had.
- My parents have told me you have to create your own opportunities. Nobody hands them to you.

### Self-transcendence: Altruism

- I would be willing to have fewer luxuries (like nice cars, clothes, or fancy houses) if that would help starving people in other countries.

- I would be willing to have fewer luxuries if that would preserve the earth for future generations.
- Before I make a decision I try to think about how it will affect others.
- In the future when I'm an adult, I would be willing to pay taxes to help the poor or homeless.
- I get mad if I see someone being treated badly.
- In the future when I'm an adult, I would be willing to work fewer hours and earn less income if that would create jobs for unemployed people.

Self-enhancement: Materialism

When you think about your life and your future, how important is each of the following for you personally to achieve?

- Earning a lot of money
- Having nice clothes
- Having a nice home

## Chapter 7

The data for this chapter are drawn from the three-year longitudinal study discussed in Chapter 5. My colleagues and I set out to learn more about social trust and how it develops in a longitudinal study of more than 1,000 early, middle, and late adolescents and their parents whom we followed for three years. In Year 1, the teens were between the ages of ten and eighteen and came from a broad range of social backgrounds and communities—rural and urban, from different racial or ethnic backgrounds, and with family incomes ranging from less than $10,000 to greater than $100,000.

Measures (using Likert-type strongly disagree to strongly agree scales). Cronbach's alphas for scales ranged from .70 to .86.

### TRUST

Social trust (The same items were asked of adolescents and of parents)

- In general, most people can be trusted.
- Most people are fair and don't take advantage of you.

## Interpersonal trust

- My friends can count on me to keep a secret.
- I stick up for my friends when somebody says something mean about them.
- I have friends that I can trust to keep a secret.
- I have friends that I can trust to keep their promises.

## SCHOOL CLIMATE VARIABLES

## Civil climate for learning at school

In my school . . .

- Students can disagree with teachers as long as they are respectful.
- Students have an opportunity to debate and discuss issues.
- Students are encouraged to voice their opinions, even if they are different from what most people think.
- Teachers expect students to respect one another.
- If some students threaten other students, adults will put a stop to it.
- Teachers give all students a fair chance.
- Teachers treat students as individuals, not as members of groups.
- Teachers won't let students make fun of other students.

## Students' feelings of school solidarity

In my school . . .

- Students feel like they are an important part of the school.
- Everyone tries to keep the school looking good.
- Most students take pride in our school.
- Most students seem to care about each other, even people they don't know well.
- Students have a lot of school spirit.

## FAMILY VARIABLES

### Adolescents' reports of democratic parenting in their families

- My parents let me have a say even if they disagree.
- My parents respect my opinions.
- I can talk to my parents about what is bothering me.
- My parents trust me to do what they expect without checking up on me.

### Parents' values of social responsibility and openness toward other people

(N.B. The same wording was used in items for parents and for adolescents [My parents tell me . . . ])
I tell my children . . .

- To be helpful to others, especially the less fortunate.
- To respect people no matter who they are.
- To be aware of other people's feelings and needs.
- To treat everyone equally.
- Not to judge people before you get to know them.
- To stand up for others, not just yourself.
- That everyone deserves a fair chance.

### Parents' values of vigilance/caution toward other people

(N.B. The same wording was used in items for parents and for adolescents (My parents tell me . . . )

- I warn my children that you can't always trust people.
- I warn my children that people sometimes take advantage of you.
- I encourage my children to stick up for their rights if someone tries to push them around.
- I warn my children that there may be times that people will judge you before they get to know you.

## HOW PARENTS DISCUSSED 9/11 WITH THEIR CHILDREN

The following open-ended item was included in the survey that was sent home to parents. The prompt was framed broadly in order to provide parents an opportunity to express the diverse array of potential reactions and interpretations they used with their children.

*Many people have said that September 11th changed everything in the United States. But nobody has asked parents if it had any effect on the way they are raising their children. As a parent, what are your thoughts? Have you talked to your child about it?*

## Chapter 8

In two studies in my program of work—the project on intergroup relations and beliefs about social justice (discussed in Chapter 3) and the longitudinal study (discussed in Chapter 7)—I included items asking teens about their involvement in community service projects. I use the longitudinal data to compare the trajectories over time in social trust and social responsibility for teens who had engaged in community service with their peers who had not. However, the lion's share of the data reported in this chapter were drawn from teens' reports in the first study.

Thus, the analyses for this paper are based on the responses of 1,031 twelve- to eighteen-year-olds who completed surveys in their schools. Those schools were located in low-middle income communities that differed in their racial or ethnic mix. The majority of the students were Caucasian, but there were approximately 350 students from African-American, Arab-American, and Latino backgrounds. Adolescents answered three items about their involvement in extracurricular and volunteer activities: First, they simply checked whether, during the past year, they had been involved in any clubs or volunteer work. Second, if they said that they had done some volunteer work, they were asked to state what they had done. And third, if they had indicated that they had done some volunteer work, they were asked, "Did you learn anything about yourself, about others, or about your community by doing this volunteer work?" Those who indicated that they had learned something from volunteering were asked to report what they had learned.

Of the 1,031 teens who responded to the three previously given items, 567 reported that they were both a member of at least one club and had volunteered during the past year; 116 reported volunteering but no club membership, 211 reported that they belonged to some club but had not volunteered during the past year, and 137 claimed they were neither members of clubs nor had volunteered.

Of those who had done some type of volunteer work, 70 percent said that they had learned something from their experience, and 30 percent said that they had not. According to chi-square tests, there was a significant relationship between the frequency of an individual's volunteering and the likelihood that s/he had learned something: whereas 37 percent of those who viewed volunteering as a learning experience had volunteered once a week for about a year, among those who did not learn from the experience, only 25 percent volunteered at least once a week.

## Measures

Adolescents also responded to items using Likert-type strongly disagree (1) to strongly agree (5) scales. N.B. The social trust and social responsibility scales used in this chapter have been described in earlier chapters. Based on adolescents' reports, the following items factored into three *perceptions of my community* scales:

### COMMUNITY CLIMATE SCALES

## Caring

In my community . . .

- There are people I can ask for help when I need it.
- People trust each other.
- If someone has a problem, they can usually count on others to help them out.
- Most people try to make this a good place to live.
- Most people feel safe.

## Effective in solving our problems

- If there is a problem getting some service from the government, people could get the problem solved.

- People pull together to help each other.
- Every town has some problems. In general, people in my town work together to solve our problems.

## Open

- When someone moves here, people are pretty nice to them.
- People like to meet others from different races and cultures.
- When someone moves here, people make them feel welcome.

# Notes

## Introduction

1. Michael Walzer, "Citizenship," in *Political Innovation and Conceptual Change,* ed. T. Ball, J. Farr, and R. L. Hanson (New York: Cambridge University Press, 1989), 211.

2. Charles Mills, *The Racial Contract* (Ithaca, NY: Cornell University Press, 1997); Carole Pateman, *The Sexual Contract* (Stanford, CA: Stanford University Press, 1988).

3. Constance A. Flanagan and Jacquelynne S. Eccles, "Changes in Parental Work Status and Adolescents' Adjustment at School," *Child Development* 64 (1993): 246–257; Constance A. Flanagan, "Change in Family Work Status: Effects on Parent-Adolescent Decision-making," *Child Development* 61 (1990): 163–177.

4. Jacob S. Hacker, *The Great Risk Shift: The Assault on American Jobs, Families, Health Care, and Retirement and How You Can Fight Back* (Oxford: Oxford University Press, 2006).

5. Jonathan Gould, ed., "Guardian of Democracy: The Civic Mission of Schools," Leonore Annenberg Institute for Civics of the Annenberg Public Policy Center at the University of Pennsylvania and the Campaign for the Civic Mission of Schools, 2010, http://civicmission.s3.amazonaws.com/118/f0/5/171/1/Guardian-of-Democracy-report.pdf.

6. Timothy E. Cook, "The Bear Market in Political Socialization and the Costs of Misunderstood Psychological Theories," *American Political Science Review* 79 (1985): 1080.

## 1. Adolescents' Theories of the Social Contract

1. Jean-Jacques Rousseau, *The Social Contract and the Discourses (Everyman's Library)*, translated by G. D. H. Cole (London: J. M. Dent & Sons, Ltd, 1762/1920), 11.

2. John Locke, *Two Treatises of Government* (Oxford: C. and J. Rivington, 1690/1824).

3. Carole Pateman, *The Sexual Contract* (Cambridge, UK: Polity Press, 1988); Charles Mills, *The Racial Contract* (Ithaca, NY: Cornell University Press, 1997).

4. John T. Jost, M. R. Banaji, and B. A. Nosek, "A Decade of System Justification Theory: Accumulated Evidence of Conscious and Unconscious Bolstering of the Status Quo," *Political Psychology* 25 (2004): 881–920.

5. Stéphane Baldi, Marianne Perie, Dan Skidmore, Elizabeth Greenberg, and Carole Hahn, *What Democracy Means to Ninth-graders: U.S. Results from the International IEA Civic Education Study* (Washington, DC: National Center for Educational Statistics, U.S. Department of Education, 2001).

6. Judith Torney-Purta, John Schwille, and Jo-Ann Amadeo (eds.), *Civic Education across Countries: Twenty-four Case Studies from the IEA Civic Education Project* (Amsterdam: International Association for the Evaluation of Educational Achievement, 1999).

7. Jost, Banaji, and Nosek, "A Decade of System Justification Theory."

8. David Easton, *A Systems Analysis of Political Life* (New York: John Wiley, 1965), 21.

9. Constance Flanagan, Patreese Ingram, Erika M. Gallay, and Erin E. Gallay, "Why Are People Poor? Social Conditions and Adolescents' Interpretation of the 'Social Contract'" in *Social and Emotional Adjustment and Family Relations in Ethnic Minority Families*, ed. Ronald D. Taylor and Margaret C. Wang, (Mahwah, NJ: Erlbaum, 1997), 53–62.

10. The Social Contract Press, www.thesocialcontract.com; Marta Tienda, "Demography and the Social Contract," *Demography* 39 (2002): 587–616.

11. Sheri R. Levy, Chi-yue Chiu, and Ying-yi Hong, "Lay Theories and Intergroup Relations," *Group Processes and Intergroup Relations* 9, no. 1 (2006): 5–24.

12. Donald R. Kinder and Susan T. Fiske, "Presidents in the Public Mind," in *Political Psychology,* ed. Margaret G. Hermann (San Francisco: Jossey-Bass, 1998), 193–218.

13. Constance A. Flanagan and Corinna J. Tucker, "Adolescents' Explanations for Political Issues: Concordance with Their Views of Self and Society," *Developmental Psychology* 35, no. 5 (1999): 1198–1209, doi:10.1037/0012–1649.35.5.1198.

14. Nicholas Emler and Julie Dickinson, "Children's Understanding of Social Class and Occupational Groupings," in *Children's Understanding of Society,* ed. Martin Barrett and Eithne Buchanan-Barrow (East Sussex, UK: Psychology Press, 2005), 191.

15. Guy Standing, *The Precariat: The New Dangerous Class* (London: Bloomsbury Academic, 2011).

16. Henry M. Wellman and Susan Gelman, "Knowledge Acquisition in Foundational Domains," in *Handbook of Child Psychology, Vol. 2. Cognition, Perception, and Language,* 5th ed., ed. D. Kuhn and R. S. Siegler (New York: John Wiley), 523–574.

17. Lev S. Vygotsky, *Mind in Society: The Development of Higher Psychological Processes* (Cambridge, MA: Harvard University Press, 1978).

18. Martyn Barrett, *Children's Knowledge, Beliefs, and Feelings about Nations and National Groups* (East Sussex, UK: Psychology Press, 2007).

19. Judith Torney-Purta, Britt Wilkenfeld, and Carolyn Barber, "How Adolescents in Twenty-seven Countries Understand Support and Practice Human Rights," *Journal of Social Issues* 64, no. 4 (2008): 857–880.

20. Jacqueline J. Goodnow, "Merging Cultural and Psychological Accounts of Family Contexts," in *Bridging Cultural and Developmental Psychology: New Syntheses in Theory, Research and Policy,* ed. Lene Arnett Jensen (New York: Oxford University Press, 2011), 73–91.

21. John L. Sullivan and John E. Transue, "The Psychological Underpinnings of Democracy: A Selective Review of Research on Political Tolerance, Interpersonal Trust, and Social Capital," *Annual Review of Psychology* 50 (1999): 625–650.

22. David Easton and Jack Dennis, "The Child's Acquisition of Regime Norms," *American Political Science Review* 61, no. 1 (1967): 25.

23. Giyoo Hatano and Keiko Takahashi, "The Development of Societal Cognition: A Commentary," in *Children's Understanding of Society,* ed. M. Barrett and E. Buchanan-Barrow (East Sussex, UK: Psychology Press, 2005), 287–303.

24. David S. Crystal, Melanie Killen, and Martin D. Ruck, "Fair Treatment by Authorities Is Related to Children's and Adolescents' Evaluations of Interracial Exclusion," *Applied Developmental Science* 14, no. 3 (2010): 125–136.

25. Timothy E. Cook, "The Bear Market in Political Socialization and the Costs of Misunderstood Psychological Theories," *American Political Science Review* 79 (1985): 1080.

26. Albert Bandura, *Self-efficacy: The Exercise of Control* (New York: W. H. Freeman, 1997), 491.

27. Larry M. Bartels, *Unequal Democracy: The Political Economy of the New Gilded Age* (New York: Russell Sage Foundation / Princeton, NJ: Princeton University Press, 2008); Cathy Cohen and Michael C. Dawson, "Neighborhood Poverty and African American Politics," *American Political Science Review* 87 (1993): 286–302.

28. Judith G. Smetana and Myriam Villalobos, "Social-cognitive Development during Adolescence," in *Handbook of Adolescent Psychology,* ed. Richard L. Lerner and Laurence Steinberg, 3rd ed., vol. 1 (New York: Wiley-Blackwell, 2009), 187–208.

29. For a longer discussion of groupways, see Constance Flanagan, M. Loreto Martinez, Patricio Cumsille, and Tsakani Ngomane, "Youth Civic Development: Theorizing a Domain with Evidence from Different Cultural Contexts," *New Directions for Child and Adolescent Development* 134 (2011): 93–110.

30. Erik H. Erikson, *Identity: Youth and Crisis* (New York: W. W. Norton, 1968), 190.

31. Emler and Dickinson, "Children's Understanding of Social Class," 191.

32. Nancy Eisenberg and Amanda Sheffield Morris, "Moral Cognitions and Prosocial Responding in Adolescence," in *Handbook of Adolescent Psychology,* ed. R. M. Lerner and L. Steinberg, 2nd ed. (Hoboken, NJ: John Wiley, 2004), 155–188.

33. Shalom H. Schwartz and Tammy Rubel, "Sex Differences in Value Priorities: Cross-cultural and Multimethod Studies," *Journal of Personality and Social Psychology* 89, no. 6 (2005): 1010–1028, doi:10.1037/0022–3514.89.6.1010.

34. Sara Jaffee and Janet Shibley Hyde, "Gender Differences in Moral Orientation: A Meta-analysis," *Psychological Bulletin* 126 (2000): 703–726.

35. Vaclav Havel, "Politics, Morality, and Civility," in *Summer Meditation,* trans. P. Wilson (New York: Knopf, 1992), 7.

36. David Easton, *The Political System: An Inquiry into the State of Political Science* (New York: Knopf, 1953); David Easton, *A Systems Analysis of Political Life* (New York: John Wiley, 1965), 21.

37. Shalom H. Schwartz and Wolfgang Bilsky, "Toward a Universal Psychological Structure of Human Values," *Journal of Personality and Social Psychology* 53 (1987): 551.

38. Erikson, *Identity,* 233–235.

39. Shalom H. Schwartz, "Value Priorities and Behavior: Applying of Theory of Integrated Value Systems," in *The Psychology of Values: The Ontario Symposium,* ed. C. Seligman, J. M. Olson, and M. P. Zanna, vol. 8 (Hillsdale, NJ: Erlbaum, 1996), 1–24.

40. Michael J. Sandel, *Democracy's Discontent: America in Search of a Public Philosophy* (Cambridge, MA: Belknap Press, 1996); Rogers M. Smith, "American Conceptions of Citizenship and National Service," *Responsive Community* 3 (Summer 1993): 14–27.

41. M. Kent Jennings, "Generation Units and the Student Protest Movement in the United States: An Intra- and Intergenerational Analysis," *Political Psychology* 23 (2002): 303–324.

42. Howard Schuman and Jacqueline Scott, "Generations and Collective Memories," *American Sociological Review* 54 (1989): 351–381.

43. See the special issue of *Parliamentary Affairs,* 65, 2012, doi:10.1093/pa /gsr056.

44. Robert D. Putnam, *Bowling Alone: The Collapse and Revival of American Community* (New York: Simon & Schuster, 2000).

45. Roderick J. Watts, Matthew A. Diemer, and Adam M. Voight, "Critical Consciousness: Current Status and Future Directions," in "Youth Civic Development: Work at the Cutting Edge," ed. Constance A. Flanagan and Brian D. Christens, special issue, *New Directions for Child and Adolescent Development* 134 (Winter 2011): 43–57.

46. Matthew A. Diemer, "Pathways to Occupational Attainment among Poor Youth of Color: The Role of Sociopolitical Development," *Counseling Psychologist* 37, no. 1 (2009): 6–35. See also contributions by Christens and Kirshner; Seif; and Watts, Diemer, and Voight in the special issue of *New Directions for Child and Adolescent Development* 134 (Winter 2011).

47. Sidney Verba, Nancy Burns, and Kay Lehman Schlozman, "Unequal at the Starting Line: Creating Participatory Inequalities across Generations and among Groups," *American Sociologist* 34, nos. 1–2 (2003): 45–69.

48. Erikson, *Identity,* 258.

49. Erik H. Erikson, *Insight and Responsibility: Lectures on the Ethical Implications of Psychoanalytical Insight* (New York: W. W. Norton, 1964), 126.

## 2. Teens from Different Social Orders

1. David S. Mason, "Justice, Socialism, and Participation in Post-Communist States," in *Social Justice and Political Change: Public Opinion in Capitalist and Post-Communist States,* ed. James R. Kluegel, David S. Mason, and Bernd Wegener (New York: Aldine Degruyter, 1995), 49–80.

2. M. D. R. Evans, Jonathan Kelley, and Tamas Kolosi, "Images of Class: Public Perceptions in Hungary and Australia," *American Sociological Review* 57 (1992): 461–482.

3. Petr Maček, Constance Flanagan, Leslie Gallay, L. Kostron, Luba Botcheva, and Benö Csapó, "Post-Communist Societies in Times of Transition: Perceptions of Change among Adolescents in Central and Eastern Europe," *Journal of Social Issues* 54, no. 3 (1998): 547–560.

4. Ibid.

5. Constance A. Flanagan and Bernadette Campbell, with Luba Botcheva, Jennifer Bowes, Benö Csapó, Peter Maček, and Elena Sheblanova, "Social Class and Adolescents' Beliefs about Justice in Different Social Orders," *Journal of Social Issues* 59, no. 4 (2003): 711–732.

6. Jacqueline Goodnow, Peggy J. Miller, and Frank Kessel, eds., *Cultural Practices as Contexts for Development* (San Francisco: Jossey-Bass, 1995); Peggy J. Miller, "Instantiating Culture through Discourse Practices: Some Personal Reflections on Socialization and How to Study It," in *Ethnography and Human Development: Context and Meaning in Social Inquiry,* ed. R. Jessor, A. Colby, and R. Shweder (Chicago: University of Chicago Press, 1996), 183–204.

7. Jennifer M. Bowes, Constance Flanagan, and Alan J. Taylor, "Adolescents' Ideas about Individual and Social Responsibility in Relation to Children's Household Work: Some International Comparisons," *International Journal of Behavioral Development* 25 (2001): 60–68.

8. Melvin Kohn, "Cross-national Research as an Analytic Strategy," in *Cross-national Research in Sociology,* ed. M. Kohn (Newbury Park, CA: Sage, 1989): 77–103.

9. Constance A. Flanagan, Jennifer Bowes, Britta Jonsson, Benö Csapó, and Elena Sheblanova, "Ties That Bind: Correlates of Adolescents' Civic Commitments in Seven Countries," *Journal of Social Issues* 54, no. 3 (1998): 457–475.

10. Kenneth L. Roberts, "Unemployment without Social Exclusion: Evidence from Young People in Eastern Europe," *International Journal of Sociology and Social Policy* 21 (2001): 118–144.

11. Ibid.

12. Olga Toth, "Hungarian Adolescents' Attitudes toward Their Future, Peace, and the Environment," in *Families as Educators for Global Citizenship,* ed. Judith A. Myers-Walls and Peter Somlai, with Robert Rapoport (Aldershot, UK: Ashgate, 2001): 131–138.

13. Lynne Chisholm and Siyka Kovacheva, *Exploring the European Youth Mosaic: The Social Situation of Young People in Europe* (Strasbourg: Council of Europe, 2002); Claire Wallace, "Young People in Post-Communist Countries: Vanguard of Change or Lost Generation?" in *From Pacesetters to Dropouts: Post-Soviet Youth in Comparative Perspective,* ed. T. Horowitz, B. Kotiik-Friedgut, and S. Hoffman (Lanham, NY: University Press of America, 2003), 3–26.

### 3. We the People

1. National longitudinal studies of high school students in the United States find that public performance is the form of extracurricular involvement that is most predictive of political participation in young adulthood. See D. McFarland and R. Thomas, "Bowling Young: How Youth Voluntary Associations Influence Adult Political Participation," *American Sociological Review* 71 (2006): 401–425.

2. Michael Walzer, *What It Means to Be an American: Essays on the American Experience* (New York: Marsilio, 1992), 23, 27.

3. A total of 569, or 47.5 percent, of the first responses were assigned to a discrete code. The three thematic categories captured 90 percent of these discrete

codes. Fifty-two percent of the respondents either did not answer the question or provided an uncodable response, primarily the former.

4. Michael J. Sandel, *Democracy's Discontent: America in Search of a Public Philosophy* (Cambridge: Harvard University Press, 1996).

5. Percentages discussed in the text reflect the percent of valid (nonmissing and coded) responses.

6. John Updike, "The Individual," *Atlantic Monthly* (November 2007): 14.

7. Marti Hope Gonzales, Eric Riedel, Ian Williamson, Patricia G. Avery, John L. Sullivan, and Angela Bos, "Variations of Citizenship Education: A Content Analysis of Rights, Obligations, and Participation in High School Civic Textbooks," *Theory and Research in Social Education* 32 (2004): 301–325.

8. It is important to remember that this category includes such "error," so to speak, that is, the civic republican/common good category includes respondents who interpret American identity within a liberal framework as well. These two public philosophies need not be at odds; they can be combined, one moderating the other.

9. Sandel, *Democracy's Discontent.*

10. Azar Nafisi, "Sivilization," *Atlantic Monthly* (November 2007): 15, 19.

11. The percentage of responses in the civic republican category were the result of collapsing several discrete codes into one larger category.

12. Rick Kosterman and Seymour Feshbach, "Toward a Measure of Patriotic and Nationalistic Attitudes," *Political Psychology* 10 (1989): 257–274.

13. Michael Walzer, "Civility and Civic Virtue," in *Radical Principles: Reflections of an Unreconstructed Democrat* (New York: Basic Books, 1980), 71.

14. Walzer, *What It Means to Be an American,* 31.

15. Rogers M. Smith, "American Conceptions of Citizenship and National Service," *Responsive Community* 3, no. 3 (Summer 1993): 14–27.

16. Kay Deaux, "To Be an American: Immigration, Hyphenation, and Incorporation," *Journal of Social Issues* 64, no. 4 (2008): 937.

17. Samuel P. Huntington, *Who Are We? The Challenges to America's National Identity* (New York: Simon & Schuster, 2004).

18. Y. J. Huo and L. E Molina, "Is Pluralism a Viable Model of Diversity? The Benefits and Limits of Subgroup Respect," *Group Process and Intergroup Relations* 9 (2006): 359–376.

19. Lene Arnett Jensen, "Immigrant Youth in the United States: Coming of Age among Diverse Civic Cultures," in *Handbook of Research on Civic Engagement in Youth,* ed. L. Sherrod, J. Torney-Purta, and C. Flanagan (Hoboken, NJ: Wiley, 2010), 425–444.

20. Kimber L. Bogard and Lonnie R. Sherrod, "Citizenship Attitudes and Allegiances in Diverse Youth," *Cultural Diversity and Ethnic Minority Psychology* 14, no. 4 (2008): 286–296.

21. Hinda Seif, "The Civic Life of Latina/o Immigrant Youth: Challenging Boundaries and Creating Safe Spaces," in *Handbook of Research on Civic Engagement in Youth,* ed. Lonnie Sherrod, Judith Torney-Purta, and Constance Flanagan (Hoboken, NJ: Wiley, 2010), 445–470.

22. Percentages of first and second responses that fell into the three categories: liberalism/individual rights: 54.3, 45.3; civic republican/common good: 22.2, 35.2; patriotism/loyalty: 23.5, 16.5.

23. A. Valenzuela, *Subtractive Schooling: U.S.-Mexican Youth and the Politics of Caring* (Albany: State University of New York Press, 1999); Hinda Seif, " 'Wise up!' Undocumented Latino Youth, Mexican-American Legislators, and the Struggle for Higher Education," *Latino Studies* 2 (2004): 210–230.

24. Robert N. Bellah, Richard Madsen, William M. Sullivan, Ann Swidler, and Steven M. Tipton, *Habits of the Heart: Individualism and Commitment in American Life* (Berkeley: University of California Press, 1985).

25. In international studies, Torney-Purta and her colleagues also find positive relationships between teens' endorsement of immigrants' rights and their exposure to international topics and open classroom climates at school, and to their general knowledge of human rights. See Judith Torney-Purta, Britt Wilkenfeld, and Carolyn Barber, "How Adolescents in 27 Countries Understand, Support, and Practice Human Rights," *Journal of Social Issues* 64, no. 4 (2008): 857–880, doi:10.1111/j.1540–4560.2008.00592.x.

26. Jean S. Phinney, S. DuPont, C. Espinosa, J. Revill, and K. Sanders, "Ethnic Awareness and American Identification among Ethnic Minority Youths," in *Journeys into Cross-cultural Psychology: Selected Papers from the Eleventh International Association for Cross-Cultural Psychology,* ed. A. Bouvy, F. J. R. van de Vijer, P. Boski, and P. Schmitz (Berwyn, PA: Swets & Zeitlinger, 1994), 167–183. Note, however, that school practices that encourage celebrations of our many diverse cultural roots do enable young people with roots in Europe to appreciate their culture. After sharing with her second-grade classmates the Hungarian history and crafts that her grandfather had supplied, Maggie, our granddaughter, reflected, "I just love our culture."

27. Jean S. Phinney, A. Ong, and T. Madden, "Cultural Values and Intergenerational Value Discrepancies in Immigrant and Non-immigrant Families," *Child Development* 71 (2000): 528–539.

28. Clarence Page, *Showing My Color: Impolite Essays on Race and Identity* (New York: HarperCollins, 1996), 27.

29. Rogers M. Smith, "American Conceptions of Citizenship and National Service," *Responsive Community* 3, no. 3 (Summer 1993): 14–27.

30. Alejandro Portes and Rubén G. Rumbaut, *Legacies: The Story of the Immigrant Second Generation* (Berkeley: University of California Press / New York: Russell Sage Foundation, 2001).

31. Robert L. Selman, "Social-cognitive Understanding: A Guide to Educational and Clinical Practice," in *Moral Development and Behavior: Theory, Research, and Social Issues,* ed. T. Lickona (New York: Holt, Rinehart and Winston, 1976).

32. C. S. Brown and R. S. Bigler, "Children's Perceptions of Discrimination: A Developmental Model," *Child Development* 76 (2005): 533–553.

33. Virginia W. Huynh and Andrew J. Fuligni, "Perceived Ethnic Stigma across the Transition to College," *Journal of Youth and Adolescence* 40, no. 12 (2011), doi:10.1007/s10964-011-9731-x.

34. Beverly Daniel Tatum, *Why Are All the Black Kids Sitting on One Side of the Cafeteria? And Other Conversations about Race* (New York: Basic Books, 1997).

35. Diane Hughes, J. Rodriguez, E. P. Smith, D. J. Johnson, H. C. Stevenson, and P. Spicer, "Parents' Ethnic-racial Socialization Practices: A Review of Research and Directions for Future Study," *Developmental Psychology* 42 (2006): 747–770.

36. Jelani Mandara, Maryse H. Richards, Noni K. Gaylord-Harden, and Brian L. Ragsdale, "The Effects of Changes in Racial Identity and Self-Esteem on Changes in African American Adolescents' Mental Health," *Child Development* 80, no. 6 (2009): 1600–1675; Hughes et al., "Parents' Ethnic-racial Socialization Practices."

37. Diane Hughes and L. Chen, "Parents' Race-related Communications to Children: A Developmental Perspective," in *Child Psychology: A Handbook of Contemporary Issues,* ed. L. Balter and C. S. Tamis-LeMonda (New York: Psychology Press, 1999), 467–490.

38. H. D. Fishbein, *Peer Prejudice and Discrimination: Evolutionary, Cultural, and Developmental Dynamics* (Boulder, CO: Westview, 1996).

39. Jacqueline J. Goodnow, "Merging Cultural and Psychological Accounts of Family Contexts," in *Bridging Cultural and Developmental Psychology: New Syntheses in Theory, Research and Policy,* ed. Lene Arnett Jensen (New York: Oxford University Press, 2011), 73–91.

40. J. S. Phinney and V. Chavira, "Parental Ethnic Socialization and Adolescent Coping with Problems Related to Ethnicity," *Journal of Research on Adolescence* 5 (1995): 31–53.

41. Clark McKown and Michael J. Strambler, "Developmental Antecedents and Social and Academic Consequences of Stereotype-Consciousness in Middle Childhood," *Child Development* 80, no. 2 (2009): 406–417. See also S. M. Quintana, P. Castaneda-English, and V. C. Ybarra, "Role of Perspective-taking Ability and Ethnic Socialization in the Development of Adolescent Ethnic Identity," *Journal of Research on Adolescence* 9 (1999): 161–184.

42. Eleanor K. Seaton, Tiffany Yip, and Robert M. Sellers, "A Longitudinal Examination of Racial Identity and Racial Discrimination Among African American Adolescents," *Child Development* 80 (November–December 2009): 1643–1659.

43. D. Hughes, D. Witherspoon, D. Rivas-Drake, and N. West-Bey, "Received Ethnic-racial Socialization Messages and Youth's Academic and Behavioral Outcomes: Examining the Mediating Role of Ethnic Identity and Self-Esteem," *Cultural Diversity and Ethnic Minority Psychology* 15, no. 2 (2009): 112–124.

44. Deborah Rivas-Drake, "Ethnic-racial Socialization and Adjustment among Latino College Students: The Mediating Roles of Ethnic Centrality, Public Regard, and Perceived Barriers to Opportunity," *Journal of Youth and Adolescence* 40 (2011): 606–619.

45. Phinney et al., "Ethnic Awareness."

46. A similar argument has been made by Margaret Beale Spencer in her article, "American Identity: Impact of Youths' Differential Experiences in Society on Their Attachment to American Ideals," *Applied Developmental Science* 15, no. 2 (2011): 61–69, doi:10.1080/10888691.2011.560806.

47. Rosalind A. Mickelson, "The Attitude-Achievement Paradox among Black Adolescents," *Sociology of Education* 63 (1990): 44–61.

48. Hinda Seif, "The Civic Life of Latina/o Immigrant Youth: Challenging Boundaries and Creating Safe Spaces," in *Handbook of Research on Civic Engagement in Youth,* ed. Lonnie Sherrod, Judith Torney-Purta, and Constance Flanagan (Hoboken, NJ: Wiley, 2010), 445–470.

49. Constance Flanagan, Amy Syvertsen, Sukhdeep Gill, and Leslie Gallay, "Ethnic Awareness, Prejudice, and Civic Commitments in Four Ethnic Groups of American Adolescents," *Journal of Youth and Adolescence* 38, no. 4 (2009): 500–518.

50. M. A. Diemer and D. L. Blustein, "Critical Consciousness and Career Development among Urban Youth," *Journal of Vocational Behavior* 68, no. 2 (2006): 220–232.

51. Robert Pinsky, "Pudd'nheads," *Atlantic Monthly* (November 2007): 42.

52. Congresswoman Barbara Jordan, statement made on July 25, 1974, before the House Committee on the Judiciary.

53. John Dewey, *The Public and Its Problems* (New York: Holt, 1927), 149.

54. Aristotle, "Nicomachean Ethics," in *Introduction to Aristotle,* ed. Richard McKeon, trans. S. D. Ross (New York: Random House, 1947).

55. Constance Flanagan, Patricio Cumsille, Sukhdeep Gill, and Leslie Gallay, "School and Community Climates and Civic Commitments: Processes for Ethnic Minority and Majority Students," *Journal of Educational Psychology* 99, no. 2 (2007): 421–431.

56. J. Torney-Purta, R. Lehmann, H. Oswald, and W. Schulz, *Citizenship and Education in Twenty-eight Countries: Civic Knowledge and Engagement at Age Fourteen* (Amsterdam: International Association for the Evaluation of Educational Achievement, 2001), 138. For more on open classroom climates, see Carole L. Hahn, *Becoming Political: Comparative Perspectives on Citizenship Education* (New

York: State University of New York Press, 1998). For a discussion of handling controversy in classrooms, see Diana Hess, *Controversy in the Classroom: The Democratic Power of Discussion* (New York: Routledge, 2009).

57. Patrick Deneen, *Democratic Faith* (Princeton, NJ: Princeton University Press, 2005), xx.

58. Dewey, *The Public and Its Problems*, 22, 24.

## 4. Democracy

Portions of this chapter were published in Constance A. Flanagan, Leslie S. Gallay, Sukhdeep Gill, Erin E. Gallay, and Naana Nti, "What Does Democracy Mean? Correlates of Adolescents' Views," *Journal of Adolescent Research* 20, no. 2 (2005): 193–218, a SAGE journal.

1. W. Churchill, Speech before the House of Commons on the Parliament Bill, November 22, 1947, in *Churchill by Himself: The Definitive Collection of Quotations*, ed. Richard Langworth (New York: Public Affairs, 2008), 574.

2. Abraham Lincoln, annual message to Congress, December 1, 1862, in *The Collected Works of Abraham Lincoln, Vol. 5* (Piscataway, NJ: Rutgers University Press, 1953), 537.

3. Robert Post, "Democracy and Equality," Yale Law School, Faculty Scholarship Series, Paper 177 (2005), http://digitalcommons.law.yale.edu/fss_papers/177, doi: 10.1177/0002716205282954.

4. R. L. Hanson, "Democracy," in *Political Innovation and Conceptual Change*, ed. T. Ball, J. Farr, and R. L. Hanson (New York: Cambridge University Press, 1989), 69.

5. Erik H. Erikson, *Identity: Youth and Crisis* (New York: W. W. Norton, 1968).

6. When presenting an adolescent's verbatim response, I have included some background information about the individual both to help the reader to imagine the speaker and to emphasize that the teen's social background matters for his or her knowledge and interest in politics.

7. Lev S. Vygotsky, *Mind in Society: The Development of Higher Psychological Processes* (Cambridge, MA: Harvard University Press, 1978).

8. Judith G. Smetana and M. Villalobos, "Social-cognitive Development during Adolescence," in *Handbook of Adolescent Psychology,* ed. Richard L. Lerner and Laurence Steinberg, 3rd ed., vol. 1 (New York: Wiley-Blackwell, 2009), 187–208.

9. Larry M. Bartels, *Unequal Democracy: The Political Economy of the New Gilded Age* (Princeton, NJ: Princeton University Press, 2008); Cathy Cohen and Michael C. Dawson, "Neighborhood Poverty and African American Politics," *American Political Science Review* 87 (1993): 286–302.

10. Hugh McIntosh, Daniel Hart, and James Youniss, "The Influence of Family Political Discussion on Youth Civic Development: Which Parent Qualities Matter?" *PS: Political Science and Politics* 40, no. 3 (2007): 495–499.

11. Molly W. Andolina, Krista Jenkins, Cliff Zukin, and Scott Keeter, "Habits from Home, Lessons from School: Influences on Youth Civic Development," *PS: Political Science and Politics* 36, no. 2 (2003): 275–280; Sidney Verba, Kay Lehman Schlozman, and Henry Brady, *Voice and Equality: Civic Voluntarism in American Politics* (Cambridge, MA: Harvard University Press, 1995).

12. Richard G. Niemi and Jane Junn, *Civic Education: What Makes Students Learn?* (New Haven, CT: Yale University Press, 1998); Diane Owen and Jack Dennis, "Preadult Development of Political Tolerance," *Political Psychology* 8 (1987): 547–561; S. Santoloupo and M. Pratt, "Age, Gender, and Parenting Style Variations in Mother-Adolescent Dialogues and Adolescent Reasoning about Political Issues," *Journal of Adolescent Research* 9 (1994): 241–261.

13. Lake Snell Perry and Associates, *Short-Term Impacts, Long-Term Opportunities: The Political and Civic Engagement of Young Adults in America,* analysis and report for the Center for Information and Research on Civic Learning and Engagement, 2002, available at http://www.civicyouth.org/research/products/National_Youth_Survey/summary.pdf.

14. Julie S. Pacheco, "Political Socialization in Context: The Effect of Political Competition on Youth Voter Turnout," *Political Behavior* 30 (2008): 415–436.

15. Hans Kelsen, *General Theory of Law and State*, translated by Anders Wedberg (New York: Russell and Russell), 285–288, cited in Post, "Democracy and Equality," 28.

16. B. J. Fallon and T. V. P. Bowles, "Family Functioning and Adolescent Help-seeking Behavior," *Family Relations* 50 (2001): 239–245, doi:10.1111/j.1741–3729.2001.00239.x.

17. W. Andrew Collins and Brett Laursen, "Parent-Adolescent Relationships and Influences," in *Handbook of Adolescent Psychology,* ed. Richard M. Lerner and Laurence Steinberg, 2nd ed. (Hoboken, NJ: John Wiley, 2004), 331–361.

18. Carol E. Franz and David C. McClelland, "Lives of Women and Men Active in the Social Protest Movements of the 1960s: A Longitudinal Study," *Journal of Personality and Social Psychology* 66 (1994): 196–205.

19. C. Chapman, M. Nolin, and K. Kline, *Student Interest in National News and Its Relation to School Courses,* NCES 97-970, U.S. Department of Education, National Center for Education Statistics, 1997; M. K. Jennings, "Generation Units and the Student Protest Movement in the United States: An Intra- and Intergenerational Analysis," *Political Psychology* 23 (2002): 303–324; Niemi and Junn, *Civic Education*; Santoloupo and Pratt, "Age, Gender, and Parenting Style Variations"; J. Torney-Purta, "The School's Role in Developing Civic Engagement: A Study of Adolescents in Twenty-eight Countries," *Applied Developmental Science* 6, no. 4 (2002): 203–212; D. McFarland and R. Thomas, "Bowling Young: How Youth Voluntary Associations Influence Adult Political Participation," *American Sociological Review* 71 (2006): 401–425.

20. Joseph Kahne and Ellen Middaugh, "Democracy for Some: The Civic Opportunity Gap in High School," in *Engaging Young People in Civic Life,* ed. James Youniss and Peter Levine (Nashville, TN: Vanderbilt University Press, 2009), 29–58.

21. Robert Atkins and Daniel Hart, "Neighborhoods, Adults, and the Development of Civic Identity in Urban Youth," *Applied Developmental Science* 7, no. 3 (2003): 156–164.

22. Sidney Verba, Nancy Burns, and Kay Lehman Schlozman, "Unequal at the Starting Line: Creating Participatory Inequalities across Generations and Among Groups," *American Sociologist* (Spring–Summer 2003), 45–69.

23. Michael J. Sandel, *Democracy's Discontent: America in Search of a Public Philosophy* (Cambridge, MA: Belknap Press, 1996).

24. Martha C. Nussbaum and Amartya Sen, eds., *The Quality of Life* (Oxford: Oxford University Press, 1993); Amartya Sen, "Well-Being, Agency, and Freedom: The Dewey Lectures," *Journal of Philosophy* 82, no. 4 (1984): 169–221.

25. Walt Whitman, *Democratic Vistas*, with an Introduction by John Valente (New York: Liberal Arts Press, 1888/1949), 21, 26, 21, 29.

26. John L. Sullivan and John E. Transue, "The Psychological Underpinnings of Democracy: A Selective Review of Research on Political Tolerance, Interpersonal Trust, and Social Capital," *Annual Review of Psychology* 50 (1999): 625–650. See also Jean Bethke Elshtain, *Democracy on Trial* (New York: Basic Books, 1995).

27. David Easton, *A Systems Analysis of Political Life* (New York: John Wiley, 1965), 21.

28. Erik H. Erikson, *Identity: Youth and Crisis* (New York: W. W. Norton, 1968), p. 31, p. 187.

29. Ibid.

30. James Youniss and Miranda Yates, *Community Service and Social Responsibility in Youth* (Chicago: University of Chicago Press, 1997).

31. Shalom H. Schwartz, "Are There Universal Aspects in the Structure and Contents of Human Values?" *Journal of Social Issues* 50 (1994): 19–45.

32. Joan E. Grusec and Jacqueline J. Goodnow, "Impact of Parental Discipline Methods on the Child's Internalization of Values: A Reconceptualization of Current Points of View," *Developmental Psychology* 30 (1994): 4–19, doi:10.1037 /0012-1649.30.1.4; Laura Wray-Lake, Constance Flanagan, and Jennifer Maggs, "Examination of a Process Model Linking Maternal Value Socialization and Adolescent Substance Use in a Social Responsibility Framework," under review, 2012.

33. M. W. Pratt, B. Hunsberger, M. Pancer, and S. Alisat, "A Longitudinal Analysis of Personal Values Socialization: Correlates of a Moral Self-ideal in Late Adolescence," *Social Development* 12 (2003): 563–585, doi:10.1111/1467-9507 .00249; B. Verplanken and R. W. Holland, "Motivated Decision Making: Effects

of Activation and Self-centrality of Values on Choices and Behavior," *Journal of Personality and Social Psychology* 82 (2002): 434–447, doi:10.1037/0022-3514 .82.3.434.

34. Abraham H. Maslow, *Motivation and Personality,* 3rd ed. (New York: Harper & Row, 1954); Ronald Inglehart and Paul R. Abramson, "Measuring Postmaterialism," *American Political Science Review* 93, no. 3 (1999): 665–667.

35. Tim Kasser, R. M. Ryan, M. Zax, and A. J. Sameroff, "The Relations of Maternal and Social Environments to Late Adolescents' Materialistic and Prosocial Values," *Developmental Psychology* 31 (1005): 907–914.

36. Robert N. Bellah, Richard Madsen, William M. Sullivan, Ann Swidler, and Stephen M. Tipton, *Habits of the Heart: Individualism and Commitment in American Life* (Berkeley: University of California Press, 1985).

37. Michael Schudson, *The Good Citizen: A History of American Civic Life* (New York: Simon & Schuster, 1998).

38. Whitman, *Democratic Vistas*, 30, 33.

## 5. Laws and Public Health

1. For additional details about methods, see the Appendix.

2. Trends for the past thirty years of increasing motorcyclist deaths and decreasing state mandates for helmet use are documented at http://www.fair warning.org/2012/06/despite-death-toll-motorcycle-groups-strive-to-muzzle-u-s -regulators/.

3. Jeffrey Fagan and Tom R. Tyler. "Legal Socialization of Children and Adolescents," *Social Justice Research* 18, no. 3 (2005), 217–242, DOI:10.1007/ s11211-005-6823-3.

4. Charles Helwig, "Children's Conceptions of Fair Government and Freedom of Speech," *Child Development* 69 (1998): 518–531.

5. Joseph Adelson and Robert P. O'Neil, "Growth of Political Ideas in Adolescence: The Sense of Community," *Journal of Personality and Social Psychology* 4 (1966): 295–306.

6. Philip E. Tetlock, "A Value Pluralism Model of Ideological Reasoning," *Journal of Personality and Social Psychology* 50 (1986): 819–827.

7. Fagan and Tyler, "Legal Socialization of Children."

8. Gustavo Carlo, Lisa J. Crockett, Brandy A. Randall, and Scott C. Roesch, "A Latent Growth Curve Analysis of Prosocial Moral Reasoning," *Journal of Research on Adolescence* 17 (2007): 301–324.

9. Martin D. Ruck and Stacey S. Horn, eds., "Young People's Perspectives on the Rights of the Child: Implications for Theory, Research, and Practice," *Journal of Social Issues* 64, no. 4 (2008): 685–920.

10. Lonnie R. Sherrod, "Adolescents' Perceptions of Rights as Reflected in Their Views of Citizenship," *Journal of Social Issues* 64, no. 4 (2008): 771–790.

11. Charles Helwig, "The Role of Agent and Social Context in Judgments of Freedom of Speech and Religion," *Child Development* 66 (1997): 484–495.

12. Constance Flanagan, Michael Stout, and Leslie Gallay, "It's My Body and None of Your Business: Developmental Changes in Adolescents' Perceptions of Rights concerning Health," *Journal of Social Issues* 64, no. 4 (2008): 815–834.

13. Celia B. Fisher, Adam L. Fried, and Andrea Anushko, "Development and Validation of the College Drinking Influences Survey," *Journal of American College Health* 56 (2007): 217–230, doi:10.3200/JACH.56.3.217-230.

## 6. Inequality

1. Robert L. Leahy, "Development of the Conception of Economic Inequality: II. Explanations, Justifications, and Concepts of Social Mobility and Change," *Developmental Psychology* 19, no. 1 (1983): 111–125.

2. Jacob S. Hacker, *The Great Risk Shift: The Assault on American Jobs, Families, Health Care, and Retirement and How You Can Fight Back* (Oxford: Oxford University Press, 2006).

3. In 1960, the top income tax rate was 91 percent; in 1980, 70 percent; in 1986, 50 percent; in 2000, 39.6 percent; and currently is 35 percent.

4. David S. Johnson, Timothy M. Smeeding, and Barbara Boyce Torrey, "Economic Inequality through the Prisms of Income and Consumption," *Monthly Labor Review* 128 (2005): 11–24; Emmanuel Saez, "Striking It Richer: The Evolution of Top Incomes in the United States," *Pathways Magazine,* Stanford Center for the Study of Poverty and Inequality (Winter 2008): 6–7, updated July 17, 2010, from work in 2003 with Thomas Piketty, http://elsa.berkeley.edu/~saez/saez-UStopincomes-2008.pdf. See also updates by Saez with 2009 and 2010 estimates at http://elsa.berkeley.edu/~saez/saez-UStopincomes-2010.pdf.

5. These data were collected before the market crash of 2008 and the Troubled Asset Relief Program bailout. For additional details, see Constance A. Flanagan and Corinna J. Tucker, "Adolescents' Explanations for Political Issues: Concordance with Their Views of Self and Society," *Developmental Psychology* 35, no. 5 (1999): 1198–1209, doi:10.1037/0012-1649.35.5.1198.

6. Philip Tetlock, "A Value Pluralism Model of Ideological Reasoning," *Journal of Personality and Social Psychology* 50 (1986): 819–827. See also P. Suedfeld, P. E. Tetlock, and S. Streufert, "Conceptual/Integrative Complexity," in *Motivation and Personality: Handbook of Thematic Content Analysis*, ed. C. P. Smith, J. W. Atkinson, D. C. McClelland, and J. Veroff (New York: Cambridge University Press, 1992), 393–400.

7. Shanto Iyengar, "How Citizens Think about National Issues: A Matter of Responsibility," *American Journal of Political Science* 33, no. 4 (1989): 878–900.

8. John G. Nicholls, M. Patashnick, and Susan B. Nolen, "Adolescents' Theories of Education," *Journal of Educational Psychology* 77 (1985): 683–692.

9. Jennifer L. Hochschild, *Facing Up to the American Dream: Race, Class and the Soul of the Nation* (Princeton, NJ: Princeton University Press, 1995). According to Hochschild, these themes of family responsibility echo those found in national opinion polls in which the American public holds parents, and especially mothers, responsible for how children turn out.

10. Charles Murray, *Coming Apart: The State of White America, 1960–2010* (New York: Crown Forum, 2012).

11. Siobhan Austen, "An International Comparison of Attitudes to Inequality," *International Journal of Social Economics* 29, no. 3 (2002): 218–237.

12. Kevin P. Phillips, *Wealth and Democracy: A Political History of the American Rich* (New York: Broadway, 2002).

13. Katherine S. Newman, *Falling from Grace: Downward Mobility in the Age of Affluence* (Berkeley: University of California Press, 1999).

14. Hochschild, *Facing Up to the American Dream*; Jennifer Hochschild, *What's Fair? American Beliefs about Distributive Justice* (Cambridge, MA: Harvard University Press, 1981).

15. Diana Kendall, *Framing Class: Media Representations of Wealth and Poverty in America* (Lanham, MD: Rowman & Littlefield, 2005).

16. Shanto Iyengar, *Is Anyone Responsible?* (Chicago: University of Chicago Press, 1991); M. Sotirovic, "How Individuals Explain Social Problems: The Influence of Media Use," *Journal of Communication* (March 2003): 122–137.

17. Larry M. Bartels, *Unequal Democracy: The Political Economy of the New Gilded Age* (Princeton, NJ: Princeton University Press, 2008), 297; Barbara Ehrenreich, *Nickle and Dimed: On (Not) Getting By in America* (New York: Metropolitan, 2001).

18. John T. Jost, Mahzarin R. Banaji, and Brian A. Nosek, "A Decade of System Justification Theory: Accumulated Evidence of Conscious and Unconscious Bolstering of the Status Quo," *Political Psychology* 25 (2004): 881–920.

19. Joseph E. Kahne and Susan E. Sporte, "Developing Citizens: The Impact of Civic Learning Opportunities on Students' Commitment to Civic Participation," *American Educational Research Journal* 45, no. 3 (2008): 738–766.

20. Tim Kasser, R. M. Ryan, M. Zax, and A. J. Sameroff, "The Relations of Maternal and Social Environments to Late Adolescents' Materialistic and Prosocial Values," *Developmental Psychology* 31 (1995): 907–914; Ronald Inglehart, "Post-materialism in an Environment of Insecurity," *American Political Science Review* 75 (1981): 880–900.

21. Kristin Laurin, Grainne M. Fitzsimons, and Aaron C. Kay, "Social Disadvantage and the Self-Regulatory Function of Justice Beliefs," *Journal of Personality and Social Psychology* 100, no. 1 (2010): 149–171, doi:10.1037/a0021343.

22. John T. Jost, B. W. Pelham, O. Sheldon, and B. N. Sullivan, "Social Inequality and the Reduction of Ideological Dissonance on Behalf of the System:

Evidence of Enhanced System Justification among the Disadvantaged," *European Journal of Social Psychology* 33 (2003): 13–36; Kristin Laurin, Grainne M. Fitzsimons, and Aaron C. Kay, "Social Disadvantage and the Self-Regulatory Function of Justice Beliefs," *Journal of Personality and Social Psychology* 100, no. 1 (2011): 149–171.

23. Danielle A. Crosby and Rashmita S. Mistry, "Children's Causal Attributions for Economic Inequality: Relation to Age and Socioeconomic Environments," manuscript under review.

24. Leahy, "Development of the Conception of Economic Inequality," 113–116. Leahy's sample was much younger (6–18). He coded statements that I consider descriptive (the poor don't have jobs) and ambiguous statements (the poor are not well trained) as references to equity. Thus, there are methodological issues with his claims.

25. Jacob S. Hacker and Paul Pierson, *Winner-Take-All Politics: How Washington Made the Rich Richer—And Turned Its Back on the Middle Class* (New York: Simon & Schuster, 2011).

26. Hacker, *The Great Risk Shift*, 65.

27. Richard Sennett, *The Corrosion of Character: The Personal Consequences of Work in the New Capitalism* (New York: W. W. Norton, 1998), 31.

28. For an argument about the different responses of younger generations to a world ruled by flexible capital, see Constance A. Flanagan, "Private Anxieties and Public Hopes: The Perils and Promise of Youth in the Context of Globalization" in *Figuring the Future: Globalization and the Temporalities of Children and Youth*, ed. Jennifer Cole and Deborah Durham (Santa Fe, NM: School of Advanced Research Press, 2008), 125–150.

29. Sennett, *The Corrosion of Character*, 135.

## 7. Trust

1. Paul Krugman, "Moment of Truth," *New York Times*, October 10, 2009, A29.

2. Megan Tschannen-Moran and Wayne K. Hoy, "A Multidisciplinary Analysis of the Nature, Meaning, and Measurement of Trust," *Review of Educational Research* 70, no. 4 (2000): 547–593.

3. Eric Uslaner, *The Moral Foundations of Trust* (Cambridge: Cambridge University Press, 2002); Tom W. Smith, "Generation Gaps in Attitudes and Values from the 1970s to the 1990s," in *On the Frontier of Adulthood: Theory, Research, and Public Policy*, ed. Richard A. Settersten, Frank F. Furstenberg, and Rubén G. Rumbaut (Chicago: University of Chicago Press, 2005), 177–221.

4. Wendy M. Rahn and John E. Transue, "Social Trust and Value Change: The Decline of Social Capital in American Youth, 1976–1995," *Political Psychology* 19 (1998): 545–565.

5. Morris Rosenberg, "Misanthropy and Political Ideology," *American Sociological Review* 21, no. 6 (1956): 690–695. See also C. Douglas Lummis, *Radical Democracy* (Ithaca, NY: Cornell University Press, 1996).

6. Trudy Grovier, *Social Trust and Human Communities* (Montreal: McGill-Queen's University Press, 1997).

7. Alejandro Portes, "Social Capital: Its Origins and Applications in Modern Sociology," *Annual Review of Sociology* 24 (1998): 1–24.

8. Michael J. Sandel, *Democracy's Discontent: America in Search of a Public Philosophy* (Cambridge, MA: Belknap Press, 1996); Rogers M. Smith, "American Conceptions of Citizenship and National Service," *Responsive Community* 3, no. 3 (1993): 14–27.

9. John L. Sullivan and John E. Transue, "The Psychological Underpinnings of Democracy: A Selective Review of Research on Political Tolerance, Interpersonal Trust, and Social Capital," *Annual Review of Psychology* 50 (1999): 625–650.

10. Julian B. Rotter, "Interpersonal Trust, Trustworthiness, and Gullibility," *American Psychologist* 35, no. 1 (1980): 1–7.

11. Toshio Yamagishi, "Trust as a Form of Social Intelligence," in *Trust in Society,* ed. Karen S. Cook, vol. 2, The Russell Sage Foundation Series on Trust (New York: Russell Sage Foundation, 2001), 121–147.

12. Ken J. Rotenberg, "The Trust-value Basis of Children's Friendships," in *Children's Interpersonal Trust: Sensitivity to Lying, Deception, and Promise Violations,* ed. Ken J. Rotenberg (New York: Springer-Verlag, 1991), 160–172; Ken J. Rotenberg, "Loneliness and Interpersonal Trust," *Journal of Social and Clinical Psychology* 13, no. 2 (1994); 152–173.

13. Uslaner, *The Moral Foundations of Trust*, 14–50. The two types of trust—strategic and moralistic—are discussed in the chapter on these pages.

14. Mark Granovetter, "The Strength of Weak Ties," *American Journal of Sociology* 78 (1973): 1360–1380.

15. In his Youth-Parent Socialization panel study, the political scientist Kent Jennings followed a national high school senior cohort from 1965 into midlife and found that, as adult life settles into somewhat predictable patterns, beliefs about people tend to harden.

16. Robert V. Robinson and Elton F. Jackson, "Is Trust in Others Declining in America? An Age-Period-Cohort Analysis," *Social Science Research* 30 (2001): 117–145; Constance Flanagan and Peter Levine, "Civic Engagement and the Transition to Adulthood," *The Future of Children* 20, no. 1 (Spring 2010): 159–170, doi: 10.1353/foc.0.0043; Laine Briddell, Laura Wray-Lake, Amy K. Syvertsen, Constance A. Flanagan, D. Wayne Osgood, Jerald G. Bachman, Lloyd D. Johnston, Patrick M. O'Malley, and John E. Schulenberg, "Role Transitions and Social Trust: A Study of Late Adolescence," paper presented at the meetings of the Society for Research on Child Development, Denver, April 2009.

17. Erik H. Erikson, *Identity: Youth and Crisis* (New York: W. W. Norton, 1968), 96, 97.

18. Ibid., 96.

19. Ibid., 82.

20. Erik Erikson, *Insight and Responsibility: Lectures on the Implications of Psychoanalytical Insight* (New York: W. W. Norton, 1964), 117. Eric Uslaner also notes the connection between trust and hope and the sense that one is part of a supportive community that is the foundation for both. According to Uslaner, social trust which he refers to as moralistic trust is based on feelings of optimism which has four components—view of future as better than the past; belief that we can control and improve our environment; sense of personal well-being; and of a supportive community. "Optimists believe that tomorrow will be better than today because *they can make it better*" (Uslaner, *The Moral Foundations of Trust*, 81).

21. Jean Piaget, *The Moral Judgment of the Child* (London: Free Press. 1932/1965).

22. Morton Deutsch, "Trust and Suspicion," *Journal of Conflict Resolution* 2 (1958): 265–279.

23. Lummis, *Radical Democracy*, 145.

24. Ibid., 146.

25. Ken J. Rotenberg and Carrie Cerda, "Racially Based Trust Expectancies of Native American and Caucasian Children," *Journal of Social Psychology* 134, no. 5 (1994): 621–631; Ken J. Rotenberg, "Same-sex Patterns and Sex Differences in the Trust-value Basis of Children's Friendships," *Sex Roles* 15, nos. 11–12 (1986): 613–626.

26. Lummis, *Radical Democracy*, 153.

27. In discussing these two sets of values, I use the terms "compassion" and "social responsibility" interchangeably, and likewise the terms "caution," "vigilance," and "guardedness" are understood to refer to the same characteristic.

28. National studies within the United States also find that social trust is higher in more homogeneous communities and states.

29. Constance A. Flanagan and Michael Stout, "Developmental Patterns of Social Trust between Early and Late Adolescence: Age and School Climate Effects," *Journal of Research on Adolescence* 20, no. 3 (2010): 748–773.

30. Julian B. Rotter, "Interpersonal Trust, Trustworthiness, and Gullibility," *American Psychologist* 35, no. 1 (1980): 1–7. See also Yamagishi, "Trust as a Form of Social Intelligence."

31. Lummis, *Radical Democracy*, 153.

32. Toshio Yamagishi, *Trust: The Science of the Mind* (Tokyo: Springer, 2011), 107–131.

33. M. K. Johnson, "Social Origins, Adolescent Experiences, and Work Value Trajectories during the Transition to Adulthood." *Social Forces* 80 (2002): 1307–1341.

34. Briddell et al., "Role Transitions and Social Trust."

35. Jeffrey Jensen Arnett, "Emerging Adulthood: A Theory of Development from the Late Teens through the Twenties," *American Psychologist* 55 (2000): 469–480.

36. Roy F. Baumeister and Mark R. Leary, "The Need to Belong: Desire for Interpersonal Attachments as a Fundamental Human Motivation," *Psychological Bulletin* 117 (1995): 497–529.

37. Robert D. Putnam, *Bowling Alone: The Collapse and Revival of American Community* (New York: Simon & Schuster, 2000), 138.

38. Tom Smith, "Factors Related to Misanthropy in Contemporary American Society," *Social Science Research* 26 (1997): 170–196. Since 1972 the General Social Survey has conducted research on the structure and development of American society with data collection designed to monitor change within the United States and to compare the United States with other nations.

39. Uslaner, *The Moral Foundations of Trust.*

40. Constance Flanagan, Patreese Ingram, Erika Gallay, and Erin Gallay, "Why Are People Poor? Social Conditions and Adolescents' Interpretation of the 'Social Contract,'" in *Social and Emotional Adjustment and Family Relations in Ethnic Minority Families,* ed. Ronald D. Taylor and Margaret C. Wang (Mahwah, NJ: Erlbaum), 53–62.

41. Grazyna Kochanska and Ross A. Thompson, "The Emergence and Development of Conscience in Toddlerhood and Early Childhood," in *Parenting and Children's Internalization of Values: A Handbook of Contemporary Theory,* ed. Joan E. Grusec and Leon Kuczynski (New York: Wiley, 1997), 53–77; Nancy Eisenberg and Amanda Sheffield Morris, "Moral Cognition and Prosocial Responding in Adolescence," in *Handbook of Adolescent Psychology,* ed. Richard M. Lerner and Laurence Steinberg, 2nd ed. (Hoboken, NJ: Wiley, 2004), 155–188; S. D. Madsen, "Parents' Management of Adolescents' Romantic Relationships through Dating Rules: Gender Variations and Correlates of Relationship Qualities," *Journal of Youth and Adolescence* 37 (2008): 1044–1058, doi: 10.1007/s10964-008-9313-8.

42. Hava Rachel Gordon, "Gendered Paths to Teenage Political Participation: Parental Power, Civic Mobility, and Youth Activism," *Gender and Society* 22 (2008): 31–55.

43. I have decided to summarize the data for mothers as more mothers than fathers responded to the surveys.

44. Laura Wray-Lake and Constance Flanagan, "Parenting Practices and the Development of Adolescents' Social Trust," *Journal of Adolescence* 35, no. 3 (2012): 549–560, doi: 10.1016/j.adolescence.2011.09.006.

45. Joan E. Grusec and Jacqueline J. Goodnow, "Impact of Parental Discipline Methods on the Child's Internalization of Values: A Reconceptualization of Current Points of View," *Developmental Psychology* 30 (1994): 4–19, doi: 10.1037/0012-1649.30.1.4.

46. Alfonso J. Damico, Margaret M. Conway, and Sandra B. Damico, "Patterns of Political Trust and Mistrust: Three Moments in the Lives of Democratic Citizens," *Polity* 32, no. 3 (2002): 377–400; Uslaner, *The Moral Foundations of Trust*.

47. Gallup, "Confidence in Congress: Lowest Ever for Any U.S. Institution," June 20, 2008, http://www.gallup.com/poll/108142/Confidence-Congress-Lowest-Ever-Any-US-Institution.aspx.

48. Dewey G. Cornell, *School Violence: Fears vs. Facts* (Mahwah, NJ: Erlbaum, 2006).

49. Tara Stoppa and Constance Flanagan, "School Trust and the Civic Incorporation of Youth: Perceptions of Schools as Institutions and Local Entities," manuscript under review, 2012.

50. Reasons given by the 37 percent of parents who felt that schools were equally or more trustworthy included more teacher involvement, increased security and policy changes that had improved the climate for learning, and better laws and community involvement.

51. Robert D. Putnam, *Making Democracy Work: Civic Traditions in Modern Italy* (Princeton: Princeton University Press, 1993).

52. Uslaner, *The Moral Foundations of Trust*.

53. John Dewey, *The Public and Its Problems* (New York: Holt, 1927), 142.

54. For a review of relevant studies, see Flanagan and Stout, "Developmental Patterns of Social Trust."

55. Uslaner, *The Moral Foundations of Trust*.

56. Baumeister and Leary, "The Need to Belong"; Tschannen-Moran and Hoy, "The Nature, Meaning, and Measurement of Trust."

57. Flanagan and Stout, "Developmental Patterns of Social Trust."

58. Damico, Conway, and Damico, "Patterns of Political Trust and Mistrust"; Uslaner, *The Moral Foundations of Trust*.

59. Deborah Meier, *In Schools We Trust: Creating Communities of Learning in an Era of Testing and Standardization* (Boston: Beacon, 2002), 14.

60. J. M. Orbell, A. van de Kragt, and R. M. Dawes, "Explaining Discussion-induced Cooperation," *Journal of Personality and Social Psychology* 54 (1988): 811–819.

61. We found convergent evidence for these positive relationships between teens' social trust and their reports of student solidarity and civil climates at school in the aforementioned civic education study conducted over one semester.

62. Amy K. Syvertsen, Constance A. Flanagan, and Michael D. Stout, "Code of Silence: Students' Perceptions of School Climate and Willingness to Intervene in a Peer's Dangerous Plan," *Journal of Educational Psychology* 101 (2009): 219–232.

63. Michael D. Resnick, P. S. Bearman, R. W. Blum, K. E. Bauman, K. M. Harris, J. Jones, J. Tabor, T. Beuhring, R. E. Sieving, M. Shew, M. Ireland, L. H.

Bearinger, and J. R. Udry, "Protecting Adolescents from Harm: Findings from the National Longitudinal Study on Adolescent Health," *Journal of the American Medical Association* 278, no. 10 (1997): 823–832.

64. Naomi N. Duke, C. L. Skay, S. L. Pettingell, and Iris W. Borowsky, "From Adolescent Connections to Social Capital: Predictors of Civic Engagement in Young Adulthood," *Journal of Adolescent Health* 44 (2008): 161–168.

65. Joseph E. Kahne and Susan E. Sporte, "Developing Citizens: The Impact of Civic Learning Opportunities on Students' Commitment to Civic Participation," *American Educational Research Journal* 45, no. 3 (2008): 738–766.

66. Tara Stoppa, Laura Wray-Lake, Amy K. Syvertsen, and Constance A. Flanagan, "Defining a Moment in History: Parent Communication with Adolescents about September 11th, 2001," *Journal of Youth and Adolescence* 40, no. 12 (2011): 1691–1704, doi: 10.1007/s10964-011-9676-0.

67. J. A. Davis, "Did Growing Up in the 1960s Leave a Permanent Mark on Values and Attitudes?" *Public Opinion Quarterly* 68, no. 2 (2004): 161–183.

68. J. Greenberg, S. Solomon, and T. Pyszczynski, "Terror Management Theory of Self-esteem and Cultural World Views: Empirical Assessments and Conceptual Refinements," *Advances in Experimental Social Psychology* 29 (1997): 61–139.

69. Christia Spears Brown, Rashmita S. Mistry, and Rebecca S. Bigler, "Hurricane Katrina: African American Children's Perceptions of Race, Class, and Government Involvement amid a National Crisis," *Analyses of Social Issues and Public Policy* 7 (2007): 191–208.

70. Erikson, *Identity*, 235–236.

71. Richard Sennett, *The Corrosion of Character: The Personal Consequences of Work in the New Capitalism* (New York: W. W. Norton, 1998), 135.

72. Lummis, *Radical Democracy*, 151, 153.

### 8. Community Service

1. I use the terms "community service," "service learning," and "volunteer work" interchangeably in this chapter. Although scholars make distinctions between these terms, those distinctions are not relevant to the arguments put forth in this chapter.

2. Andrew Furco and Susan Root, "Research Demonstrates the Value of Service Learning," *Phi Delta Kappan* 91, no. 5 (2010): 16–20; J. A. Schmidt, L. Shumow, and H. Kackar, "Adolescents' Participation in Service Activities and Its Impact on Academic, Behavioral, and Civic Outcomes," *Journal of Youth and Adolescence* 36, no. 2 (2007): 127–140.

3. Daniel Hart, Thomas M. Donnelly, James Youniss, and Robert Atkins, "High School Community Service as a Predictor of Adult Voting and Volunteering," *American Educational Research Journal* 44, no. 1 (2007): 197–219.

4. Hart et al., "High School Community Service as a Predictor."

5. Miranda Yates and James Youniss, "Community Service and Political-Moral Identity in Adolescents," *Journal of Research on Adolescence* 6 (1997): 271–284.

6. Sidney Verba, Kay Lehman Schlozman, and Henry Brady, *Voice and Equality: Civic Voluntarism in American Politics* (Cambridge, MA: Harvard University Press, 1995).

7. Toby Walker, "Service as a Pathway to Political Participation: What Research Tells Us," *Applied Developmental Science* 6, no. 4 (2002): 183–188.

8. Sara M. Evans and Harry C. Boyte, *Free Spaces: The Sources of Democratic Change in America* (Chicago: University of Chicago Press, 1992).

9. Jane Addams, *Twenty Years at Hull House* (New York: Macmillan, 1910).

10. William A. Galston, "Political Knowledge, Political Engagement, and Civic Education," *Annual Review of Political Science* 4 (2001): 217–234.

11. Shelley H. Billig, "Research on K–12 School-Based Service-Learning: The Evidence Builds," *Phi Delta Kappan* 81, no. 9 (2000): 658–664.

12. It also is noteworthy that many new models of youth training programs, such as Youth Build and the National Guard Youth ChalleNGe program, include service to the community as part of the training. The implication is that young people have something to contribute right away, that their training may enhance their skills but that they need not wait to finish training before they are able to make a contribution. Further, by combining service with training, these new youth development models may communicate that civic contribution and work can go hand in hand.

13. Jacquelynne S. Eccles and Bonnie L. Barber, "Student Council, Volunteering, Basketball, or Marching Band: What Kind of Extracurricular Participation Matters?" *Journal of Adolescent Research* 14, no. 1 (1999): 10–43.

14. For a review, see Constance Flanagan and Matthew Bundick, "Civic Engagement and Psychosocial Well-being in College Students," *Liberal Education* 97, no. 2 (2011): 20–27.

15. P. A. Thoits and L. N. Hewitt, "Volunteer Work and Well-being," *Journal of Health and Social Behavior* 42 (June 2001): 115–131.

16. N. Pearce and R. Larson, "The Process of Motivational Change in a Civic Activism Organization," *Applied Developmental Science* 10, no. 3 (2006): 121–131.

17. A. M. Omoto, M. Snyder, and J. D. Hackett, "Personality and Motivational Antecedents of Activism and Civic Engagement," *Journal of Personality* 78 (2010): 1703–1734.

18. S. G. Post, "Altruism, Happiness and Health: It's Good to Be Good," *International Journal of Behavioral Medicine* 12, no. 5 (2005): 66–77.

19. Tim Kasser and Richard M. Ryan, "Be Careful What You Wish For: Optimal Functioning and the Relative Attainment of Intrinsic and Extrinsic

Goals," in *Life Goals and Well-Being: Towards a Positive Psychology of Human Striving,* ed. P. Schmuck and K. M. Sheldon (Seattle: Hogrefe, 2001), 116–131.

20. Verba, Schlozman, and Brady, *Voice and Equality,* 10–23.

21. Robert A. Emmons and Michael E. McCullough, "Counting Blessings versus Burdens: An Experimental Investigation of Gratitude and Subjective Well-being in Daily Life," *Journal of Personality and Social Psychology* 84, no. 2 (2003): 377–389.

22. Lev S. Vygotsky, *Mind in Society: The Development of Higher Psychological Processes* (Cambridge, MA: Harvard University Press, 1978), 163.

23. John Dewey, *Democracy and Education: An Introduction to the Philosophy of Education* (New York: Macmillan, 1916), 83.

24. Bill Bishop, *The Big Sort: Why the Clustering of Like-minded Americans Is Tearing Us Apart* (New York: Houghton Mifflin, 2008); Larry M. Bartels, *Unequal Democracy: The Political Economy of the New Gilded Age* (New York: Russell Sage Foundation/Princeton, NJ: Princeton University Press, 2008).

25. Robert D. Putnam and David E. Campbell, *American Grace: How Religion Divides and Unites Us* (New York: Simon & Schuster, 2010).

26. David Myers and Helmut Lamm, "The Group Polarization Phenomenon," *Psychological Bulletin* 83, no. 4 (1976): 602–627; Serge Moscovici and Marissa Zavaloni, "The Group as a Polarizer of Attitudes," *Journal of Personality and Social Psychology* 1, no. 2 (1969): 125–135; Cass R. Sunstein, *Why Societies Need Dissent* (Cambridge, MA: Harvard University Press, 2003).

27. Cass R. Sunstein, *Republic.com 2.0* (Princeton, NJ: Princeton University Press, 2007).

28. Martyn Barrett, *Children's Knowledge, Beliefs, and Feelings about Nations and National Groups* (New York: Psychology Press, 2007); Ken J. Rotenberg, "Same-sex Patterns and Sex Differences in the Trust-Value Basis of Children's Friendship," *Sex Roles* 15, nos. 11–12 (1986): 613–626; K. J. Rotenberg and C. Cerda, "Racially Based Trust Expectancies of Native American and Caucasian Children," *Journal of Social Psychology* 134, no. 5 (1994): 621–631.

29. Thomas F. Pettigrew, "Inter-group Contact Theory," *Annual Review of Psychology* 49 (1998): 65–85; Thomas F. Pettigrew and Linda R. Tropp, "Does Inter-group Contact Reduce Prejudice: Recent Meta-analytic Findings," in *Reducing Prejudice and Discrimination*, ed. Stuart Oskamp, Claremont Symposium on Applied Social Psychology Series (Mahwah, NJ: Erlbaum, 2000), 93–114; Barrett A. Lee, Chad R. Farrell, and Bruce G. Link, "Revisiting the Contact Hypothesis: The Case of Public Exposure to Homelessness," *American Sociological Review* 69 (February 2004): 40–63.

30. Eric Uslaner, *The Moral Foundations of Trust* (Cambridge: Cambridge University Press, 2002).

31. Ed Metz and James Youniss, "Longitudinal Gains in Civic Development through School-based Required Service," *Political Psychology* 26 (2005): 413–437.

32. Morris Rosenberg, "Misanthropy and Political Ideology," *American Sociological Review* 24 (1956): 690–695.

33. Paul A. Miller, Nancy Eisenberg, Richard A. Fabes, and Rita Shell, "Relations of Moral Reasoning and Vicarious Emotion to Young Children's Prosocial Behavior toward Peers and Adults," *Developmental Psychology* 32 (1996): 210–219.

34. Carmen Hamilton and Constance Flanagan, "Reframing Social Responsibility within a Technology-based Youth Activist Program," *American Behavioral Scientist* 51, no. 3 (2007): 444–464.

35. Rogers M. Smith, "American Conceptions of Citizenship and National Service," *Responsive Community* (Summer 1993): 14–26: 25, 26.

36. Franklin D. Gilliam Jr. and Susan Nall Bales, "Strategic Frame Analysis: Reframing America's Youth," *Society for Research in Child Development Social Policy Report* 15, no. 3 (2001): 1–15.

37. Jacquelynne S. Eccles and Bonnie L. Barber, "Student Council, Volunteering, Basketball, or Marching Band: What Kind of Extracurricular Involvement Matters?" *Journal of Adolescent Research* 14, no. 1 (1999): 10–43.

38. Roy F. Baumeister and Mark R. Leary, "The Need to Belong: Desire for Interpersonal Attachments as a Fundamental Human Motivation," *Psychological Bulletin* 117 (1995): 497–529.

39. Michael Resnick, Peter Bearman, Robert Blum, Karl Bauman, Kathleen Harris, Jo Jones, Joyce Taboe, Trish Beuhring, Renee Sieving, Marcia Shew, Marjorie Ireland, Linda H. Bearinger, and J. Richard Udry, "Protecting Adolescents from Harm; Findings from the National Longitudinal Study of Adolescent Health," *Journal of the American Medical Association* 278, no. 10 (1997): 823–832; Jacquelynne S. Eccles and Jennifer A. Gootman, *Community Programs to Promote Youth Development* (Washington, DC: National Academy Press, 2002).

40. Naomi N. Duke, Carol L. Skay, Sandra L. Pettingell, and Iris W. Borowsky, "From Adolescent Connections to Social Capital: Predictors of Civic Engagement in Young Adulthood," *Journal of Adolescent Health* 44, no. 2 (2009): 161–168.

41. Allen M. Omoto, Mark Snyder, and J. D. Hackett, "Personality and Motivational Antecedents of Activism and Civic Engagement," *Journal of Personality* 78 (2010): 1703–1734.

42. Edward Metz, Jeffrey McLellan, and James Youniss, "Types of Voluntary Service and Adolescents' Civic Development," *Journal of Adolescent Research* 18, no. 2 (2003): 188–203.

43. Daniel A. McFarland and R. Jack Thomas, "Bowling Young: How Youth Voluntary Associations Influence Adult Political Participation," *American Sociological Review* 71 (2006): 416.

44. Uslaner, *The Moral Foundations of Trust.*

45. The terms "club" and "vol." are used as shorthand in Figure 8.4.

46. Mark Pancer, Michael Pratt, Bruce Hunsberger, and Susan Alisat, "Community and Political Involvement in Adolescence: What Distinguishes the Activists from the Uninvolved?" *Journal of Community Psychology* 35, no. 6 (2007): 741–759.

47. Shep Zeldin, A. K. McDaniel, D. Topitzes, and M. Calvert, *Youth in Decision-Making: A Study on the Impacts of Youth on Adults and Organizations* (Chevy Chase, MD: National 4-H Council, 2000).

48. Ben Kirshner, "Guided Participation in Three Youth Activism Organizations: Facilitation, Apprenticeship, and Joint Work," *Journal of the Learning Sciences* 17, no. 1 (2008): 60–101.

49. Jean-Jacques Rousseau, *The Social Contract or Principles of Political Right, 1762,* trans. Maurice Cranston (London: Penguin, 1953), 36.

50. Erik Amnå and Par Zetterberg, "A Political Science Perspective on Socialization Research: Young Nordic Citizens in a Comparative Light," in *Handbook of Research on Civic Engagement in Youth,* ed. L. Sherrod, J. Torney-Purta, and C. Flanagan (Hoboken, NJ: Wiley, 2010), 43–66.

51. Laura Wray-Lake, Constance A. Flanagan, and D. Wayne Osgood, "Examining Trends in Adolescent Environmental Attitudes, Beliefs, and Behaviors across Three Decades," *Environment and Behavior* 42, no. 1 (2010): 61–85.

52. David Easton, *The Political System: An Inquiry into the State of Political Science* (New York: Knopf, 1953); David Easton, *A Systems Analysis of Political Life* (New York: John Wiley, 1965), 21.

53. Peter Levine and Ann Higgins-D'Alessandro, "Youth Civic Engagement: Normative Issues," in *Handbook of Research on Civic Engagement in Youth,* ed. Lonnie Sherrod, Judith Torney-Purta, and Constance Flanagan (Hoboken, NJ: Wiley, 2010), 115–138.

54. Hannah Arendt, *The Human Condition* (Chicago: University of Chicago Press, 1958), 50.

## Coda

1. Timothy E. Cook, "The Bear Market in Political Socialization and the Costs of Misunderstood Psychological Theories," *American Political Science Review* 79 (1985): 1080.

2. Michael McDevitt and Spiro Kiousis, "Experiments in Political Socialization: Kids Voting USA as a Model for Civic Education Reform," Working Paper No. 49, Center for Information and Research on Civic Learning and Engagement, University of Maryland, College Park, MD, 2006, http://www.civicyouth.org.

3. Sarah M. Evans and Harry C. Boyte, *Free Spaces: The Sources of Democratic Change in America* (Chicago: University of Chicago Press, 1992).

4. Stephen T. Russell, Anna Muraco, Aarti Subramaniam, and Carolyn Laub, "Youth Empowerment and High School Gay-Straight Alliances," *Journal of Youth and Adolescence* 38 (2009): 891–903.

5. Michael Schudson, *The Good Citizen: A History of American Civic Life* (New York: Simon & Schuster, 1998), 309.

6. David G. Myers and Helmut Lamm, "The Polarizing Effect of Group Discussion," *American Scientist* 63 (1975): 297–303.

7. John Dewey, *Democracy and Education: An Introduction to the Philosophy of Education* (New York: Macmillan, 1916), 83.

8. Barrett A. Lee, Chad R. Farrell, and Bruce G. Link, "Revisiting the Contact Hypothesis: The Case of Public Exposure to Homelessness," *American Sociological Review* 68 (2004): 40–63.

9. David E. Campbell, "Sticking Together: Classroom Diversity and Civic Education," *American Politics Research* 35, no. 1 (2007): 57–78; David E. Campbell, "Voice in the Classroom: How an Open Classroom Environment Facilitates Adolescents' Civic Development," Working Paper No. 28, Center for Information and Research on Civic Learning and Engagement, Medford, MA, February 2005, http://www.civicyouth.org/circle-working-paper-28-voice-in-the-classroom-how-an -open-classroom-environment-facilitates-adolescents-civic-development/.

10. Diana E. Hess, *Controversy in the Classroom: The Democratic Power of Discussion* (New York: Routledge, 2009).

11. James Youniss and Miranda Yates, *Community Service and Social Responsibility in Youth* (Chicago: University of Chicago Press, 1997).

12. Public goods games are experimental economics games used to assess participants' allocation of resources to the self or the common or public good.

13. James H. Fowler and Nicholas A. Christakis, "Cooperative Behavior Cascades in Human Social Networks," *Proceedings of the National Academy of Sciences* 107, no. 12: 5334–5338, www.pnas.org/cgi/doi/10.1073/pnas.0913149107.

14. Peter Levine and Ann Higgins-D'Alessandro, "Youth Civic Engagement: Normative Issues," in *Handbook of Research on Civic Engagement in Youth,* ed. Lonnie Sherrod, Judith Torney-Purta, and Constance Flanagan (Hoboken, NJ: Wiley, 2010), 115–138.

## Appendix

1. Laura Wray-Lake, Constance A. Flanagan, and Jennifer L. Maggs, "Socialization in Context: Exploring Longitudinal Correlates of Mothers' Value Messages of Compassion and Caution," *Developmental Psychology* 48, no. 1 (2011): 25–56, doi: 10.1037/a0026083.

2. James R. Kluegel, David S. Mason, and Bernd Wegener, eds., *Social Justice and Political Change: Public Opinion in Capitalist and Post-Communist States* (New York: Aldine de Gruyter, 1995).

3. Amos Tversky and Daniel Kahneman, "Availability: A Heuristic for Judging Frequency and Probability," *Cognitive Psychology* 5 (1973): 207–232; Roy F. Baumeister and Brad J. Bushman, *Social Psychology and Human Nature,* 2nd ed. (Belmont, CA: Thomson Wadsworth, 2008).

# Acknowledgments

Many organizations and individuals provided support and guidance as I imagined this project and brought it to this stage. My program of work was launched with a Scholars Award from the William T. Grant Foundation. The financial support was important, but the fact that the foundation was prepared to take a chance on these ideas gave me the confidence to pursue them. The Jacobs Foundation provided support that enabled my colleagues and me to collect the data in the cross-national study. The Carnegie Corporation of New York funded the project on adolescents' views of their ethnic and American identities and theories about democracy. Other parts of the program of work were supported by CIRCLE (the Center for Information and Research on Civic Learning and Engagement), the National Institute on Drug Abuse (RO1 DA13434-01A1), the Annenberg Foundation, the Corporation for National and Community Service, the MacArthur Foundation's Network on Transitions to Adulthood, and Penn State's Children, Youth, and Families Consortium. A fellowship from Penn State's Rock Ethics Institute and a workshop on globalization and the temporalities of youth organized by Jennifer Cole and Deborah Durham at the School of Advanced Research provided opportunities to think and write on teens' theories about inequality. A resident fellowship from the Spencer Foundation provided time for an uninterrupted period of writing. It was in the supportive atmosphere at the foundation that I started to see light at the end of the tunnel.

I thank Lonnie Sherrod for his early and steady encouragement on this project and Peter Levine and Jim Youniss who helped to nurture, through countless conversations, many of the themes in this book. Mark Pancer and Mike Pratt were early advocates who introduced me to integrative complexity coding techniques. Mark also played a major role in the data analyses for the chapter on laws. I am grateful to colleagues in the cross-national study—Jenny Bowes, Luba Botcheva, Benö Csapó, Petr Maček, Britta Jonsson, Elena Sheblanova, and Irina Averina—and to Patricio Cumsille, Loreto Martinez, Tsakani Ngomane, Andy Dawes, and Linda Richter for introducing me to other cultural contexts where adolescents explore the terms of their nations' social contracts. Thanks to Jacque Eccles for encouraging me to pursue this line of work and to Toby Jayaratne, my mother, and my siblings for persistent political discussions. I am indebted to Erika MacGregor and Erin Gallay for conducting focus groups and coding data in the days prior to funding when this project was in its infancy.

Others whose insights and encouragement have nourished this work include Erik Amnå, Dennis Barr, Martyn Barrett, Debbie Belle, Dale Blythe, Lynne Borden, Mark Brennan, Christy Buchanan, Barry Checkoway, Jeremy Cohen, Ann Colby, Bill Damon, Michael Delli Carpini, Matt Diemer, Pat Dolan, Helmut Fend, Michelle Fine, Lew Friedland, Jeff Froh, Andy Furco, Shawn Ginwright, Kathleen Hall Jamieson, Steve Hamilton, Dan Hart, Diana Hess, Ann Higgins-D'Alessandro, Stacey Horn, Marc Hooghe, Lene Jensen, Joe Kahne, Ron Kassimir, Margaret Kerr, Ben Kirshner, Reed Larson, Rich Lerner, Roger Levesque, Nancy Love, Vonnie McLoyd, Alan Melchior, Rashmita Mistry, Laura Nissen, Peter Noack, Wayne Osgood, Danny Perkins, Anne Petersen, David Post, Bob Putnam, Susan Root, Martin Ruck, Stephen Russell, Hinda Seif, Scott Seider, Bob Selman, Rick Settersten, Rainer Silbereisen, Carmen Siriani, Margaret Beale Spencer, Håkan Stattin, Dietland Stolle, Judith Torney-Purta, Chico Villarruel, Rod Watts, Jon Zaff, Shep Zeldin, and Marc Zimmerman.

Research is a collaborative endeavor and I would like to acknowledge the graduate students, postdocs, and colleagues who worked on various pieces of the project: Tara Stoppa, Andrea Finlay, Mike Stout, Suet-ling Pong, Monika Buhl, Carmen Hamilton, Nakesha Faison, Jon Boateng, Sam Duo, Beth Van Horn, Bernadette Campbell, Purandhar Dhital, Susan Masters-Chyczewski, Corinna Jenkins Tucker, Elvira Elek, Taehan Kim, and Claudia Mincemoyer. I owe a special debt of gratitude to Sukhdeep Gill who went beyond the call of duty in managing the project on ethnic and American identities, and to Amy Syvertsen and Laura Wray-Lake for their dedicated work on data analyses and commitment to building the field of youth civic development. Michael Cole deserves credit for suggesting this book and Elizabeth Knoll for urging me to do it. I also am grateful to four anonymous reviewers for very helpful guidance on revising the original manuscript.

There would be no book without the insights shared by thousands of adolescents and many of their parents. I thank them as well as the teachers and principals who continue to believe in the civic purposes of public education and who welcomed us into their schools. Finally, a special thank you to Les Gallay, my steady companion whose counsel and collaboration has seen me through this and many other life projects.

# Index

Addams, Jane, 199–200

Add Health, 191

Adelson, Joseph, 125

adolescents: affective feelings for the polity, 19–21; changes in political theories between early and late adolescence, 8, 23, 228; as citizens in the making, 203; come to appreciate that there is more than one side to an issue, 131, 228, 232, 233; in community-based groups, 47–48, 93–95; community service by, 197–226; contemporary life in Central and Eastern Europe, 48–49; controversy as motivator of political interest and action, 92, 233–35; on democracy, 12–13, 87–111; from different social orders, 35–49; differing views on role of the state, 12–13, 37–39; feeling American and being aware of their ethnic roots, 68–81; identity exploration by, 33, 104, 175, 195, 198, 223, 227; on inequality, 16, 134–60, 228, 235; and laws and public health, 112–33; lay theories of politics of, 3, 16–17, 227–29; in mediating institutions, 18–19, 21–23, 229; mini-polities of, 2–3, 18–19; political identities take shape in adolescence and young adulthood, 30, 53; social contract as constructed by, 3, 6, 7, 10–34, 39–41; social trust in, 161–96, 228; stereotypes of, 217–18, 223, 229; values in theories about social contract, 45–47; on what it means to be an American, 50–86; why we should pay attention to their political development, 32–34

adult role models, 222–23

alcohol use: social consequences of, 132. *See also* drunk driving (DUI) law

allowances, 45

altruism: in civic republicanism, 66; endorsement of government role correlated with, 45–46; and meaning of democracy, 105, 106, 107, 108, 109; relational self-interest contrasted with, 225

American Dream: community service and learning about challenges to achieving, 208; erosion of, 158–60; immigrants aspire to, 79; individual responsibility for achieving, 138, 142, 150; key elements of, 150; unemployment and, 143; values and, 106, 107

Amnå, Erik, 225

Aquinas, Thomas, 11, 99

Arendt, Hannah, 71, 85, 94, 226

Aristotle, 82, 163, 172

Arnett, Jeffrey Jensen, 175

ascriptive Americanism, 62

assimilation, 63, 68

Atkins, Robert, 94

*Atlantic Monthly,* 53, 55

Australia: adolescents' views on inequality, 39, 40; adolescents' views on state's role, 38; household chores in, 45; stable institutional practices in, 7

authority figures, adolescents influenced by, 21

bad choices, law for protecting individuals from their own, 116–17

Bandura, Albert, 21

Bartels, Larry, 152–53

Bellah, Robert N., 67, 109

Bogard, Kimber, 64

Boyte, Harry, 199, 230

Brady, Henry, 206–7

Bulgaria: adolescents' views on inequality, 39, 40–41; adolescents' views on state's role, 38; household chores in, 44; winners and losers in the new order, 42–43

Burns, Nancy, 32, 95

Campbell, David, 236

caution. *See* social vigilance (caution)

Center for Information and Research on Civic Learning and Engagement (CIRCLE), 226

Central and Eastern Europe: adolescents from different social orders in, 8, 35–49; ambivalence about economic changes in, 48; civil society in, 36, 48; contemporary life in, 48–49; as security societies, 35–36, 38; sudden social change and views on social contract in, 13, 14, 36–38; views of ideal social contract in, 39–41; winners and losers in the new order, 42–43; and youth civic engagement, 30; youth organizations lacking in, 47

Christens, Brian, 31

Churchill, Winston, 87

citizenship: community service as preparatory for, 203; expanding to include developmental processes, 2; immigrants and American, 15; liberal versus civic republican views of, 28–29; liberty depends on obligations of, 59; membership as characteristic of, 1–2; rights-based, 231; Rousseau on, 10; skills for, 6; stand-by citizens, 225

civic identity: construction of, 3, 83, 92, 199, 235–36; national service and, 215

civic participation: civic norms and values as mechanism of, 235–37; class and racial divide regarding, 32, 95; controversy as motivator of, 233–35; democracy relies on, 19; ethnicity and forms of, 25; motivators of, 232; parent-child communication and, 93. *See also* community service

civic republicanism: adolescents' view of American, 57–60; and American adolescents' view of democracy, 109; and attitudes toward immigrants, 65–68; on deliberation, 163; as fundamental public philosophy, 28–29, 52, 231; liberalism drowns out, 57, 67, 109; on need for others to succeed ourselves, 84; practices seen as character flaws, 57; and values, 104

Civilian Conservation Corps (CCC), 85–86

civil liberties (rights), 54–55, 58, 65–66

civil rights movement, 36, 61, 68, 230, 231

civil society, 36, 48, 93, 163, 168

cluster analysis, 102–3

cognition: adolescents' increasing capacity for, 90; and attitudes toward state's authority, 125; cognitive development theories, 17; in justification of political and economic arrangements, 43; social, 16, 20, 74, 152, 172, 228

collective action: common good and collective work, 224–26; community connectedness and, 218; as foundational for civic domain, 23; as psychologically beneficial, 230–31; youth civic engagement and, 31

common good: adolescents' view of American, 57–60; and attitudes toward immigrants, 65–68; in civic republicanism, 28, 52, 231; and collective action, 224–26; democracy and identification with, 162–63; family values that support, 235; heterogeneous associations and commitment to, 209; laws and public health, 113, 114–15; mini-polities in negotiation of, 229; and self-transcending values, 28; in social engineering cluster, 125; and social responsibility, 203

community: community service and sense of connectedness in, 217–19; Dewey on communication and, 186, 189; learning from community service and perceptions of, 219–20; moral, 54, 164, 187; social trust boosted by, 190–91. *See also* neighborhoods

community-based organizations: adult role models in, 222–23; in community service engagement, 198, 218; correlates of

adolescents' engagement in, 47–48; democratic dispositions boosted by, 221; as mini-polities, 2–3, 18, 229, 230; opportunities for civic practice in, 93–95; parental education and access to, 90; in safety net for the privileged, 157

community service, 197–226; adult role models in, 222–23; characteristics of participants, 186; collective action and common good, 224–26; motivations for, 220; opportunities afforded by, 9; and other civic outcomes, 47–48, 198; psychosocial benefits of, 205–7, 234; for restorative justice, 217–18; sense of the public formed through, 200, 212–14; and social intelligence, 213–17; and social trust, 200, 210–11, 215–17, 221; what adolescents learn from, 201–26

compassion, 178, 179, 181, 235

competition, 28, 43, 143, 144, 174, 189, 229

Constitution of the United States: class differences in study of, 94; helmet laws and smoking taxes as issue of, 119, 121; Preamble of, 50, 81, 85, 86

contact theory, 211, 212

controversy, interest in political issues generated by, 92, 233–35

Cook, Timothy E., 9, 21, 227, 229

cultural pluralism, 58–59

current events, family discussions of, 91–93, 105, 106, 107, 108, 225, 229–30

Czech Republic: adolescents' views on inequality, 39, 40–41; adolescents' views on state's role, 38; household chores in, 44; winners and losers in the new order, 42–43

Deaux, Kay, 63

deliberation, 6, 28, 163, 169, 231, 233

democracy: adolescents' differing views on, 12–13, 87–111; core values in, 28–29, 52–53, 88, 100–101; defining, 87–90, 95–96; as developmental achievement,

democracy *(continued)*
119–20; diffuse support for, 19–20; dispositions for, 19, 163, 168–69, 180, 209, 221, 234, 235; family discussions of current events and knowledge of, 92; giving practical definition to, 81; laws and public health, 113; personal meaning of, 95–102; schools in teaching about, 187; social trust as foundation of, 162–63; taking it for granted, 110–11; themes of, 102–3; values and meaning of, 103–11, 235; younger generation becomes part of, 85
*Democratic Vistas* (Whitman), 100, 111
Deneen, Patrick, 84
Deutsch, Morton, 168
Dewey, John, 81, 85, 186, 189, 209, 234
Dickinson, Julie, 16
Diemer, Matt, 31, 79–80
diffuse support, 19–20, 21, 50
discrimination: helmet laws and smoking taxes seen as, 119–21; personal experiences with, 74–79, 228; as systemic cause for inequality, 145–46
Dostoyevsky, Fyodor, 11
Douglas, Stephen A., 111
downward mobility, 146, 176
DREAM Act, 78–79
drunk driving (DUI) law, 114; bases of defense and contestation of, 123–24; for bringing about individual change, 117–18; common good as goal of, 115; effectiveness of, 122–23; for protecting individuals from their own bad choices, 117; for protecting innocent others, 116
Duncan, Arne, 141

Eastern Europe. *See* Central and Eastern Europe
Easton, David, 14, 27, 226
Eccles, Jacquelynne, 4
education. *See* schools
effectiveness of laws, 121–23

Ehrenreich, Barbara, 152–53
elderly, community service and overcoming stereotypes about, 211–12, 224–25
Emler, Nicholas, 16
English fluency, 58, 62, 66, 70
Enron scandal, 161
environmentalism, 105, 106, 107, 109, 225, 237
equality: adolescents' views about, 39; in American founding documents, 80; civic, 95, 96, 99–102, 108, 109; civic republicanism associated with, 57, 58; as core value of democracy, 88; family values that support, 235; giving practical definition to, 81; minority adolescents and challenges of realizing, 65–66. *See also* equal opportunity; inequality
equal opportunity: adolescents' theories about inequality and beliefs about, 154–55; as American ideal, 78, 79; in civic equality, 99; and civic republicanism, 58, 68; in definitions of democracy, 95; for education, 139; and personal experience of discrimination, 79; schools in promotion of, 83, 94
Erikson, Erik: on each generation reinterpreting social contract, 34; on fidelity to values, 27; on necessity of developing standards to live by, 33; on range of alternatives for identity formation, 24, 222; on trust, 166–67, 175, 195; on youth finding concordance between individual and group ideals, 88, 104, 110
ethnicity: adolescents feeling American and being aware of their ethnic roots, 22, 68–81; in adolescents' interpretations of social contract, 25; ethnic differences in schools, 94; and groupways, 7, 232; and social networks with strong ties, 165; and social trust development, 176–78; and what it means to be an American, 50–86. *See also* race
Evans, Sarah, 199, 230

extracurricular activities: civic engagement predicted by, 94, 191, 221–22; gay-straight alliances, 230; mediating function of, 18; peer pressure to join in, 236; survey questions about, 200–201

families: adolescents' theories about inequality and discussions in, 153–54; communication, 173, 177, 195; current-events discussions in, 91–93, 105, 106, 107, 108, 225, 229–30; as formative influence, 140–41; intergenerational tensions around adolescents acting "too American," 71–72; as mediating institutions, 21–22, 110; as mini-polities, 92; social class and adolescents' political theories, 15, 24–25; in social trust development, 170, 171, 173–74, 177, 178–82, 236. See also parents
financial crisis of 2008, 161–62
framing, 212–13
Franklin, Benjamin, 63–64
freedom (liberty): adolescents' view of American, 53–57; and attitudes toward immigrants, 64–68; as core value of democracy, 88; depends on obligations of citizenship, 59; freedoms from and to, 97; giving practical definition to, 81; in personal meaning of democracy, 95, 96–98; of speech, 54, 72. See also individual rights and freedoms
free spaces, 199, 230
Freire, Paulo, 31
friendship, 82, 167–70, 172, 173

Galston, William, 200
gay-straight alliances, 230
gender: in adolescents' interpretations of social contract, 25–27, 41; in beliefs about rights associated with health risks, 131; equality, 99; and groupways, 7, 41; and social trust, 169, 177–78, 210

generational replacement, 29, 30
Gingrich, Newt, 14
globalization, 142–43
Granovetter, Mark, 164–65
groupways, 7, 41, 231–32

habits, 140
Hacker, Jacob, 159, 160
hard work: in new global economy, 143, 150; in school, 4, 140, 141, 157; success attributed to, 4, 16, 41, 78, 79, 138, 140, 141, 146, 147, 148, 151, 155, 156; value seen as lost, 142
Hart, Daniel, 94
Hatano, Giyoo, 20
Havel, Vaclav, 27
health, laws and public, 112–33
"health as an individual right" scale, 128
helmet law, 114; bases of defense and contestation of, 124; common good as goal of, 115; effectiveness of, 122, 123; as matter of individual right, 119; for protecting individuals from their own bad choices, 117; seen as discriminatory, 119–21
Hess, Diana, 234
Higgins-D'Alessandro, Ann, 237
Hobbes, Thomas, 11–12
Hochschild, Jennifer, 150
homelessness: complexities in theories about, 151–53; egalitarian measures to address, 146–47; family background in, 141; positive effects of exposure to, 234; responsibility attributed to systemic and structural factors, 142, 143, 146; responsibility attributed to the individual, 138
hope: social contract and public, 192–96; trust as foundation for, 166–67
household chores, 44–45
Hughes, Diane, 77
Hull House, 199–200

Hungary: adolescents' views on inequality, 39, 40–41; adolescents' views on state's role, 38; household chores in, 44; volunteer work in, 47; winners and losers in the new order, 42–43

hyphenated American identities, 15, 51, 55, 59, 63, 64, 69

immigrants: adolescents feeling American and being aware of their ethnic roots, 22, 68–81; and adolescents' interpretations of social contract, 25; civic republicanism and attitudes toward, 58; DREAM Act, 78–79; ideas of American identity and attitudes toward, 63–68; and the social contract, 15, 63; values and attitudes toward, 155; and what it means to be an American, 50–86

inclusion: as American ideal, 78, 79; equal treatment and sense of, 98; personal experiences of, 80; respect and immigrants' sense of, 73–74; in schools, 22, 83, 190, 230

individual rights and freedoms: adolescents' view of American, 53–57; age differences in adolescents' concern with, 128, 130; and American adolescents' view of democracy, 108, 109; in cluster analysis of democracy, 102–3; first- and second-generation American youth and, 71; gender differences regarding, 131; individual rights cluster of responses, 126, 127; in liberalism, 52, 57, 108, 231; and molding individuals cluster, 125; in personal meaning of democracy, 95, 96–98, 101–2; responsibility correlated with, 130; and risky behavior, 112, 113, 118–19; view of democracy and value of, 235

inequality: adolescents' theories about, 16, 134–60, 229, 235; belief in just world and theories about, 141–42; community service and reflecting on, 207–9;

complexities in theories about, 151–53; correlates of adolescents' theories about, 153–58; critical reflection on, 79–80; formative influences and, 139–41; gender differences in attitudes toward, 25–26; increase in, 134–35; lowering aspirations as response to, 149–51; responsibility attributed to individuals, 137–42, 150; responsibility attributed to systemic and structural factors, 142–47, 150, 235; responsibility attributed to uncontrollable forces, 148–49, 150; values and theories of, 28, 236; and views of ideal social contract, 39–41

Inglehart, Ronald, 106

innocent others, law for protecting, 115–16

integrative complexity, 126–27, 136, 152

intelligence, social, 164, 171, 173, 174, 177, 178, 214–17

International Association for the Evaluation of Educational Achievement (IEA), 12

Jensen, Lene Arnett, 64

Jordan, Barbara, 80–81

Jost, John, 12, 154

Kahne, Joseph, 154, 191

Kelsen, Hans, 92

Kids Voting USA, 230

King, Martin Luther, Jr., 14

Kirshner, Ben, 31

Kohn, Melvin, 45, 46, 47

Krugman, Paul, 162, 175

Lappé, Frances Moore, 224–25

laws: age differences in adolescents' theories about, 124–25, 129–30; for bringing about individual change, 117–18; common good as goal of, 113, 114–15; effectiveness of, 121–23; growth in adolescents' understanding of social purpose of, 8, 23; for protecting individuals from their own bad choices, 116–17; for protecting innocent others, 115–16; and public health, 112–33; and social trust, 163

Leahy, Robert, 134, 136

learning: service, 31, 197–99, 201–2, 223; trust as foundation for, 166. *See also* schools

legal socialization studies, 119

Levine, Peter, 226, 237

liberalism: and American adolescents' view of democracy, 108, 109; in American adolescents' view of freedom, 53–54, 56, 57; and attitudes toward immigrants, 64–68; civic republicanism drowned out by, 57, 67, 109; first- and second-generation American youth and, 71; as fundamental public philosophy, 28, 52, 231; the individual as conceived in, 95; tolerance of rights of others to hold their own views, 96; values and, 104

liberty. *See* freedom (liberty)

Lincoln, Abraham, 87, 111

Locke, John, 11, 99

Lowell, James Russell, 53

loyalty. *See* patriotism and loyalty

Lummis, C. Douglas, 168, 170, 173, 196

majority rule: in cluster analysis of democracy, 102–3, 108–9; in definition of democracy, 87; democracy seen as more than, 111; in personal meaning of democracy, 95, 98–99, 101

Maslow, Abraham H., 106

Mason, David S., 37

materialism, 105, 106, 107, 108, 109, 156, 235

McFarland, Daniel, 220

McIntosh, Hugh, 91

mediating institutions: adolescents' experiences in, 18–19, 21–23, 229; civil society provides space for reinvention of Central and Eastern European, 48;

defined, 7; opportunities afforded by, 9; in political stability and change, 230; politics embedded in, 2–3; routine practices of, 18–19, 43–45

Meier, Deborah, 188–89

meritocracy: acceptance of inequality associated with, 41; challenges to, 148, 151, 156; individualism associated with, 16; recognition of weaknesses of, 141; in system justification theory, 157; United States seen as, 16, 38, 142, 156, 157

Metz, Edward, 211

Mickelson, Roz, 78

mini-polities: in development of commitment to larger polity, 2, 84, 93; mediating institutions as, 2–3, 18, 229; in political stability and change, 230; schools as, 18, 84, 187, 189, 190, 229, 230

minorities. *See* ethnicity

molding individuals cluster, 125–26, 127

Monitoring the Future study, 225

Murray, Charles, 142

Nafisi, Azar, 60, 72

National Household Education Survey, 91

nationalism, 60

neighborhoods: civically engaged, 154, 191; as formative influence, 140–41; high-poverty urban, 95; increasing segregation of, 209

No Child Left Behind Act, 139

Nussbaum, Martha, 97

O'Neil, Robert P., 125

open classroom climates, 84

open-mindedness: adolescence as time for developing disposition for, 3; civic republicanism associated with, 58, 68; controversy and disposition toward, 233; in definition of democracy, 89, 100–101; as democratic disposition, 168, 175; heterogeneous associations and, 209; as self-transcending value, 28 opportunity: class and racial divide regarding, 32; creating one's own, 156; educational, 24–25, 90; opportunity societies, 38. *See also* equal opportunity

out-groups: blamed for economic decline, 145; community service disconfirms stereotypes about, 211; trustworthiness of, 169

Page, Clarence, 73, 74

Pancer, Mark, 222

Panel Study on Income Dynamics (PSID), 146

parents: democratic parenting, 93, 181; influences on adolescents' social trust, 178–82; as moral guides, 195; parental education, 24, 40–41, 42, 90, 91, 108, 154, 156; parent-child communication, 93, 174, 179; September 11, 2001, and parenting, 192–95; views of changing world, 182–86

patriotism and loyalty: in adolescents' view of what it means to be American, 52, 53, 60–63; and attitudes toward immigrants, 65–68

peers: in development of concepts of citizenship, 18; health risks and peer pressure, 132; sense of civic duty instilled by, 236; social trust and peer relations, 167–70; solidarity among, 46, 82

perspective taking, 23, 84, 127–28, 230

Phillips, Kevin, 148

Phinney, Jean S., 69, 78

Piaget, Jean, 167

Piketty, Thomas, 135

Pinsky, Robert, 80

Plato, 84

political socialization studies, 17, 19–20, 21, 29, 227, 229

politics: adolescents' lay theories of, 3, 16–17, 227–29; affective feelings for the polity, 19–21; awareness that there is more than one side to an issue, 131, 228,

232, 233; changes in theories between early and late adolescence, 8, 23, 228; community membership in, 2; community service as bridge to, 199–200; controversy as motivator of interest and action, 92, 233–35; declines in conventional forms of participation, 30–31; developmental mechanisms underlying stability and change, 229–31; as domain of experience and knowledge, 17, 228; family discussions of current events, 91–93, 105, 106, 107, 108, 225, 229–30; groupways link personal and political, 231–32; identities take shape in adolescence and young adulthood, 30, 53; political significance of friendship, 82; psychologists ignore, 1; religion and polarization of, 209; theories about what it means to be American as political idea, 68; values and, 27–29, 46, 103–4, 226, 235–37; why we should pay attention to adolescents' political development, 32–34. *See also* democracy; majority rule; representative government; social contract

Portes, Alejandro, 74

Post, Robert, 87, 88, 92, 93, 98, 233

poverty: community service and learning about, 208–9, 212; complexities in theories about, 151–53, 228; family background in, 140–41; increase in, 135–36; lowering aspirations as response to, 149–51; media portrayal of, 152; responsibility attributed to the individual, 137–38; responsibility attributed to systemic and structural factors, 142–47; responsibility attributed to uncontrollable forces, 148–49; as systemic cause for inequality, 145

prearming, 76–77

promises, 168

public health, laws and, 112–33

"public health beliefs" scale, 128

Putnam, Robert, 30, 176, 186

race: in adolescents' interpretations of social contract, 25; in defining American identity, 70; divide in civic opportunities, 32; equality, 100; fair treatment for racial minorities, 23; racially mixed schools, 234–35; racial socialization, 23, 25, 75–77, 79, 176; and social trust, 169, 210; stereotypes, 77; as systemic cause for inequality, 145

rational choice theory, 132

reactive identification, 74

representative government: in cluster analysis of democracy, 102–3; in definition of democracy, 95; in personal meaning of democracy, 98–99, 101; politics as broader than, 17, 31

responsibility: attributing to individuals for inequality, 137–42; attributing to systemic and structural factors for inequality, 142–47; individual rights correlated with, 130; reciprocal, 115. *See also* social responsibility

restorative justice, 217–18

risks, privatization of, 158–60

risky behaviors: age differences in adolescents' views of, 128–33; as individual right, 118–19; legitimacy of state setting parameters on, 115; school environment and, 187

Rivas-Drake, Deborah, 77

Roosevelt, Franklin D., 14

Roosevelt, Theodore, 64

Rosenberg, Morris, 162, 175, 212

Rotter, Julian, 173

Rousseau, Jean-Jacques, 10–11, 224

routine practices, 18–19, 43–45

Rumbaut, Rubén G., 74

Saez, Emmanuel, 135

safety net: in Central and Eastern Europe, 39; erosion of, 14–15, 16, 134, 158–60; gender differences in concern about, 26; for the privileged, 157–58; seen as promoting dependency, 155; values and support for, 46; world without, 156, 158

Sandel, Michael J., 59, 67

Schlozman, Kay Lehman, 32, 95, 206–7

schools: in Central and Eastern Europe, 36, 37, 40–41, 48; civil climate for learning in, 22, 83–84, 184, 187, 188–90, 234–35; education for employment, 48, 139, 144, 146; encourage identification with dominant culture, 18, 19; ethnic and class differences in, 94; gay-straight alliances in, 230; increasing segregation of, 209; and inequality, 139–40; and materialist values, 156; as mediating institutions, 2, 18, 22–23, 48, 230; as mini-polities, 18, 84, 187, 189, 190, 229, 230; opportunities for civic practice in, 93–94; parents' declining trust in, 182, 183–86; racially mixed, 234–35; in safety net for the privileged, 157, 158; service learning in, 201–2; social class and choice of, 24–25, 90; social class and views of, 42–43; in social trust development, 22, 174, 186–90; student solidarity, 8, 19, 22, 32, 46–47, 82–83, 187–90, 234

Schudson, Michael, 110–11, 231

Schwartz, Shalom H., 28, 104–5, 109

security societies, 35–36, 38

self-determination: age differences in adolescents' views of, 125, 130–31; in American adolescents' view of freedom, 19; in Central and Eastern Europe, 36; changes in theories between early and late adolescence, 8, 23; family discussions of current events and construction of, 92; and law as bringing about individual change, 118; in personal meaning of democracy, 95, 97, 98; as post-materialist value, 106; schools in, 43

self-interest, relational, 224–25

self-reliance, 57, 156, 158, 177

Sen, Amartya, 97

Sennett, Richard, 159–60

September 11, 2001, 192–95

service learning, 31, 197–99, 201–2, 223

Sherrod, Lonnie, 64

Smith, Rogers M., 73, 78, 214

Smith, Tom, 176, 177

smoking tax, 113–14; bases of defense and contestation of, 124; for bringing about individual change, 117, 118; common good as goal of, 115; effectiveness of, 122; as matter of individual right, 119; for protecting individuals from their own bad choices, 117; for protecting innocent others, 116; seen as discriminatory, 119–21

social change: alternative theories of "good society" during, 40; media portrayals of, 230; mediating institutions contribute to, 22; social contract and, 13–15, 36–38; social trust affected by, 162; structural economic change, 134–35, 142–47

social class: and adolescents' ability to define democracy, 90; adolescents from different social orders, 35–49; in adolescents' interpretations of social contract, 15, 24–25; in adolescents' theories about inequality, 153–54, 156–58; in adolescents' views of state's role, 42; in Central and Eastern Europe, 8, 49; class consciousness, 147–48; class differences in schools, 94; in differences in adolescents' reports of values, 106–7; divide in civic opportunities, 32; and educational opportunities, 24–25, 90; and groupways, 7, 232; and opportunities for civic practice, 94–95; segregation on basis of, 209; and social networks with strong ties, 165. See also inequality; poverty; wealth

social contract, 3–4; adolescents' buy in, 20–21; adolescents' construction of, 3, 6, 7, 10–34; adolescents' theories about inequality and beliefs about, 154–55; adolescents' views of ideal, 39–41; age and adolescents' appreciation of, 130; anxiety about unraveling of, 161; in

Central and Eastern Europe, 36; community service and interpretation of, 210, 212, 224–25; experiences of discrimination and beliefs about, 79; factors in interpretation of, 24–27; historical roots of, 11; immigrants and, 15, 63; intergenerational compact, 4, 5–6; laws and public health, 113; on managing risk, 159; mediating institutions as settings for, 22, 229; and molding individuals cluster, 126; as not applying equally to all groups, 21; and people "like us," 15, 21, 41, 42, 49, 73–75, 78–80, 155–57, 231; perceptions of basic fairness of, 156–57; and public hope, 192–96; on revoking authority of government, 11, 99; and right way to organize society, 12, 39; Rousseau on, 10–11, 224; routine practices and, 18–19, 43–45; social change and, 13–15, 16; values in adolescents' theories about, 45–47; winners and losers in the new order, 42–43

Social Contract Press, 15

social engineering cluster, 125, 127

social justice, 31, 198, 200

social responsibility: adolescents' differing endorsement of, 108–9, 110; civic republicanism associated with, 59, 68; and community service, 47, 198, 203–5; as goal of education, 139; regarding health risks and view of state's role, 131–33; household chores teach, 44–45; in measuring adolescents' values, 105, 106, 107; Mexican families inculcate, 65; and parental influence on adolescents' social trust, 178, 179, 180, 236; as predictor of civic and public interest goals, 46; as self-transcending value, 106; and social trust, 8, 19; substance use versus endorsement of, 132; view of democracy and value of, 235

social trust, 161–96; communities boost, 190–91; and community service, 200,

210–11, 215–17, 221; correlated with
stands on social policies, 212; decline of,
162; declines with age, 8, 172–75, 214,
215, 228; as democratic disposition, 19,
163; developmental foundations of,
165–67; as foundation of democracy,
162–63; friendship and, 167–70; and
groups at periphery of society, 176–78;
as it develops in adolescence, 170–76;
out-groups seen as less trustworthy, 169,
210; parental influence on adolescents',
178–82, 236; parents' declining, 182–86;
schools boost, 22, 174, 186–90
social vigilance (caution): parental
influences on adolescents' social trust,
178, 179, 180, 181; as self-enhancing
value, 106; after September 11, 2001,
192, 194; values and meaning of
democracy, 105, 107, 108, 109, 110
social welfare: gender differences regarding,
41; moral hazards attributed to, 38;
reform, 134; social welfare cluster of
responses, 126, 127; in United States,
12. See also safety net
Sporte, Susan E., 154, 191
sports, 84
standing up for principle, 57, 59–60, 61,
89, 233
state, the: adolescents' differing views on
role of, 12–13, 37–39; gender differences
in attitudes toward role of, 26; relationship between personal action and
government accountability, 225–26;
social class and views of role of, 42; social
responsibility regarding health risks and
view of role of, 131–33; values and views
of role of, 46
status quo, 12, 14, 40, 59, 61, 68, 157
stereotypes: community service and
questioning, 209–11; and intergroup
contact, 211–12; racial, 77; of youth,
217–18, 223, 229
strategic trust, 164

strong democracy. See civic republicanism
structural economic change, 134–35,
142–47
Sullivan, John, 19, 100
Sweden, 7, 38–39, 40, 44, 47
system justification theory, 40, 157

Takahashi, Keiko, 20
Tatum, Beverly Daniel, 75
Thomas, R. Jack, 220
tolerance: adolescence as time for developing
disposition for, 3; adolescents from
minority backgrounds on, 15, 25, 79; as
American ideal, 78; civic republicanism
associated with, 57, 58, 68; controversy
and disposition toward, 233; and cultural
pluralism, 59; as essential for democracy,
100; in liberal philosophy, 96; as
psychological disposition to democracy,
19; schools in promotion of, 83, 230;
as self-transcendent value, 28; and
September 11, 2001, 194–95
Torney-Purta, Judith, 84
Transue, John, 19, 100
trust: interpersonal, 165, 167, 171–72, 173,
228; strategic, 164. See also social trust

unemployment: complexities in theories
about, 151–53; in downward mobility,
146; family background in, 141;
responsibility attributed to the individual,
137–38, 141, 235; responsibility
attributed to systemic and structural
factors, 142–45; responsibility attributed
to uncontrollable forces, 148; seen as
healthy, 143, 157
United Nations Convention on the Rights
of the Child, 30, 130
United States: adolescents' attitudes toward
state's role, 38; adolescents on what
it means to be an American, 50–86;
adolescents' views on inequality, 39;
household chores in, 44, 45; how

United States *(continued)*
"We the People" takes shape, 81–86; inequality in, 134–60; as meritocracy, 16, 38, 142, 156, 157; risk shouldered by individuals in, 158–60; seen as equitable society, 155; September 11, 2001, 192–95; stable institutional practices in, 7; taking democracy for granted in, 110–11. *See also* American Dream; Constitution of the United States
Updike, John, 55–56, 72
upward mobility, 143, 144
Uslaner, Eric, 164

values: in adolescents' theories about inequality, 153–54; in adolescents' theories about social contract, 45–47; and civic norms as mechanism of civic participation, 235–37; as functional, 107; gender differences regarding, 26; and meaning of democracy, 103–11, 235; mediating institutions reflect, 18; in parental influence on adolescents' social trust, 178–82; personal and family, 7, 8, 27, 45, 87, 88, 106, 155–58, 235; political parties allocate, 14, 27; and politics, 27–29, 46, 103–4, 226, 235–37; social class in differences in adolescents' reports of, 106–7
value socialization theory, 105
Verba, Sidney, 32, 95, 206–7
vigilance (caution). *See* social vigilance (caution)

Voight, Adam, 31
volunteer work. *See* community service
Vygotsky, Lev, 17, 21, 76, 89, 90, 127, 208, 228, 233

Walzer, Michael, 1–2, 8, 51, 52, 58, 59, 61, 63, 86
Watts, Roderick, 31
wealth: class conscious views of, 147–48; complexities in theories about, 151–53, 228; education and, 139, 140; family background in, 140, 141; lowering aspirations as response to inequality, 149–51; media attention to, 152; responsibility attributed to the individual, 138; responsibility attributed to uncontrollable forces, 148–49; as systemic cause for inequality, 145
welfare. *See* social welfare
Whitman, Walt, 100, 111
work: in intergenerational compact, 5; as source of purpose and meaning, 6; work ethic, 141, 144. *See also* hard work; unemployment

Yamagishi, Toshio, 173
Yates, Miranda, 104, 198, 235
Youniss, James, 104, 198, 211, 235
youth. *See* adolescents
youth activism, 31
youth civic engagement, 7, 29–32, 221, 237

Zeldin, Shep, 223